Tom Ashley, Sam McGee, Bukka White

Tom Ashley

Sam McGee

Bukka White

TENNESSEE TRADITIONAL
SINGERS
Edited by Thomas G. Burton

KNOXVILLE ᵾ THE UNIVERSITY OF TENNESSEE PRESS

Clothbound editions of University of Tennessee Press books are printed on paper designed for an effective life of at least 300 years, and binding materials are chosen for strength and durability.

LIBRARY OF CONGRESS CATALOGING IN PUBLICATION DATA
Main entry under title:

Tom Ashley, Sam McGee, Bukka White, Tennessee tradi-
    tional singers.

    Bibliography: p.   ; Discography: p.
    Includes index.
    CONTENTS: Burton, T. G. Introduction. — Manning,
A. N., and Miller, M. M. Tom Ashley. — Wolfe, C. K.
Sam McGee. [etc.]
    1. Ashley, Thomas Clarence, 1895–1967. 2. McGee,
Sam, 1894–1975. 3. White, Bukka, 1909–1977. 4. Singers — Tennessee
— Biography.   5. Folk music, American — Tennessee —
History and criticism.   I. Burton, Thomas G.
II. Title.   III. Title: Tennessee traditional singers.
ML400.T6   784′.092′2 [B]   79-19655
ISBN 0-87049-260-8

Contents

Illustrations

Acknowledgments

Publication of this book was possible because of the efforts of many individuals and several institutions. The authors thank them all, even though only a few are named below. To Anne Burton, who has been essentially a coeditor, we are particularly grateful.

For help with the chapter on Tom Ashley, we owe a special debt of thanks to Eva Ashley Moore, daughter of the singer, who lent her patient assistance from the time the work on this section began. We are indebted as well to the family of Sam McGee and to Mary Dean Wolfe, who helped in the interviews with Sam. Our thanks also to the Research Development Committee at East Tennessee State University, which provided for typing of the final draft, John B. Tallent, former chairman of the English department of this institution, who lightened our load, David Hatcher, who assisted in checking copyrights of the music, Peggy Henry, who helped in proofing the manuscript, Al Tanner, who first introduced Charles Wolfe and Sam McGee, and to Fuller Arnold, a close friend and associate of Sam. In addition, we appreciate the counsel and other assistance of the following individuals: Bill Harrison, Steve Davis, Doug Tuchman, Bob Nobley, Frank Scott, and Doug Taylor.

Thomas G. Burton

Introduction

BY THOMAS G. BURTON

All of Tennessee may be divided into three parts, as in fact the Tennessee River cuts it and as it exists in the minds of many people—even the official flag displays three stars "representing the three grand divisions of the state." Tennessee does not yield easily to such simplistic geographic divisions, however; it has great scope and diversity: it rises in the lofty Appalachian Mountains; stretches for almost 500 miles westward across the Great Valley, the Cumberland Plateau, the Central Basin, the Gulf Coastal Plain; and finally settles in the Mississippi River.

The traditional music of Tennessee is also sometimes conceived as being divided into three categories: Anglo-American folksongs in East Tennessee, country music in Middle Tennessee, and black blues in West Tennessee. The state's traditional music, however, is certainly much richer and more complex than these broad categories would suggest. The three groups are not mutually exclusive and do not sufficiently emphasize sacred music, work chants, children's songs, and folk music of various other types and countries. They also suggest a false restriction of particular traditions to specific areas—Anglo-American folksongs are not confined to the Unakas and Great Smoky Mountains, nor is country music to the Nashville Basin, nor are black blues to the Gulf Coastal Plain of West Tennessee. Unquestionably, to bind up Tennessee's traditional music into these three categories would arbitrarily restrict and belie its great scope and diversity; yet there is some basis for this classification in people's minds.

The eastern part of Tennessee is in the center of the Southern Appalachians, midway between the Eastern Panhandle of West Virginia to the north and the northeast corner of Alabama to the south, as well as midway between the Blue Ridge slopes to the east and the Central Cumberland Plateau to the west. That the old British tradition is associated with this area is due to various circumstances, including the proliferation of fanciful notions about mountaineers and the exclusion of other traditions in the early collecting of Appalachian folksongs. The area's geography and cultural development have of course been especially significant in making this identification. The Southern Appalachian region was populated principally by British settlers, dominantly Scottish, who came (as described by W. D. Weatherford and Wilma Dykeman) in two tributaries: the first, Scotch-Irish, starting from Delaware Bay, went westward and at Harper's Ferry forked, one branch going to West Virginia, Ohio, and westward, the other branch running down the Shenandoah Valley into the Holston River country of East Tennessee and from there flowing into Kentucky, North Georgia, and North Alabama. The second stream, Scottish Highlanders, starting from Wilmington, Charleston, and Port Royal, ran up the Great Pee Dee, Neuse, and Cape Fear rivers into North Carolina and over into Tennessee and Kentucky, merging there with the Scotch-Irish. The music of this region consequently was predominantly, but not exclusively, that which these settlers held in common, the traditional tunes and songs of the British Isles, a music that found rich soil. Its vitality, however, is not simple to explain; much of the explanation surely has to do with the character of the music itself, but much also with the fact that the region remained a frontier for longer than have many other regions in America. Long isolated from erratic changes, the Southern Appalachians formed a matrix of Anglo-American folksong, and in the center of this matrix lies East Tennessee.

Country music — variously labeled, including such other terms as *hillbilly, old-time,* and *western* — has grown from the British folksong tradition; and in Middle Tennessee between the folds of the Tennessee River lies the giant itself of country music, Nashville. The prodigious potential of Nashville in country music began to manifest itself in the years following the First World War, most significantly in 1925, when the WSM barn dance show (later named the Grand Ole Opry) came into being. This program in the years following the Second World War became universally recognized as the nation's number one barn-dance radio show and America's strongest magnet of country music talent. In 1942 Acuff-Rose Publications, the first publishing house in the United States to issue country music exclusively, was established in Nashville. Other commercial publishers swarmed to the area. Also in the 1940s Nashville's recording prowess began to emerge. The Decca Company in 1945 under Paul Cohen was the first to record its hillbilly artists there, but later other companies followed, and by 1960 Nashville studios had completely dominated the recording of country music. Nashville produced the country pop and the "Nashville Sound" associated with the country music of the 1950s and 1960s. Furthermore, it has become the homesite of many stars and satellites of country music as well as of their booking agencies and professional organizations. Indisputably, the heart of country music beats in Middle Tennessee.

How, when, or where the blues originated, no one knows exactly, but in the story of the blues, West Tennessee has figured large. The blues apparently came into being among rural blacks in the South sometime near the end of the nineteenth century; and even though the birthplace of the blues is uncertain, it may have been the fertile fields of the Mississippi Delta (Memphis, Tennessee, south to Vicksburg, Mississippi, and east to the Yazoo River). There the engendering elements were present: a concentration of black field workers, an isolation in many ways from white society, and a developed tradition of rhymed work-song material. Then, as large numbers of blacks moved off plantations seeking employment, the blues began to be propagated by cities as well as by countrysides, particularly ports such as Memphis and New Orleans that had many jobs available. Not until the early part of the twentieth century, however, did the blues gain recognition, and much of that originated in Memphis. It was there in 1912 that one of the first compositions ever to be labeled "blues" ("The Memphis Blues") was published, and by a man whose name became synonymous with the genre: W. C. Handy, a bandleader who was in some respects, as he styled himself, the "father of the blues." Memphis performed an important role in the recognition of the blues not only during the early years but also throughout the history of the blues, both in and out of the Delta. It produced, for example, many of the popular jug bands recorded in the late 1920s and the 1930s, and it created many individual blues singers. It has served as a recording center for the blues; it is one of some half-dozen cities that are of primary importance to blues style; and it continues to be alive with blues activity as well as to function as a meeting place for bluesmen from within the Delta and without, especially from places west (e.g., Texas, Oklahoma, Louisiana, Arkansas, and Missouri). In addition, it has been through Memphis principally that bluesmen have migrated on their way north to Chicago from other parts of the Delta, from the hill country of Mississippi, and from the rural areas of Alabama. Memphis has always been vital to the blues.

It is a distinctive feature of Tennessee's traditional music that East, Middle, and West Tennessee are springs of Anglo-American folksongs, country music, and black blues, respectively; and it is in part to provide some perspective on these three major streams of music in Tennessee and the diversity within them that we present the following portraits of Tom Ashley, Sam McGee, and Bukka White, each a significant folk musician associated with one of these traditions and with that section of the state to which the tradition is sometimes related.

Even with a view to representative qualities, the choice of individuals for the portraits could reasonably have been a number of persons who are more or less widely known or who more nearly characterize either distinctly Tennessean subtypes (for example, Memphis blues) or simply different subtypes (such as old-time fiddle music). Any representative selection, however, would have its limitations, each person perhaps being in his own way both more and less nearly characteristic of Tennessee folk musicians than are these three men by birth, residence, nature, or definition of terms, and the music of another perhaps being more and less nearly typical of a particular tradition (both its stock and its multifaceted characteristics).

To provide some perspective on the Anglo-American folksong, country music, and black blues traditions in Tennessee is, however, only one aim of these portraits. In some ways Ashley, McGee, and White are individually characteristic of a type of traditional musician in Tennessee, but in other ways each is unique. We would do violence to these men if we included or deleted biographical details, statements, or repertory pieces in order to force them into any preconceived mold. Uninformed readers might accept in varying degrees the sop of a shoeless Tom Ashley, sitting on a porch of his log cabin, picking out on his fretless banjo quaint-sounding songs of forlorn love and bloodshed while the copper coil at his side dripped corn liquor into his jug and while his aged mother, who taught him songs sought by the British folksong collector Cecil Sharp, accompanied her son on a homemade dulcimer that she fretted with the stem of her corncob pipe. Or a Sam McGee, bandanna stuck in the hip pocket of his bib-overalls rolled high over brogans and white socks, straw hat on the back of his head, hayseed in his mouth, slopping hogs and entuning in his enlarged nasal cavities the "Great Speckle[d] Bird." Or a muscular, soiled, shiny-black Bukka White in some tar-papered shack near the field where he had picked cotton until sundown, crying out for his woman who just walked out and left him alone with his guitar, bottleneck, and plate of chitlins.

But even though such romanticized and brutalized sketches might satisfy some, any preconceived moldings would betray the men because not one of them is purely a traditional singer or simply a stock performer. Tom Ashley, Sam McGee, and Bukka White did receive rich, vital folk-music heritages (as the result in part of the geographic and social isolation of their forefathers) — traditional songs, traditional instruments, and traditional styles (a musical matter and a manner) were passed on to them by oral-aural means and demonstration. Nevertheless, their music cannot be described simply as a repository of tradition in a vacuum; rather, the traditional music that they inherited is only one aspect of their musical careers and is influenced by many factors, including inner physical, mental, and emotional properties and outer cultural forces. Each life is musically a repository of traditional music and of much more — one sees in each a professional who refines his craft, an entertainer who is responsive to his audience, an artist who creates and shapes sound, and a musician who has varied tastes. From selected reeds in their agrarian backgrounds they carved themselves a profession and skillfully piped their tunes, not one achieving the laurel crown, but their music sounding and being echoed across the land.

Although professionally they have much in common, these singers vary considerably relative to the specific traditions of which they are part. Bukka White was black; and in general his music—in subject, structure, rhythmic pattern, type of instrument, and playing style—is Southern rural black, a music that has retained in its manner an African heritage. This African heritage (as discussed by Bruno Nettl) is manifested in the importance of rhythm, instruments, improvisation, and call-and-response, as well as in the use of the voice in a relaxed, open, yet sometimes purposefully harsh way. Specifically, Bukka White's music is what may be called *Delta country blues*, a category of blues the distinguishing features of which (as analyzed by Charles Keil) are drones, moans, bottleneck techniques on an unamplified guitar, repetition of melodic figures, heavy sound, and rough intensity. Obviously, Bukka White's music is distinctly different from that of the other two men; but a distinction is not immediately clear between the music of Tom Ashley and of Sam McGee. Both Ashley and McGee stem from the Anglo-American folksong tradition; furthermore, the music of both is eclectic—it comes from both traditional (British and American folksongs, hymns, and tunes, and white and black blues or bluesy music) and popular music (music from the traveling show and Tin Pan Alley). They also have in common the manner in which their music is produced, a manner that may be called old-time style. Ashley's style tends to be more conservative than McGee's (that is, less influenced by later tunings, picking and playing styles, and vocal techniques). Ashley, at least in his later years, was adamant in his attempt to maintain a certain sound and adhere to a certain style, but his stylistic conservatism was perhaps somewhat affected by his ceasing for a long period to depend financially upon his musical profession, whereas McGee never stopped being active in a changeable market. In Ashley's later career, his audience demanded a conservative style and repertory since he was identified with an area that represented, in the minds of many, a "pure" folk tradition—he in fact reemerged in his profession as an Appalachian folk musician during the "revival" of that music in the late 1950s and the 1960s. One might describe the difference in the music of Tom Ashley and Sam McGee (using terms for forms of early hillbilly music that have been suggested by Bill Malone) by saying that Ashley's music leans more toward *mountain* and McGee's more toward *country*; the difference, however, is a matter of degree.

Rather than force Tom Ashley, Sam McGee, or Bukka White into any mold, we note what each has done, what he voices, and what those who knew him say about him; in this way, perhaps, we may produce at least a measure of harmony between the portrait and the man himself. The procedure demanded by this kind of portrait relies heavily, though not solely, on personal interviews with both the principal subjects and those who knew them well. In the case of Tom Ashley, since this book was begun after his death and since only a few of his comments are available on taped recordings, the writers rely heavily on personal recollection as well as on the testimony of many cooperative friends and members of the Ashley family.

The interviews and other sources did not provide all the answers, but we attempted to pursue the right questions—for example, what is the subtle mixture in each singer of the traditional and nontraditional? of universality and provinciality?—as well as to deal with the matters of self-concept, skill, style, relationship between singer and repertory, the significance of the singer's own explications of the text, and the influence by and on other performers.

In any written sketch of a person, interpretation is manifested even in selection of details; and the following three portraits by design go beyond selection in interpreting material. The focus, however, is upon revelation of the men, which includes interpretation, rather than upon extensive analysis or theory.

To reveal another person completely is of course a herculean task. Even if the vision were present to understand another perfectly, its expression would transcend language. To produce the man, one would have to produce the life, to re-create him; for no part of the whole *is* the whole. Nevertheless, one means of understanding an object is to place its parts in perspective and at the same time to remember that the whole, especially in respect to people, may be more than the sum of its parts. Every man is complex and in each of the three presented here "there is much music, excellent voice," and we do not pretend to "pluck out the heart" of his mystery. What we do attempt, from the vantage point of propitious access to these men, is to reflect images of lives rather than to re-create lives; images only of individuals, individuals with interesting careers, and not images of personified abstractions of traditional singers of Tennessee; and, we hope, images of reality, in place of the shadows of any fanciful imagination. Each of these men, who are not of one piece, is worthy of study as an individual musician; yet as true as it is that to know an individual is to know much of humanity, to perceive something of each of these singers is to perceive much of the tradition from which he comes and that tradition of which he is a part.

Tom Ashley, Sam McGee, and Bukka White are presented here because each had an interesting, varied life and musical career that has not already been well documented; each has made a contribution to the history of traditional music; each manifests the intricate influences of tradition, heredity, domestic culture, country and city life, temporal setting, professional opportunities, commercial media, national tastes in music, and chance. And before his death, each fortunately drew the concern of these scholars, who can thus share knowledge and perceptions that would otherwise not exist of three Tennessee traditional singers.

PART ONE

Tom Ashley

BY AMBROSE N. MANNING AND MINNIE M. MILLER

Music Notation by Annette L. Burton

The place could be any of a number of stages in cities across the country during the first part of the 1960s: Newport, Chicago, Los Angeles. Or it could even be a city in England. The audience is hushed; then everyone's attention falls on a small mountain man just over five feet tall, perhaps dressed somewhat as a Raleigh reporter once described him, "the coat of the brown suit open, exposing a pair of suspenders even redder than the shirt . . . sporty brown hat . . . perched jauntily on his head and . . . a big Gibson banjo on his lap."

He might look up and say (as he did in 1966 at the East Tennessee State University Folk Festival):

Now, I'm going to offer you an old tune here that I started out thumbing with about sixty-one year ago. Now, I don't deny my age —I'm seventy-one year old, and very proud to be kicking around with the people as healthy as I am. I'm very thankful. Now, this old tune that I'm going to do I did back sometime during the twenties. I was honored that Columbia recorded it. Well, it went along as the average tune; and during a certain period of time, well, it faded out just like a lot of others—a lot of my tunes and other people's tunes. They faded out; they was in the old tradition, and the modern music pushed them out. Along about '61, this old record was found in the Music Library of Congress, and some of the people were studying the old folksongs. They went to checking up on me to see if I was a-living, and they wanted me to go back to New York and record it once again in '61 on Folkways. Well, it's been going around the country. It's a little different, but I noticed in the last few months that a very popular and well-known group from the Grand Ole Opry is a-doing the same song although in a modern tune. Now, they fixed their own tune, which is all right; they had a perfect right to do it and they do a good job. They use the old words that I used, and the old title, but they fixed the tune to suit their music. Now, I'm a-going to try my best to do this just the way I did it years and years ago.

Or, he might give a little more background for the song (as he once did for a folklore class at East Tennessee State University).

I've got one more here that I'm a-going to do on the banjer. I'll have to tell you a little about this'n. I used to sit around and try to fix me some songs to suit myself. I'm no songwriter now — don't misunderstand me — and I'm no music writer. I don't know enough about it. But I kindly put one together by taking — now, the real old song is an old English tune, came out of England many years ago. I used to hear my mother sing hit, but I never cared for it — it didn't appeal to me. If anything don't appeal to you, you're not apt to learn it. But I took a few words from hit and made me one of my own.

Well, this is one that is a-living its second life. I recorded this — I can very well remember when I recorded it — for Columbia, Frank Walker. And hit done all right, but nothing — never burnt up the world. None of them did back in those days, 'cause them old two-faced records, you know — two songs on a record — they sold for about seventy-five cents, and most of them were like me and didn't have the seventy-five. But anyhow, hit sold a little. So this is, I guess, part of what caused some of the folks, people that's such in folk music come a-looking for me. They found this old record, and they wanted to find the fellow that made it if they could. And they found me. Now, hit has become very popular. Hit's been on the top of the folksongs and around the top for some time. Although they's been a lot of other people has done it, but they don't hardly get my version exactly. They get the words and the tune pretty well, but they's one part of it they don't get. And I'll let you be the judge.

Then again, this old gentleman might feel more like playing than talking and might simply say (as he did at the University of Chicago Folk Festival in 1962): "I set this old bird a-flying back in the twenties, and she's been flying around the country ever since. People sing this song all over. It's called 'The Coo Coo Bird.'"

THE COO-COO BIRD (The Cuckoo Bird)
Words and Music by Clarence Ashley
TRO — © Copyright 1976 LUDLOW MUSIC, INC., New York, N.Y.
USED BY PERMISSION.

Goin'   to   build   me   log   cab - in   on   a   moun - tain   so   high

. Goin' to build me log cabin on a mountain so high
So I can see Willie as he goes on by.

. Oh, the coo coo is a pretty bird; she wobbles as she flies.
She never hollers "coo coo" till the fourth day July.

. I've played cards in England, I've played cards in Spain;
I'll bet you ten dollars I beat you next game.

4. Jack of Diamonds, Jack of Diamonds, I've known you from old;
Now you rob my poor pockets of my silver and my gold.

5. I've played cards in England, I've played cards in Spain;
I'll bet you ten dollars I beat you this game.

6. Oh, the coo coo is a pretty bird; she wobbles as she flies.
She never hollers "coo coo" till the fourth day July.

Roy Acuff has his "Wabash Cannonball," Bill Monroe his "Uncle Pen"; similarly, this man had his "Coo Coo Bird." When he started the gentle rolling of his fingers across the strings of his banjo and picked out the familiar notes of this song, audiences knew they were about to hear Tom Clarence Ashley.

"The Coo Coo Bird" was certainly among Tom Ashley's favorites, as those with whom he played music know. One of them, Clint Howard, comments, "He felt like that was his trademark. That was the one that put him back in music in the sixties, as far as he was concerned. Every new town we went to, he would always play that song first, on the first show." Doc Watson, now nationally known in his own right, concurs. "'The Coo Coo Bird' was by far Clarence's favorite." Although this song (as Ashley suggests) is a medley of "traveling stanzas" from other ballads and folksongs, the unified sentiments make all the verses seem appropriate. It was perhaps the pervasive sense of sadness, loss, and defeat—but at the same time of love, beauty, and hope—that made the verses "sound to suit" Ashley.

After Folkways Records brought "The Coo Coo Bird" out of

Some of Tom's associates early in his career: the Greer Sisters, G. B. Grayson, and Henry Whitter (standing).

"Now I certainly don't want you to expect too much from me. I'm very backwoodsy, as you can readily see — uneducated — and I know a few songs in the old tradition."

Tom Ashley and Tex Isley at the East Tennessee State University Folk Festival in 1966.

Tom and Hettie with their daughter Eva.

Byrd Moore and His Hot Shots: Byrd Moore, Clarence Greene,
Tom Ashley.

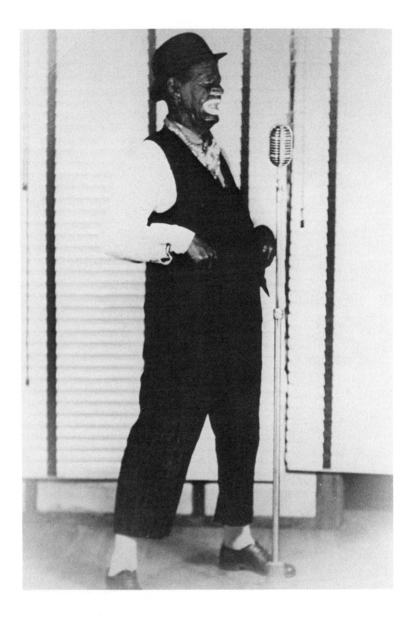

"I'm from the hills and mountains of East Tennessee. I'm a back-woodsman. The farther back you get, the deeper the woods, and I live in the last house."

Tom as "Rastus."

Tom Ashley performing.

"A lot of people in the city are playing old-time music these days. But country people play their feeling and feel their playing. That's the big difference."

Tom.

history and back into life, various bluegrass and old-time musicians tried to emulate the sounds Ashley was able to create; but as Ashley aptly put it, "They don't hardly get my version exactly." In fact, according to Tex Isley, Ashley's back-up man during the later years, only Doc Watson and he were ever able even to play the guitar accompaniment for this particular song to Ashley's satisfaction.

One difference Tom noticed between his version and others was in the tuning. "It's been modernized like many an old tune, but if my hearing is correct, I don't think they play it in a minor key." And on another occasion he said, "With modern people it's one tuning and you've got it, but in the old days we had special different tunings." With "The Coo Coo Bird" the "special different tuning" he used is often referred to as a G-modal tuning (d′ c′ g d g′);* Tom had another name for it. "I'll tell you from the beginning, I don't tune a banjer like the modern banjo pickers tunes their banjos. I tune in what I call the old-timey 'sawmill' tuning. I'm in a minor key of some kind — I don't know what. I don't write no music, although I've put some old songs together; but I didn't write the music, I just fixed the tunes to sound to suit myself."

How Ashley came to name his tuning "sawmill" is an interesting story. Fred Price, a neighbor and member of one of Tom's bands during the sixties, is one of those who tell it.

> He said that they went to a fiddlers' convention. Tom said they was a-tuning up and they was a-tuning maybe up in A or something and one of the boys in another band come by and said, "Boys, you're getting her up now in sawmill key, ain't you?" He said, "Yes, we're getting her up now in sawmill key; we're gonna saw you-uns right out of it tonight." And when they got through playing, why, they'd won first prize on everything. They'd beat 'em all. He often used that expression about "sawmill tuning."

Although Tom had his own particular style in playing the banjo, in general the style he used is called "frailing"; Ashley used the term "clawhammer." Basically, frailing is striking down on

---

*The letter notations of banjo and guitar tunings begin with the bottom string as the instrument is held by the musician. Octaves are differentiated in the following manner: pitches below middle c are capital letters, those above are lower case, and the distance is indicated by primes; e. g., F′ is in the second octave below middle c, F is just below, f is just above, and f′ is in the second octave above.

the strings with the fingernails. Ashley struck the first (bottom) and second strings with his middle finger and the third and fourth strings with his index finger. His style in "The Coo Coo Bird," and that which he used most of the time, was primarily single-note picking. As Richard Blaustein, a folklorist at East Tennessee State University, observes, Ashley didn't do any "drop-thumbing" or "double-thumbing" in "The Coo Coo Bird"; that is, he did not place his thumb below the drone string onto the four other strings to produce additional notes. He did use drop-thumbing, however, in certain other songs — for example, "Little Sadie." Another stylistic feature used in "The Coo Coo Bird" and typical of Ashley's playing style is the use of a "brush." He would pick a few licks with his thumb and finger, and then he would "brush it off" with all of his fingers. "I've seen him do that very often," says Fred Price; "before he would start a tune he'd usually do that a lot of times." Whether it was because other banjo players were unable to match his accuracy, speed, and smoothness, or to pick up on his peculiar timing, or because they failed to match his style or to reproduce the feeling of the piece, after Tom Ashley "The Coo Coo Bird" never soared quite as high again.

Although Thomas Clarence Ashley gained most of his renown as a folk musician after he had reached sixty-five years of age, singing songs like "The Coo Coo Bird," he had gained a measure of popularity as a recording personality more than thirty years earlier (both singly and as a member of bands such as Byrd Moore and His Hot Shots, the Carolina Tar Heels, and the Blue Ridge Mountain Entertainers). Even before that, as a very young man, he was recognized as a talented entertainer in medicine shows and as a skillful local professional musician. Tom began his musical career singing the old ballads and other folksongs he had learned as a boy. He also ended his career singing these songs, and as one gathers from his comments in later years, he had a strong commitment to the old folksongs because he felt they were a vital part of his heritage.

October 1929 had a profound impact on Tom Ashley as well as on the nation. Six days before the stock market crash on Wall Street, Tom Ashley recorded "The Coo Coo Bird" for Columbia Records (Co 15489), a significant recording individually and, according to some students of folk music, also an important one (through its rediscovery) in that period of renewed interest in folk music during the late 1950s and early 1960s.

When Ashley recorded "The Coo Coo Bird" in 1929, he was thirty-four years old. He had grown up and lived in an atmosphere of traditional music that had traveled across the Atlantic from the British Isles. The Ashley family, "part Dutch," as Tom's daughter Eva Moore says, left Ireland and arrived in the United States in the 1690s. Part of the family remained in East Virginia and part went on west to North Carolina. It was in Ashe County, soon after the Civil War, that Enoch Ashley (son of Tom's great-grandfather Joe Ashley) was married to Tas Robinson's daughter Martha (Mat or Maddy). The young couple frequently sang old ballads, and their three daughters came to love the old songs as did their parents. One of the daughters, Rosie Belle, developed a good singing voice and was often asked to sing in churches; the two older girls, Ira (pronounced Arey) and Daisy, were instrumentalists.

The family did not remain in North Carolina, however; Tom said, "My people left Ashe County, North Carolina, about 1892, and went to Bristol where my mama and daddy were married." The marriage took place in 1894, against the wishes of Rosie Belle's parents. The groom, known as One-Eyed Fiddling George McCurry, had a bar in Bristol. The two were together only for about a year, because McCurry had another wife and he was asked to move. Rosie Belle returned home to her parents; and about two weeks later, on 29 September 1895, in Bristol, Virginia, she gave birth to a son, Clarence Earl McCurry. In a matter of months Enoch Ashley left Bristol and took his family back to Ashe County; they soon moved again, to Shouns, Tennessee, in Johnson County, where they stayed. Enoch took a job at a lumberyard and began a boarding house at Shouns.

Although Rosie Belle named her son Clarence Earl McCurry, no one knew him by that name. The lively and playful young boy was nicknamed by his grandfather and the boarders "Tommy Tiddy Waddy." As Clarence grew older the "Tiddy Waddy" was dropped, but "Tommy" stuck; and because he was reared by his grandparents, "Ashley" became the surname he used. Eventually he dropped the "Earl" and used "Thomas Clarence," signing as either Thomas C. Ashley or Tom C. Ashley. In Johnson County, however, he was known simply as Tom Ashley. Some people have believed that Tom Ashley and Clarence Ashley were two different men, partly because he recorded under both names. Adding to this confusion is the use on record labels of various combinations of his given names, as well as the use of pseudonyms Oscar Brown and Tom Hutchinson.

It was not until Tom Ashley was well into adulthood that he saw his father for the first time. All his life, he had wondered where his father was, what he was like; and he had hoped that some day he would be able to meet him. That day came. As Eva tells the story, Tom was with the medicine show in Greeneville, Tennessee, at the time.

> Daddy was sitting on the porch of an evening with the man who ran the hotel where he was staying. When he found out the man was a McCurry, he asked him if he knew Fiddling One-Eyed George, and the man said that he was his brother. Daddy asked if he was living, and the man said he was, and he agreed to take Daddy over there the following Sunday to see him. He got in touch with George Mc-Curry, then, but he didn't tell him who it was that he was bringing with him. When they got there on Sunday, Daddy's father was sitting across a little branch under a big oak tree, as Daddy told it; and as Daddy and his uncle were crossing the little bridge over the branch he came and grabbed Daddy and said to him, "How in the hell can a man get so old in thirty-nine years?" He recognized him immediately, and he knew exactly how old Daddy was. He hadn't known if he was a boy or girl till then.

As Tom's son JD tells the story, it is slightly different. McCurry's half-sister invited Ashley and the Doc of the medicine show out to her home for dinner. They accepted the invitation, and when they arrived at her house, McCurry was there. The first words McCurry spoke to his son were, "My God, how can a man get that ugly in thirty-nine years!" At any rate, Tom and his father became friends after that meeting, even though there were harsh feelings toward McCurry among part of the Ashley family; and McCurry became "Granddaddy" to Eva and JD.

Tom attended school only five years. The same year he dropped out of school, his mother married a man by the name of Tom Walsh. Tom and his stepfather got along well together, but Ashley continued to live with his grandparents.

Tom got his first banjo when he was eight. As Karl Dallas

learned from an interview with Ashley in 1966, Tom's grandfather brought a banjo "home when he was given it as a free gift
with a sack of peanuts." Tom himself commented: "I started
fooling with an old banjer at about eight years old. I had two
aunts was good banjer pickers, and my mother—they was my
mother's two sisters—my mother was a fine singer. I used to fool
with their old banjer and messed around a-listening at them
play. I had one aunt that was just a wizard on the banjer, and the
other one played fairly well." Although Aunt Ira and Aunt Daisy
both instructed Tom on the instrument, Ralph Rinzler (a man
professionally devoted to folk music and the one principally responsible for what is generally known about Tom Ashley) suggests that rather than adopting Aunt Ira's style of picking up on
the thumb-string, Tom followed Aunt Daisy's style, which was
similar to that of others in the area. According to Eva, Tom
talked more of learning from Aunt Ira—by sitting on the floor
and listening to her music.

A few years after he got his first banjo, when he was about
twelve, Tom obtained a guitar and subsequently broadened his
instrumental skill. (The guitar that Tom played for almost half a
century, however, was one he bought in the twenties in Boise,
Idaho, while on a trip with his "musicianer" buddies, which took
him as far west as Oregon and Washington, playing mostly at
dances.)

Tom bought a homemade banjo, shortly after he was married,
from a man in West Jefferson, North Carolina (Tom's widow,
Hettie, remembered his name—Dryce Bare [?]—but did not recall the spelling). Later he bought another banjo, a small one,
from a man who lived at Cove Creek, North Carolina. In the
1960s Tom bought a Gibson Mastertone from a pawnshop in
North Carolina; this was the banjo that old-time musician
Charlie Poole had played until his death in 1931. The history of
this banjo was a source of pleasure to Tom as long as he lived,
and he kept a 1927 photograph showing Poole with the Gibson
in his lap. The story is told that when Tom showed the newly acquired banjo to the more practical Hettie, she was upset at the
cost. Ashley told her it was worth much more than he had paid
for it, but she did not waver in her opposition. Tom then arranged with JD's wife, Hazel, for her to offer him twice what it
cost him and to beg him to sell it to her for her son, Joe Dean,

who was showing an interest in playing music. The plan was carried out on the night when Hazel came to visit, and it worked well: Hettie refused to let Tom sell the banjo. (Joe Dean has this instrument now, as well as another smaller one that Tom bought at a little store in Trade, Tennessee.) There were long periods of time in Tom's life when he did not own a banjo, however; in fact, on many of his early records Tom is heard playing a borrowed instrument. Sometimes he even went to contests without an instrument; for example, Clint Howard tells of one occasion when Tom commandeered a banjo. As the story runs, Ashley watched all the competitors come on and go off the stage until he spotted a really fine banjo. Ashley went backstage and asked to borrow it long enough to enter the contest. The owner refused, saying he had enough competition without lending his instrument to someone else. Ashley told him that it was a "mighty fine banjo" and asked if he could just look at it for a minute. The man handed Ashley the banjo, and Ashley, with a grin on his face, ran onto the stage, started playing, and won first place in the contest.

It is only natural that Tom responded to music early in his life since his family on both sides enjoyed music. Tom said that everyone in his family played an instrument, from his great-grandmother on down, and according to Tom, although many people sang in his "boyhood days, they wasn't too many people who played music." Apparently his family was a little uncommon in this respect. "Well, they's a few people who played music, but they wasn't at every house like they are now." Frequently the Ashleys invited the neighbors in for an evening of music-making; and he also had occasion to use his musical talent at social gatherings, because the people of Mountain City and Shouns — like those of most rural areas of the United States — combined their work and fun. "I used to like to go to the corn shuckings, and I'd sing and dance to get my supper, you know. They always had something good to eat." He even commonly called many of his old songs "lassy-making tunes," from times songs were sung as people got together to make molasses. These musical activities at home and in the community encouraged Tom to continue playing and singing, learning all the old songs he could.

In 1911, at the age of sixteen and with Enoch Ashley's permission, Tom joined a medicine show that had camped at Mountain

City. The Doc, publicized as a full-blooded Indian, was known as White Cloud; with him were various musicians who also performed as comedians. It was Doc White Cloud's Medicine Show that gave Tom his start as a professional musician, a career that, with the exception of a seventeen-year lapse, would last until his death fifty-five years later.

The medicine show, as Eva describes it, "would pick up different ones for a few days at a time, or a month or two at a time." Tom began as one of these "different ones." Generally in the summer the group would consist of between three and six members, and they would play outside on a portable stage. In the winter they played inside, often at tobacco warehouses, in Greeneville, Morristown, Knoxville (Tennessee), and Abingdon (Virginia); then the group was reduced in number. As Tom once said, "Old Doc cut them down to one man — me — in wintertime." Eva adds that, during her father's more than thirty years with the show, it was "the bigger part of the time just Daddy and Doc." The circuit not only covered the area of East Tennessee and Southwest Virginia but also extended sometimes into West Virginia and North Carolina. Hettie suggested that the extent and duration of the circuit was determined greatly by the weather; nevertheless, Tom returned home for a few days every week or two when possible.

White Cloud's show, like most of the others, stopped in rural communities and stayed as long as the towns or villages could support it. The Doc sold tonic, salve, soap, and candy. He regularly set up his show near a fair, a carnival, or a tobacco or cattle sale, where an audience could wander by from other attractions. Since there were no seats, the audience generally stood around the platform, which was attached to a covered wagon. The performances consisted of playing and singing, telling jokes, and sometimes presenting comic skits such as the now outdated (but then widely accepted) blackface routine known usually as "Rastus." "Tommy Tiddy Waddy" became Rastus. Quick with a quip and easily outthinking a straight man he gave a performance extremely popular on the medicine show circuit.

After the entertainment had attracted the crowd, the Doc would begin his sales talk. He was an old-fashioned orator. He told tear-jerking stories about how they had found a little baby whose parents had been killed and who had consequently gone for days without any nourishment. When they found the child, the Doc would say, it was so weak that it was barely alive; however, after only a few days on his medicine, it became lively and healthy again. Another of Doc's tales described a small girl whose entire body had become infested with worms but who was cured within days by the elixir. This medicine, which sold for about a dollar for a half-pint bottle, was sometimes reportedly nothing more than colored water; but Eva remembers helping gather wild cherries, mullein, and wild horehound for the mixture. It was supposed to heal everything from headaches to gout. Doc's candy sold for ten cents a box.

Prior to coming out on the stage, White Cloud rubbed a solution on his hands that caused his eyes to burn and to water when he put his hands near his face. As he told his stories, he rubbed his eyes, and the tears flowed. By the time he finished two or three stories, many in the audience as well would be in tears. Anyone who wanted a bottle of his medicine held up his hand; then the entertainers, including Ashley, would go out into the audience, distribute the medicine, and collect the money. In the meantime, Doc continued to narrate his sad tales, rub his eyes, and wipe the tears. At the end of the show, Doc and the entertainers met in the wagon to count the take for the night.

In his early days as a musician with the show, Tom traveled in a wagon with the equipment, while the Doc rode in a fashionable buggy. In addition to his duties as singer, comedian, banjoist, guitarist, and salesman, Tom was also responsible for hauling water and feeding the horses. Later on, Tom, the rest of the troupe, and the equipment moved from place to place in trucks and a house trailer.

Although ownership of the medicine show changed several times during the thirty years Tom was with it, the only two docs that the people of Johnson County can generally remember are Doc White Cloud and Doc Hauer from Knoxville. Eva remembers a few details regarding the latter. "He was part German . . . an odd man, actually; I mean, he didn't believe in anything much. He was a big, broad-built man, slightly older than Daddy." One incident that occurred when Tom was with Doc Hauer has become one of Eva's favorite anecdotes. "Daddy was a-playing with the medicine show in Greeneville—could possibly have been Knoxville—and Doc Hauer came out and told him one day that he had this boy that wanted to play with them some — he might have played some before but not out very much." The young man was Roy Acuff, later to gain fame with the Grand Ole Opry. Ralph Rinzler describes the incident in much the same way. "Tom had not been with Doc Hower long before a young boy was brought into the troupe and the Doc asked Tom to teach him the ropes — songs, skits, jokes and all. The two boys got on well together, for the new fellow had a fine voice and learned tunes quickly; and so Tom and Roy Acuff met as youngsters and have remained friends for life." Apparently both descriptions of the incident are from Tom's point of view, and both may even reflect the manner in which he told the story himself. "Just before one summer the Doc told me he had a neighbor boy who could sing a little and play a little and said he'd like to take him along. He asked if I'd train him, and I said I would. That boy stayed with us two summers and I taught him some songs, and after that he went off on his own and did right well. He was Roy Acuff." On another occasion Tom said, "Roy wanted to learn the worst of any young man I ever saw." Elizabeth Schlappi, a biographer of Roy Acuff, gives another view. "According to Roy's recollection, when he joined the medicine show in the summer of 1932 [when Roy would have been 27 and Tom 36] besides Doc Hauer . . . there was Jake Tindell. Jake was a veteran of many summers with the Doc and he showed Roy the ropes. Later that summer they were joined by a man they called Tom Ashley." Acuff writes in a letter dated 23 December 1974:

> Dr. Hauer employed Tom Ashley, Jake Tindell and me to go with him during the summer to entertain on his medicine show. I suppose I was the least experienced of the three, but not one of them taught me fiddling or singing. Tom Ashley played the guitar, black-face comedy and sang his songs; Jake Tindell played the guitar, black-face comedy and sang his songs; and I played the fiddle and sang my songs. It was a variety show and each of us did a separate act in his own individual style of entertainment. Dr. Hauer was emcee of the show.
>
> In late years, I have performed one of Tom Ashley's songs, "The Greenback Dollar," which he used on the show. Tom and I were always good friends. In fact, Dr. Hauer, Tom Ashley, Jake Tindell and I remained friends down through the years. I learned a lot from all of them, and hopefully they picked up something entertaining from me.

Since Ashley had been associated with the medicine show for more than twenty years when Acuff began, perhaps Tom was in Shouns at the particular time Acuff first arrived on the scene; not enough information is available, however, about the show, its owners, members, or schedules to reconcile the apparent discrepancy in the accounts of the Ashley/Acuff relationship. The medicine show did not provide the income or the opportunity for either man to become wealthy; Tom at the time was earning thirty-five dollars a week and Acuff was taken on at twenty dollars.

During the part of the year when he was not with the Doc, Tom's activities included organizing a band to play wherever there was the possibility of making a few dollars. One of the bands he organized was a brass band (Tom played trombone). He and four other musicians from Johnson County gave shows for which they charged, and they even paid a music instructor to come to Shouns School to give them lessons. They also earned enough to pay for their uniforms and instruments, and they had a little cash left over. Nevertheless, during his first years with the medicine show Ashley could not earn a living by playing music; consequently he took almost any job he could find.

While working for the J. Walter Wright Lumber Company in Shouns, Tennessee, Tom became friends with a man named Osborne from Ashe County, North Carolina. Osborne introduced Tom to his sister Hettie; a year or so later, on 19 July 1914, Tom married her. Tom was only three years older than his pretty fifteen-year-old bride and didn't have much with which to make a start; yet he managed to rent a small tract of land in Shouns. There Tom and Hettie began their fifty-three-year marriage.

In 1915 their first child, Frank, was stillborn; but only eleven months later a healthy son, Ralph Earl, was born. This child died at the age of fifteen months from "brain fever" when he was teething, and the young couple was especially grieved: "it just about killed them." Eva was born in 1919, JD in 1921. During World War I Tom was turned down for service in the armed forces because of his poor vision. He "went to have his eyes straightened," but although the operation (performed in a doctor's office with no anesthesia) improved his vision, it was insufficient to qualify him in the eyes of the military.

During the early years of the marriage, with Tom working

away from home much of the time, it became Hettie's responsibility to care for the farm and the children. They lived modestly but never in want. They had vegetables from Hettie's garden, fresh in the summer and canned in the winter; they had a cow for milk and chickens for eggs and meat. The family moved often in the twenties and thirties; Eva recalls living in at least five different communities in West Virginia during those years: Cherokee, Indian Ridge, Fair Day, Berwind, and Caretta. In Caretta Tom worked at a logging camp, but during most of the time the family spent in West Virginia, he worked in the mines. Still, Shouns was always home.

When there was no better way to earn a little cash, Ashley went "busting," also known as "ballying"—performing at land sales, at fairs, at carnivals, at the mines on payday, at cattle sales, at tobacco auctions, or occasionally on a city street corner. Traveling as he did, Tom had the opportunity to meet many of the best musicians of quite a sizable area; and with one of these musicians, blind fiddler George Banman Grayson from Laurel Bloomery, Tennessee, he frequently went busting in the coalfields. There on Fridays, he and Grayson would attract a large group of appreciative listeners who would pitch in a little money to hear the old mountain songs that they enjoyed.

About 1917 or 1918, when these two men, along with their occasional companion Ted Bear, were playing a carnival in Saltville, Virginia, they met Hobart Smith, a local banjoist and fiddler. Before a week passed, many songs had been exchanged among them. Tom told Ralph Rinzler years later that the local ballad "Claude Allen" (Laws E 6) was one of the songs he had taught Smith, who in turn had recorded it for Alan Lomax in 1942. (Lomax called Ashley on several occasions but never visited or recorded him, although he did adapt "The Coo Coo Bird" for his *Folk Songs of North America*.)

The first group with a professional name that Ashley performed with, Eva says, was in West Virginia; it was called, appropriately, the West Virginia Hotfoots. "The Bell boys played with him, Dwight and Dewey Bell" from Wilkes County, North Carolina. "He had a radio program every Saturday at Emory, Virginia, right after that station got started, with the Cook sisters and the Greer sisters—they were both from North Carolina—first one and then the other would come." Tom played guitar and sang lead tenor, while the ladies provided harmony (soprano and bass) and played fiddle and mandolin. Mac Wiseman was another musician who played radio programs and "booking dates" with Tom. In addition to the Emory show, Ashley had two other regular radio programs, on WOPI and WFHG in Bristol, and he played as a guest on many other programs and stations.

Tom was a professional musician, but he also played for pleasure, which included competing. At least as early as May 1925 he played in a fiddlers' convention in Mountain City, and he continued to enjoy these events as long as he lived — and to win. Eva recalls: "One time they were having a fiddlers' convention in Mountain City and they called and told him they wanted him to come up there that night and play in the contest. He first told them he couldn't come, that he had no band together. They wanted him to come on anyway; so me, and him, and my brother JD went — and not boasting, but we got all three of the first prizes. JD and Daddy played the guitars, and I sung."

At another fiddlers' contest in 1925, at Boone, North Carolina, he met Dock Walsh; this meeting led to Tom's association with the Carolina Tar Heels, a group originally consisting of two men, Dock Walsh and Gwen Foster. The Tar Heels had already made five records in 1927 before Tom recorded with them in 1928 in Atlanta and 1929 in Camden, New Jersey. In these two sessions Dock played banjo and shared with Tom the vocal lead; Tom played guitar; and Garley Foster (of no kin to Gwen, according to folklorist Archie Green) played harmonica and guitar. Tom traveled for some time with the Carolina Tar Heels. About their "playing booking dates," Eva says, "when Garley couldn't go, Gwen went; and when Gwen couldn't go, Garley went." She also recalls references to the discomfort of long, slow recording trips and of traveling in cars packed with men and instruments. Association with the Carolina Tar Heels contributed significantly not just to Tom's profession in general but to his career as a traditional performer as well. Ralph Rinzler observes:

> Although they performed more than a few tunes which are of little interest to the folklorist . . . , they had their own interesting versions of several old standbys (i.e., "Rude and Rambling Man", "The Old Gray Goose", "My Home's Across the Blue Ridge Mountains").
> . . . Some of Tom's finest recordings are the duets with Gwen Foster on Vocalion in the early '30s. . . . Here the perfect blending

of voice and harmonica is unique among the varied sounds to be heard in recorded American traditional music.

It was in February 1928, however — before Tom recorded with the Tar Heels — that he apparently made his first record (with Dwight Bell on banjo): a ballad, "Four Nights Experience" (Child 274), and a comic popular song, "You're a Little Too Small" (which was recorded again eight months later with the Tar Heels). Even earlier than 1928, Tom had made the long trip to New York to record. The song he took, ready after months of hard work researching, composing, even waking Hettie in the middle of the night to write verses down, was a ballad about the murder of "little Marion Parker," which took place in Los Angeles in 1927. The recording company, Eva says, refused to proceed without his obtaining a written release from the girl's parents, however, and Tom rejected the idea of bothering them at that time. He returned home disappointed. When a ballad about the murder did come out later (Blind Andy Jenkins recorded his famous version in Memphis in February 1928), Tom felt somewhat cheated. In 1929, as a member of Byrd Moore and His Hot Shots, Tom recorded for Columbia (Moore on banjo and lead guitar, Clarence Greene on fiddle and guitar, and Ashley on banjo and guitar). This trio had been together on the medicine show circuit, and Ashley had also traveled a great deal to booking dates with Moore, along with Roy Dowell and young JD. It was after this session that Ashley volunteered, according to Ralph Rinzler, some "lassy-making tunes," one of which was the now classic "Coo Coo Bird"; others were "Dark Holler Blues" (later recorded with Gwen Foster on Vocalion under the title "East Virginia Blues"), "Poor Omie" (Laws F 4), and "Little Sadie" (Laws I 8). The "lassy-making tunes" caught the fancy of the recording company, which later wired Tom to record more of them, and in Atlanta during April of the following year Tom recorded a group of songs from which were issued "The House Carpenter" (Child 243) and "Old John Hardy" (Laws I 2).

Tom continued to record with his friends in various combinations. One important band, the Blue Ridge Mountain Entertainers, featured Tom on the guitar, Clarence Greene on the fiddle, Gwen Foster on the harmonica, Will Abernathy on the autoharp and harmonica, and Walter Davis on lead guitar. A few of this band's titles are "I Have No Loving Mother Now," "Bring Me a Leaf from the Sea," "Washington and Lee Swing," "Goodnight Waltz," "Honeysuckle Rag," and "Cincinnati Breakdown." Particularly interesting is "Over at Tom's House," which begins:

> TOM: Hey, hey—I sort o' got the blues. Hettie, give me that old guitar over here—I believe I'll play a little tune.
> [Tom plays guitar and sings] "Oh, they ain't no use for me hanging 'round this town."
> [Knocking sounds]
> Come in, come in—why, it's ol' Gwen Foster.
> [Sound of barking dog]
> GWEN: Hello, Tom.
> TOM: Hettie, why don't you put that dog out o' here? Gwen, come in and have a seat. Where've you been so long?
> GWEN: I've been down to Sam Hanlin's Dance Hall. Say, Tom, they're gonna have a dance down there Saturday night.
> TOM: Is that right? Well, we'll go down, won't we?
> GWEN: Yeah boy.
> TOM: Come over to go with us to the fiddlers' contest tomorrow night?
> GWEN: Yeah.
> TOM: Well, you got your harp and guitar?
> GWEN: Oh, yeah.
> TOM: How 'bout doin' a little number for my wife and babies, then?
> [Gwen plays harmonica with guitar—more knocking sounds]
> TOM: Come in. Why, it's ol' Clarence Greene. Come in, Clarence.
> CLARENCE: Hello, Tom. Hello, Gwen.
> [Sound of barking dog]
> TOM: Hettie, why don't you get that ol' dog out o' here?
> "HETTIE": [Falsetto] Come out of here, George.
> TOM: Clarence, where you been?
> CLARENCE: I been down to Elizabethton, Tennessee, over in Cat Island with ol' Hog Moore on a home-brew party.
> TOM: Been havin' a big ol' time, I reckon.
> CLARENCE: Drinkin' lots o' liquor.

The skit, which projects and perpetuates the image of the corn-drinking, music-making hillbilly, was recorded on 1 December 1931 by the American Record Corporation and released on the Conqueror label along with "The Fiddler's Contest," which briefly presents each man playing his specialty and then the whole group playing in the supposed band contest. Both

"Over at Tom's House" and "The Fiddler's Contest" offer the modern Ashley fan a delightful experience and provide at least a glimpse of Tom's stage wit. November 30 and the next two days were busy for Tom; he and other members of the Entertainers recorded some fifteen songs that were released on seven different labels. The significance of these records is increased by the fact that they were widely distributed through Sears' mail-order service. In September 1933 Tom recorded again with one of the Entertainers, Gwen Foster.

At this time Tom considered as home a seven-acre farm that he had bought in 1930; he rented out the fields, lived in the farmhouse, and continued to travel with Doc Hauer on the medicine show circuit. After a recording career of some six years, his brief fame and satisfaction in being a recording artist came to an end—for a time, anyway. For this decline there may be several reasons. One, suggested by his son JD, is that Tom Ashley was the kind of man who did not take orders from anyone easily. He did not like the idea of being told what to do by the recording companies; so he quit. Another possible explanation relates to the Great Depression. Recording companies, like most other businesses, were operating under strained financial circumstances; they were consequently limited in the number of recordings they could produce. Some companies were also unjust in compensating their artists; in some of Ashley's personal correspondence, for example, there are references to signatures not his own that relinquish his royalties for a dollar, as well as references to royalties never received. Tom, along with many other artists, was forced to turn to means other than recording for making a living.

The depression years of the thirties were difficult for almost everyone, including the Ashleys. Since people were barely able to provide food for their families, almost no one had money to spend for entertainment. Nevertheless, when Tom discontinued his extended musical tours, it was for domestic reasons as well as national economic ones. JD became extremely ill—hemorrhaging internally—when Tom was with the medicine show in Bluefield, West Virginia. The family "notified the law" to find Tom, who by chance was already on his way home; and even though JD recovered, Eva says her father "didn't go back" ever after that (Rinzler dates the cessation of Ashley's medicine show activity in 1943, some ten years after JD's critical illness). Later, Tom gave a brief description of yet further reasons for the decline in his career.

> Now, I never offered to sing a song, to play a tune or nothing for thirty year, when the rock 'n' roll come along and pushed me out, and I thought I was out for good. Now I'm a-telling you. And they're good modern musicians—now we've got some good musicians —don't you understand me to say I'm a-criticizing anybody. Some of these bluegrass players is out of this world. But I never did take up with that, you see. Well, I didn't think that they'd ever let me even go in a building where they was having a show, a music show— because I thought I was so far out of the picture. And I was.

When Ashley's principal source of income no longer existed, he returned to West Virginia, where he again found work in the coal mines. When he had saved enough money to send for his family, Hettie closed up the house at Shouns and joined him. Then came another stroke of hard luck—the mines closed down only three days after Hettie arrived. Hettie had an ample supply of preserved food back at Shouns, but the problem for the Ashleys was that they had no money to get back to Tennessee. It was eight months before Tom had enough money for travel, earned largely by playing at dances that were occasionally held in the area. Once home, Ashley finally managed to secure a job; he hauled various commodities for the federal government from Johnson City to Mountain City, Tennessee, where they were distributed among the people of Johnson County. These hard years profoundly affected Ashley, even politically; he voted for a Democrat, although he had been a lifelong Republican.

In 1937 he got a peddler's license and bought two trucks which he and JD used to haul coal, furniture, beans, lime, and anything else they could contract for. He raised tobacco and cattle, and worked at sawmills and lumberyards. Since he had a reputation of being especially good at ricking lumber for air-drying, he often got a job ricking when as many as twenty others were waiting in line ahead of him. Tom also continued to farm, and in 1941 he sold his seven acres and bought another farm at Shouns, which he expanded to as much as eighty acres at one time and where his widow Hettie lived until she died in March 1975.

In the early forties things began to look brighter economically, and musicians began to return to their professions; people could again afford the entertainment that these singers and players provided. Charlie Monroe hired Ashley as a blackface comedian for his group, known as the "Kentucky Pardners." Thus he came to know a fellow Pardner, Lester Flatt from Overton County, Tennessee, whose name later became synonymous with bluegrass music. Another musician Ashley became acquainted with during this time was Tex Isley from Reidsville, North Carolina, who in later years toured and recorded with Tom. He also met up with the Stanley Brothers, who were working out of Bristol. Tom kept reasonably busy with the Pardners or the Stanley Brothers; it was not uncommon for one of them to call on a Friday morning, for example, and ask him to meet them in North Carolina the next night for a booking—and Tom would go.

The forties also had their black clouds for Tom. An accident proved a pivotal point in Ashley's musical career. He cut his left index finger at the lumberyard, and it stiffened as it healed. Thinking that he could no longer play, he put away his banjo and guitar. He played no instruments and he sang no songs, except for an occasional humorous song, such as "Fifty Cents," as part of his blackface act. But he did not forget the old songs. In the fifties he began to teach his songs to his grandson Tommy Moore, who had started taking piano lessons; and soon after, Tom was teaching the old music to his neighbors Clint Howard, who played the guitar, and Fred Price, who played the fiddle. As their "coach" he took them to compete at fiddlers' conventions where he could also see his old cronies, as he called them, and talk about music and old times. It is fortunate that Tom kept up this activity, for had it not been for a chance meeting in April 1960 with Ralph Rinzler at the Old Time Fiddlers Convention at Union Grove, North Carolina, thousands of people who later thrilled to Ashley's banjo playing, singing, and witticisms would probably never have heard him in person. According to Tom's daughter, Rinzler happened to pass Ashley's group tuning up; he stopped and struck up a conversation with Ashley. Learning only Tom's last name, Rinzler asked if he knew Clarence Ashley. Tom answered that he thought he had heard of him but was not quite certain. Rinzler talked about how much he liked the early recording of "The Coo Coo Bird" and told about writing letters and sending telegrams to Clarence Ashley at Mountain City only to have them returned "addressee unknown." Ashley identified himself and agreed to sing one song: "Put My Little Shoes Away," which Rinzler taped.

After writing and calling him many times, Rinzler and Eugene Earle visited Ashley's home in September 1960 in order to record him. Still, Ashley would only sing, not play, on that recording for Folkways. After Rinzler returned to New York, he mailed Tom a banjo and suggested that he keep it awhile and practice up again. Rinzler recounts the effect.

> When he learned that his old recordings of the "Coo-Coo Bird", "The House Carpenter", "Peg and Awl", and "The Farmland Blues" [this song was recorded by The Carolina Tar Heels without Tom] had been reissued by Folkways and that there was an interest in old time music in the cities, he finally decided to pick up his banjo and start playing again.

It was several years after that, however, before Tom would even tune his favorite instrument, the guitar. He did not play the guitar, for example, on the 1961 and 1962 LPs, and his guitar playing on private tapes of the mid-sixties is not polished. He does, however, play second guitar well on the 1966 LP, and he gave really fine guitar performances just prior to his death. It was the banjo, however, that Tom used principally in the very active musical career that he resumed after the meeting with Rinzler.

In March 1961 the Friends of Old-Time Music (later the Friends of Traditional Music, Inc.) sponsored Tom and his group in a concert at a public school in Greenwich Village in New York City. This group included Doc Watson. Following this successful concert they were invited to perform at the University of Chicago Folk Festival in February 1962. Ashley on the banjo and Doc on the guitar, playing their rendition of "The Coo Coo Bird," greatly moved the Chicago audience. In the following months the performances of this same group included concerts on the campuses of the University of California at Los Angeles and the University of Wisconsin, and an engagement for three weeks with Jean Ritchie, the first lady of Appalachian folksong, at the Ash Grove, a coffeehouse in Los Angeles prominent in folk-music circles.

Another pinnacle in Tom's career, as Ralph Rinzler notes, came on 21 December 1962: Ashley's group appeared at Carnegie Hall. "Their appearance at Carnegie Hall on Pete Seeger's Christmas Concert, December 21, 1962, seemed to complete the cycle distinguishing them as the only folk counterpart of the New Lost City Ramblers . . . to have established itself in the field of urban performing." When Tom was asked after this concert whether he ever realized back in his old medicine-show days that he would make it to Carnegie Hall, he characteristically replied with a grin, "Back then, I didn't know there was such a place."

The following year saw Tom Ashley and his group again at the annual University of Chicago Folk Festival and at other festivals: at UCLA and Monterey, California; at Newport, Rhode Island (recorded by Vanguard); and at Philadelphia. Various workshops at these festivals both in banjo and in gospel and religious music drew on his talent and experience. He also continued his participation in fiddlers' conventions, and in 1964 he won blue and red ribbons in guitar at the Fortieth Annual Fiddlers Convention World Championship at Union Grove. The following year at Union Grove the audience responded with a standing ovation to his unaccompanied singing of an old hymn. The year 1965 brought more blue ribbons, more festivals, and more concerts, such as the series in American Folk Music at the Tyrone Guthrie Theater in Minneapolis. By spring 1966 he had also made an educational television film, a "Voice of America" broadcast, and a promotional program for the Social Security Administration; then, at the peak of this crescendo, came a long-wished-for opportunity, a trip to England. Made with Tex Isley, the tour included eighteen engagements from London to Cornwall. Tom's pleasure in having made the tour is implicit in a comment made the following fall when he and Isley performed at the East Tennessee State University Folk Festival.

Well, the gentleman said something about us being over in England. I'd sort of like to tell you what I told the audience over there. I had a very fine audience, every night for eighteen nights straight. They received us apparently very good. They was lovely people and very nice to us. But I always told them, I said, "All right, ladies and gentlemen, you can readily see that we don't belong in this part of the country; we're from the good old United States, and if we can't come up with no song or no tune or anything that will meet with your listening pleasure, we sure come a long ways to disappoint you."

Ashley was scheduled to return to England for a series of concerts the following summer, but he discovered that he had cancer. On 2 June 1967, at the age of 71, Tom Ashley died. His grave is on the side of a hill near his home — the place where he asked to be buried and the subject of the song he had written four years earlier and recorded on his last Folkways album. The song is entitled "Little Hillside" (FA 2350).

LITTLE HILLSIDE

Well, our time is swift-ly roll-ing on When I know that I must die: My bod-y to the dust do re-turn And there for God am I.

1. Well, our time is swiftly rolling on
   When I know that I must die;
   My body to the dust do return
   And there for God am I.

2. There is not so much that I've never done;
   Now you owe me no pay.
   You take me to the little hillside
   And lower me beneath the clay.

3. You may sing the songs that I used to sing,
   Talk about the things that I've done;
   When you take me to the little hillside,
   Leave me there all alone.

4. Don't place them flowers on my grave;
   There's little that you can say
   When you take me to the little hillside
   And lower me beneath the clay.

5. Oh, there is one and a precious one;
   Why do you treat me cold?
   When no one loves you as I do,
   God in heaven knows.

6. There is one more thought that I'll leave
   with you,
   Then I'll be traveling on;
   Don't shed no tears, don't weep for me,
   Maybe I was wrong.

What evoked the melancholic tone of "Little Hillside"? Perhaps his age. Perhaps he wanted to express that he had lived a full life, had loved, had achieved a measure of artistic success, and didn't ask for anyone's pity; but at the same time he may have wished to say that, in relation to his loved ones, he might have been wrong in the choice of his profession.

Tom Ashley loved his family, and perhaps he felt at times as if he were neglecting them. He knew that his wife did not always care for his music. Tom's use of the house for practice sessions was bothersome to Hettie—occasionally she would even persuade Tom and his friends to practice in the smokehouse because their music "got on her nerves." Too, she was lonely when Ashley's music kept him away for long periods of time. She would certainly have preferred him to have a steady job that would allow him to stay at home. But Tom Ashley approached the ideal of a person who does exactly what he wants to do with his life. He was a man with a lust for wandering, for playing and singing music, and for entertaining people; and he spent a great part of his life doing these things. At the same time, Ashley was concerned about his fellow man and believed that he could help humanity through music. He loved life, and his music was a great part of his life. It is quite probable that his music helped him to endure the hardships that he experienced at times, and it is possible that it contributed to his apparent optimism and favorable outlook on life. He was not a Tennessee farmer who played a little music as an avocation; he was a musician who farmed a little on the side.

Ashley did not fit the pattern of socialization expected of the rural male in northeastern Tennessee; he consequently endured much criticism. Many of the people of Ashley's generation in his section of the country either objected to secular music entirely or objected to pursuing it as a principal means of livelihood. Ashley's community believed in doing an "honest" day's work six days a week and keeping the Sabbath "holy." Wasting time was certainly considered sinful; and, in the minds of many, spending one's life playing secular music was the same as wasting time—at least it was not respectable, productive work. Some of Ashley's contemporaries around Shouns and nearby Mountain City recall him as being a "pretty good old rascal," but one who would never hold down a job because he was "always messing around, a-picking and a-singing most of the time." Others say that he had had a few really good jobs at one time or another, but that he was always quitting after a month or two to go to his music. No doubt many pitied Mrs. Ashley because of Tom's profession, and Tom himself must have felt considerable pressure from them to find some more lucrative employment that offered greater security for his wife and children.

Nevertheless, Tom Ashley possessed the stereotyped qualities of the Southern Highlander—stubbornness, pride, and individualism —and was not subdued. He was obviously proud of his profession, as is indicated in a conversation recorded in March 1965 by Jon Pankake. "I always try to be as truthful as I know how . . . I'm not educated; I'm not an educated man . . . A man would start today as I started and took my wife, was married fifty years ago, with my education, and I'd guarantee as much money as there is now he'd starve to death . . . he couldn't make it . . . I've traveled all my life, one place to another . . . If it hadn't been for my good old guitar, we would have starved to death, sure enough."

Tom Ashley, man and music, has his special appeal. To some he represents the idealized mountain troubadour who evokes the sense of struggle for life and the flavor of independence often associated with the Appalachian mountains. He was, certainly, as one critic suggested in the *Boston Globe*, "rough, unadorned, direct and honest"; and his songs and "ballits" manifest the magic ingredient of personal involvement that the best of traditional singers possess. Ashley summed up much of his own appeal when he said: "A lot of people in the city are playing old-time music these days. But country people play their feeling and feel their playing. That's the big difference."

Tom Ashley had strong feelings about the songs he played, and he was proud to be perpetuating them during his lifetime. He felt that those songs were in danger of being forgotten altogether or, perhaps as bad, of being misappropriated; the latter is clear in a comment he once made before singing "Rising Sun Blues."

Well, this song, I put it on a Folkway about '61, I guess. Since I put it on the Folkway record in a' album, it's been done by a lot of people and some of them does a very good job. Especially, I think, Joan Baez is a good singer and I've been on a couple of shows where she was on and she's a nice person. And I'll never forget a nice party she gave me and the boys about the second or third trip we was in New York. She did take this song off the record and she's done well with it and I'm glad she has, because she can sing it better than I can. But now some of the rock 'n' roll—now, they murdered it, they murdered this song. I mean they murdered it, because it's not that type of a song; it wasn't made for that. It wasn't wrote for that. Now I don't know who wrote this; it's too old for me to talk about, because

I got it off some of my grandpeople, grandparents. I guess that I better see if I can get it, get it out of the top of the house.

Even regarding country and western music, Tom felt, as he commented to Englishman John Cooper, "It don't have that feeling. It's fine to dance by, but for your listening pleasure it's not so good." He often said, shaking his head, "I'd never have believed it if anybody'd told me I'd live to see the day they'd take the taste out of a ham, and you'd break a' egg and it'd run all over the skillet, and they'd take the tune out of a song."

This philosophy would in part explain Tom's aversion to the sound of modern bluegrass, which he implied is too slick, too often as predictable and common as packaged peas, too often performed by those who play without being aware of the words they sing or the notes they pick. One characteristic of bluegrass that bothered Tom is the matter of using only a single tuning. "We've got some wonderful musicians, wonderful talent in the bluegrass-banjo picking. They're just out of this world. But they tune one time and play all their tunes." There were also other aspects of bluegrass styling which Tom did not like; Clint Howard recalls, "Tom was a hard feller to suit when it came to accompanying him. I was always slipping in a bluegrass run once in a while, and he didn't like it. He'd get awful upset when I done it." Tom's attitude toward bluegrass is reflected in a parody he did, for friends, of a bluegrass banjo picker walking down the street, fingers working by his side as he picked away at some tune on the strings of an imaginary banjo.

Ashley not only loved the old-time music but also sensed a kindred relationship to it as though it were a personal heirloom passed down through centuries. He apparently believed that the expression of this feeling was a major purpose and function of his music, and by resisting change in his style, he helped to preserve part of the heritage of his Southern Highlands. At times he almost said as much. "I hope they keep these old folksongs alive right on and on and on, although they's a lot of them that has passed away, out of existence. Now all I can do and offer you is the real old-timey, on-back-to-the-horse-and-buggy days, when we used to go to the county fairs in the old covered wagons. I'm not the greatest musician in the world, just pick a little different in that old-timey way."

Ashley did pick "a little different in that old-timey way." Richard Blaustein suggests several differences; one is a popping effect, achieved by "pulling off" on the first string with the left hand. In conjunction with this technique Ashley moved his right hand from the fourth to the first string in an alternating pattern. He also produced a clicking or clopping sound by picking where the rim of the banjo meets the fingerboard; then, when he wished to conclude a song, at least in some cases he seems to have moved his hand up slightly, away from the bridge, so that he produced a softer, lighter, not quite as resonant tone. An additional technical feature in Ashley's playing, according to Clint Howard and Tex Isley, is that he pressed the strings close to the frets. Although it is possible to get a wide variety of tones from the banjo depending on how and where the strings are fretted, pulled, and struck, it is characteristic of Ashley's playing that he generally produced the same sound.

From another point of view, Ashley's style, as Blaustein points out, is not particularly unusual in relation to that frequently found in upper East Tennessee. For example, Ashley played a limited series of melodic motifs, commonly called "licks," "runs," or "fills," which he used as a contrapuntal accompaniment to his singing. He alternated between singing and playing a phrase, a style characteristic of mountain singing in general. It may be noted that the duration of those fills and licks at the ends of phrases and stanzas varied continually when Ashley performed alone. His phrase length seems to have been determined as much by his inclinations of the moment as by anything else, but when he was accompanied by back-up men, his timing was of necessity consistent and predictable. The quality of Ashley's picking also varied between the parts he sang and those he did not; as Doc Watson observes: "Tom would get involved in his singing and not bother with clarity in his picking. If he took a break on the banjo, it was always clear and pretty; but when he sang, he just rambled along on the banjo."

In regard to Ashley's guitar playing, Blaustein suggests that Ashley used basically a three-finger picking style. Besides playing alternating bass notes with his thumb, he produced most of the melody with the bass strings. Once in a while toward the end of the verses, he would produce a triplet by coming down hard on the treble strings. His middle finger very likely didn't leave the first string, and his index finger moved between the second and the third string. Essentially, this technique is one of the older guitar-picking styles heard in upper East Tennessee, one that might be called post–Civil War parlor music guitar in very simple form.

Similarly Ashley's vocal style was in some ways characteristic of that heard frequently among mountain singers; for example, except at the end of a song the tones at the ends of phrases were often not sustained, producing a kind of staccato effect.

A discussion of Ashley's style would not be complete without attention to his presence during the performance of the songs. Important of course was his ingratiating physical appearance, and more than one writer commented upon it; an East Tennessee reporter (in the *Elizabethton Star*) described Ashley at sixty-seven as "a middle-aged man with a physique as sturdy as a gnarled oak and a healthy rough-weather complexion." More important was his manner. His humility on stage, for example, which at times appeared to contradict his pride and personal ability, charmed his audience and left few disappointed who were fortunate enough to see him in person. "Those folks that come to hear me, I tell 'em I'm from the hills and mountains of East Tennessee. I'm a backwoodsman. The farther back you get, the deeper the woods, and I live in the last house." Even to a small group of students, he once said, "Now I certainly don't want you to expect too much from me. I'm very backwoodsy, as you can readily see — uneducated — and I know a few songs in the old tradition. Now I've never tried to change my style from my boyhood. I never tried to copy nobody else, and I don't think anybody wants to copy me." Ashley often started his shows with a statement such as "We are not professional people. We're just a group of farmers who play, pick, and sing a little in the old country way — nothing very modern — because we're farmers." Although he apparently enjoyed being on the stage and performing before the public, he seemed as he grew older to become progressively more self-effacing and low-keyed. The absence of pretense or glitter proved to be his strongest physical attraction.

Showing up for a show in either overalls or his everyday trousers held up by suspenders, rather than in gaudy sequined cowboy clothes, was natural for him; and the dress in which he appeared was not worn with affectation or ostentation. His clothes were representative of the man, his personality and his purpose. "Now, I'm a fellow that certainly don't want to brag," he told one audience, "because I don't deserve it. I don't think that I've deserved these trips that they've sent me around. I don't think I'm good enough. But they've sent me and I've went. They've paid me very well, but I didn't get rich."

Nevertheless, Tom was not ashamed of his mountain background, and he refused in his later years to play the hillbilly buffoon. That he was sensitive about his lack of education is indicated by his comments to audiences about not being an educated man; still, he was proud of his ability and avoided attempting to be humorous by ridiculing his native area.

Reflecting on the years he played with Ashley's group, Doc Watson remembers with admiration Ashley the man and performer. "There was only one Clarence Ashley, and I've heard people try to imitate him. Oh, they fell way short. Clarence Ashley's style of singing and his style of playing the banjo had its own personality just like he did. It was Clarence. His music had to be himself; and to really appreciate his style fully, I think you would have had to meet him." When Watson was asked what he regarded as Ashley's most significant contribution to folk music, the reply was, "The man himself." Doc's statement indicates that the special quality was the unification of the man with his music. Tom was a part of every song he sang, and he created a visual understanding of the music through his approach to the songs.

Tom's feeling for music, which was evident in his performance, was fostered traditionally — he didn't read music and he played entirely by ear. This quality of feeling is often mentioned by former partners such as Clint Howard. "He loved music best of any fellow I have ever seen in my life. He got the biggest difference out of his sounds, I thought, from the tuning. He knowed a lot of old tunes, tuned the banjo so many ways different, in old minor keys. Nobody couldn't hardly follow him. Doc Watson would just grit his teeth, put on his capo and everything to find them off-tunes, because Tom had always played the banjo most of the time I think by himself; and he just tuned it any way he wanted to. He tuned it to please himself. Best ear for music and best timing I've ever seen."

With Tom, music came first. Many times he would listen to the rest of his group play as he stood out on the porch or in the yard, so that he could more objectively criticize their performance and determine how they sounded from a distance where the audience would be listening. He was a perfectionist, and he expected the group to practice until everything was right. He did not have much patience with his fellow musicians when they gave priority to anything other than music. Fred Price recounts the time Clint Howard cut his finger on a corn planter and Ashley was annoyed with him for not being able to practice. Obviously irked, Ashley asked Howard, "Why in the hell were you working on a corn planter in January?"

It seems that Ashley was somewhat difficult to know well and that he had few close friends. Often he was considered short-spoken, as in the incident related above; and his short temper apparently kept most people at a distance. Things had to be done to suit him or he would have little or no part of them. Even though Ashley was uncomfortably blunt sometimes, it was characteristic for him to cushion the sharp edges with humor; for example, Doc Watson tells about the incident of Ralph Rinzler, Ashley, and his meeting Jean Redpath, a Scottish folksinger, at a train station in New York City. "She was talking to Clarence ninety mile a minute with a heavy Scottish brogue. Clarence wasn't answering except maybe a' un-huh or a huh-uh once in a while. Finally she looked at Clarence and said, 'Meester Ahshley, has the cat got yer tongue?' He answered, 'No, but if you can't understand me no better 'n I can understand you, they ain't no use for me to say a word.'"

Ashley was always up to something. A favorite anecdote told by Doc Watson and others describes Tom on the road, down and out, and with no money for a meal. While he was sitting in the depot waiting for his train home, a fly lit on his leg and he caught it. He left the depot, went into a restaurant, and ordered a big dinner: steak and gravy. When he had finished eating, he placed the fly in the remaining gravy and indignantly called for the waiter to look in his plate. The waiter apologized and said Tom wouldn't have to pay; Tom replied: "Pay, hell, you ought to pay me for eating this." Another illustration of Ashley's antics is a story that Clint Howard tells about one night when Tom was scheduled to do his blackface Rastus act. He had his face blacked a long time before the show began and was eager — a bit too eager — to get his act underway. He peeped through the opening in the curtains, showed his face to the audience, and stuck out his tongue at them. He soon had everyone in stitches except the manager of the show, who canceled the Rastus act. After that incident Tom always told the members of his group: "Don't let 'em know what you got before you go on," and he would give any one of them a good talking to for strumming on an instrument or playing a little tune before the show.

Even though Tom was not often close to his musical companions and was sometimes curt, he always dealt squarely with them; for example, besides being the lead performer in his bands, he acted as local manager, but he always divided equally the amount of money the group earned.

Having experience and a reputation, Tom naturally influenced musicians coming along who wanted to play his kind of music. Roy Acuff is one case in point; Doc Watson is another. This influence was evident in a concert given by Doc Watson and his son Merle in 1973 at Appalachian State University. When Doc sang "Honey Babe Blues," he said that he learned it from Clarence Ashley (in addition, Doc gives Ashley as his source for "Dark Holler Blues," "Walking Boss," "Tough Luck Man," "Poor Omie," "The House Carpenter," and of course "The Coo Coo Bird"). Shades of Ashley's showmanship were also present when Doc told the audience the kind of performance to expect: "I don't do a flashy or artificial show. Country music expresses the simple thoughts in life."

Tom's general impact on old-time music is indicated in a number of ways. The Tom Ashley Memorial Trophy is presented each year to the outstanding single entertainer in the competition at the Old Time Fiddlers and Bluegrass Convention in Marion, Virginia. Another measure is suggested by statements such as Jon Pankake's: "Ashley is one of the rare men who first introduced honest American folk music to the mass media and began, via recordings, bridging the gap between the largely undocumented popular-folk culture and technologically preserved formal culture. Though largely unrecognized by the cultural establishment, the day that Tom Ashley decided to go for broke on music as a means of livelihood was an important one."

Tom Ashley had an extensive repertory. His discography alone is large. Not only did he know many traditional ballads and folksongs that he had learned from his family and friends, he increased his musical store greatly by traveling and performing in different parts of the country.

Analysis of Ashley's repertory suggests that it went full cycle, from traditional to popular back to traditional. He learned in his youth many traditional songs (Anglo-American ballads, American ballads, and other folksongs) from members of his family, relatives, friends, and neighbors. As he traveled with the medicine shows and performed publicly, he began to blend with those songs (as well as additional songs he learned that were similar) tunes that stemmed from the black tradition and commercial songs written for modern tastes. His expanded repertory included blues, minstrel pieces, "coon" songs, sentimental compositions, and humorous songs; and his recordings reflect this eclecticism. He recorded all kinds of songs, including instrumental tunes (fiddle and banjo songs). Finally, in the sixties, when Ashley was rediscovered and began to perform again professionally, his stage repertory consisted principally of the traditional ballads and old-time songs. Hence in broad outline he completed a cycle ranging from almost purely traditional music to highly popular and back to almost purely traditional.

Included in Ashley's repertory of traditional music of British origin were ballads of oral tradition, such as "Barbara Allen" (Child 84), "Four Nights' Experiences" (Child 274), and "House Carpenter" (Child 243); ballads from British broadsides like "London Burglar" (Laws L 16B), "Maggie Walker" (Laws P 1B), "My Pretty Fair Damsel" (Laws N 42), "Knoxville Girl" (Laws P 35), and "Rude and Rambling Man" (Laws L 12); and lyric songs, e.g., "The Coo Coo Bird." Among the American traditional songs he knew (many of which are derived at least indirectly from the British tradition) were ballads such as "On the Banks of the Ohio" (Laws F 5), "Casey Jones" (Laws G 1), "Claude Allen" (Laws E 6), "Ellen Smith" (Laws F 11), "Frankie Silvers" (Laws E 13), "Poor Omie" (Laws F 4), and "Wild Bill Jones" (Laws E 10); blues like "Tough Luck" and "Rising Sun Blues"; lyrics such as "The Old Prisoner's Song"; play-party songs like "Old Man at the Mill"; hymns and spiritual songs, e.g., "Amazing Grace"; and fiddle tunes such as "Cluck Old Hen" and "Shady Grove." Ashley's repertory drew necessarily from that of other musicians, but he also lent many of his own tunes, passing on a few to musicians like Doc Watson and Roy Acuff, and teaching many to Fred Price and Clint Howard.

At home, Tom often sang, and many times his selections were not those he used in his performances or on his recordings. He would go into the bedroom by himself, get his guitar or banjo, and sing and play for hours. Hettie could not cite many specific titles of songs Tom sang at home, but she did remember "Barbara Allen," "Knoxville Girl," and a hymn he loved, "The Old Rugged Cross." Although Tom liked to sing religious music, Hettie did not think he used any in his medicine-show performances; in the sixties, however, he usually ended his concerts with a hymn. When Tom sang hymns, he took different parts, but he insisted on singing the lead for "The Old Account Was Settled Long Ago" and "Will the Circle Be Unbroken." He and his group sang at church gatherings, but Tom felt it improper to play string instruments there. It did not bother him to sing a hymn at the close of a show in a club, but he had very definite ideas about the kind of music that should be used in church. One problem for Tom in performing at church services was the absence of audience response. After singing for a church group one night, he commented to Clint Howard, "When you get done singing, it's awful empty. Nobody claps. You don't know whether to sing another one or sit down and shut your mouth."

Eva says her father's favorite type of song was the ballad, and she recalls that her father composed a song in the ballad form which he especially liked. It was entitled "Lilly Shaw," and its subject was a Mountain City murder in 1903 and subsequent hanging in 1905. Eva mentions also "Barbara Allen" (Child 84) as special to her father, a song he learned from his mother. "Well, I can't think of anything that's any older than 'Barbry Allen.' They's about two hundred different versions of 'Barbry Allen.' I don't know which one is the right one. I learned it from my mother about sixty years ago, the way she sang it; and I've never tried to change it." Unquestionably "The House Carpenter," which he learned from his family, was another important song to Tom. "It's a real old one, one of the old ballits," he said before singing it to a university folklore class; "if you don't know it, if you haven't heard it, I'm sure you'll hear about it, or you've read after it, or something. It's the old 'House Carpenter.' Now I don't know; this is one of them that I've never heard but the one version. If they's been any more, why, I don't know where they're at."

THE HOUSE CARPENTER

"Well met, well met," said an old truelove;
"Well met, well met," said he;
"I'm just returning from the salt, salt sea,
And it's all for the love of thee."

"Come in, come in, my old truelove,
And have a seat with me.
It's been three-fourths of a long, long year
Since together we have been."

"Well, I can't come in nor I can't sit down
For I haven't but a moment's time.
They say you're married to a house
  carpenter
And your heart will never be mine."

"Now it's I could have married a king's
  daughter, dear;
I'm sure she'd 'a' married me;
But I've forsaken her crowns of gold,
And it's all for the love of thee.

"Now will you forsaken your house
  carpenter
And go along with me?

I'll take you where the grass grows green
On the banks of the deep blue sea."

6. She picked up her little babe
   And kisses gave it three,
   Sayin', "Stay right here, my darling little
     babe,
   And keep your papa company."

7. Well, they hadn't been on ship but about
     two weeks,
   I'm sure it was not three,
   Till his truelove began to weep and mourn
   And weep most bitterly.

8. Says, "Are you a-weepin' for my silver or
     my gold?"
   Says, "Are you a-weepin' for my store?
   Are you weepin' for that house carpenter
   Whose face you'll never see anymore?"

9. "No, it's I'm not a-weepin' for your silver
     or your gold
   Or neither for your store;
   I am weepin' for my darling little babe
   Whose face I'll never see anymore."

10. Well, they hadn't been on ship but about three weeks,
    I'm sure it was not four,

Till they sprung a leak in the bottom of th ship;
And it sunken for to rise no more.

After singing "The House Carpenter" to the class, he added, "Some of them old ballits that tells a story, they're pretty long; but it's like reading a book, if you don't read the last of it, you won't get much out of it."

According to commercial and available private recordings, as well as family remembrance, Tom Ashley knew as many as eight traditional and broadside ballads of British origin and as many as thirteen traditional ballads of American origin. One of his favorite American ballads was "Poor Omie" (Laws F 4) — one of those that Ashley called "lassy-making tunes" and on which he accompanied himself with the banjo tuned in sawmill tuning. He was aware of its traditional nature. "Well, here is an old one I guess you've read about, a lot of you maybe. Although it's kind of like the 'Barbry Allen' deal, they's not that many versions, but they's more than one."

OMIE WISE
Adapt. by T. Clarence Ashley

♩ = 144

Poor O - mie, poor   O - mie, poor   lit - tle O - mie Wise.

1. Poor Omie, poor Omie, poor little Omie Wise,
   How she was deluded by John Lewis's lies.

2. He promised to meet her at Adams's Springs;
   He'd bring her some money, some other fine things.

3. Her a fool-like, she met him at Adams's Springs;
   He brought her no money, no other fine things.

4. He brought her no money, but he flattere a case,
   "We will go and get married; it will be n disgrace."

5. She jumped up behind him and away the did go,
   Till he come to the river where deep wate flow.

6. "John Lewis, John Lewis, will you tell m your mind?"
   "My mind is to drown you and leave yo behind."

"Take pity on my infant and spare me my life
And let me live shamed-like if I can't be your wife."

8. He kicked her and he shoved her and he slammed her around,
Then he threw her in deep water where he knew she would drown.

Of the many lyrical folksongs from both British and American sources that Tom sang and played, one favorite over a long period of time was "East Virginia Blues" or "Dark Holler Blues" (he recorded it under both titles). "Now that's the old way I know. I can remember it sixty years, very plainly *sixty* years ago. Of course it's been modernized." "East Virginia Blues" shares a verse (the third one) with another song, "Greenback Dollar," which also has a sketchy narrative content but is principally lyrical.

EAST VIRGINIA BLUES

I was borned in East Vir - gin - ia; South Car - o - lin - er I did go.

I was borned in East Virginia;
South Caroliner I did go.
There I courted a pretty little woman,
But her age I did not know.

Well, her hair was brown and curly,
And her cheeks was rosy red.
On her breast she wore white lilies;
Oh, the tears that I have shed.

When I'm asleep, I'm dreaming about you;
When I wake I have no rest.

Every moment seems like an hour;
Oh, them pains flows through my breast.

4. I'd rather be in some dark holler,
Where the sun don't never shine,
For you to be some other man's darling
When you hain't no longer mine.

5. Papa says we can not marry,
Mama says it'll never do;
But, a-little girl, if you are willing,
I will run away with you.

This lyrical love song and "Greenback Dollar" are two of the many songs in his repertory that may be labeled "bluesy"; another bluesy tune he especially liked is "Careless Love." He also recorded black traditional blues like "Rising Sun Blues" and "Corrina, Corrina," a work song ("Walking Boss"), and other songs that stem from black tradition, including "Little Sadie," which may be termed a Negro ballad. He heard this song in the 1920s near the mining town of Welch, West Virginia, and recorded it in October 1929. There is no simple explanation for his sources for these songs, whether white or black; one would have to consider his local acquaintances and the early recordings of white singers of the blues like Jimmie Rodgers, as well as personal associations on the medicine-show circuit and in the coalfields. Too little is known of these influences upon Ashley to speak authoritatively about them. Nevertheless, a few observations may be made concerning local influences.

There are very few blacks in Ashley's home county, but he definitely had at least some association with blacks. Early in his life, for example, he learned "Trouble in Mind" from a Negro camp meeting. According to his wife and son, Tom never publicly performed with a black musician. There were occasions, however, when he did sing with a black. For example, when he was in Mountain City, he often spent time around the courthouse. Paul Everett, who was superintendent of Johnson County schools, liked to sing; and many times when Tom walked by his door, Everett would yell at Tom to come in. They would then ask Shelton ("Shelt") Jones, the black custodian of the courthouse, who also enjoyed singing, to join them. The three men would sit in the superintendent's office and sing all kinds of songs, including spirituals, with no accompaniment and only an occasional passerby for an audience. Shelt is the only black source the Ashley family suggest from whom Tom might have learned the songs he sang that are part of the black tradition. G. (Gee?) Malone was another black man in Mountain City who used to play a guitar and sing many blues songs. Since G did not have a guitar of his own, he would (during the forties) often visit Tom's son JD to play and sing. JD is not aware of his father's learning any songs from G; still G. Malone is a possible source for some of Tom's blues and bluesy songs.

A most frequently occurring type of music in Ashley's early recorded repertory is popular songs, commercial songs that he might have heard on records or from other performing musicians who had learned them by oral/aural transmission or from sheet music. In addition to the minstrel songs such as "I'm the Man That Rode the Mule around the World," there were others he performed on the medicine show circuit, songs like one of Tom's favorites, "Fifty Cents."

FIFTY CENTS

Well, I tak-en my gal to the fan-cy hall where there was a so-cial hop; We

stayed all night till the break of day-light, a-wait-ing for the mu-sic to

stop. In-to the res-taurant then we went to buy us all a treat; She

said she was-n't hun-gry, but this is what she ate: A

doz-en r-oll, a plate of sl-aw, a chick-en and a roast, A pair of doves and

ap-ple-sauce with a bob-tail crab on toast. A beef of stew and

crack-ers too; her ap-pe-tite w-as im-mense. When she called for pie, why, I

thought I would die for I just had fif-ty cents. (3rd ref. 1.4) Take

my ad-vice: don't try it twiced when you've just got fif-ty cents.

1. Well, I taken my gal to the fancy hall
   where there was a social hop;
   We stayed all night till the break of day-
   light, a-waiting for the music to stop.
   Into the restaurant then we went to buy us
   all a treat;
   She said she wasn't hungry, but this is what
   she ate:
   A dozen roll, a plate of slaw, a chicken
   and a roast,
   A pair of doves and applesauce with a
   bobtail crab on toast,
   A beef of stew and crackers too; her
   appetite was immense.
   When she called for pie, why, I thought
   I would die for I just had fifty cents.

2. You bet I wasn't hungry; now I didn't care
   to eat.
   I've got money in my clothes; I bet she's
   hard to beat.
   She taken things so cozy; she had an awful
   tank.
   She said she wasn't thirsty, but this is what
   she drank:

   A glass of ale, a gin cocktail that mad
   me shake with fear,
   A ginger pop with rum on top and fou
   or five bottles of beer,
   A whiskey skin, a glass of gin; she
   should have had more sense.
   When she called for more, well, I fell o
   the floor for I just had fifty cents.

3. You bet I wasn't thirsty; now I didn't ca
   to drink,
   Expecting every moment to be thrown ou
   on the street.
   She said she'd bring her friends around
   some day, and we'd have fun.
   I showed the man my fifty cents and this
   what he done:
   He mashed my nose, he tore my clothe
   he hit me in my jaw,
   He grabbed me by my clothing, he thre
   me in the floor,
   He caught me where my pants was loos
   and he threw me through the fence
   Take my advice: don't try it twiced wh
   you've just got fifty cents.

Another important part of Ashley's popular repertory is the parlor song, which is often sentimental. One example Tom liked is "There'll Come a Time," composed by Charles K. Harris and published in 1895. As Tom sang it, the tune varies more from the original than the lyrics do.

Tom Ashley's known repertory is large; he recorded at one time or another about one hundred songs. His complete repertory cannot be known; it certainly included more than is represented by tape and disc recordings, documented public performances, and the memory of family and friends. Other questions arise relative to his repertory: Do the songs we know about represent his musical tastes? How important were the hymns like his favorite "The Old Account Was Settled Long Ago"? Of what significance is it that he seldom recorded them? How much of his repertory was determined by public demand?

We do know that Tom Ashley was a strong-willed individual with definite musical tastes, but we also know he was a sensitive performer, conscious of his audience. If a performance in which he was participating began to lag, he would hook his fingers in his suspenders, dance a few steps, and cut loose with some saying or story that brought the audience back to life. Similarly, within certain bounds he adapted his song to his listener, but he was not the kind of man who would perform anything he did not approve of or like.

Unquestionably Tom Ashley's scope was large; he sang and played both the traditional and popular songs that he learned in his native mountains and in his professional ventures. He sang with ease, confidence, and pleasure before all kinds of audiences — agrarian and urban, poor and rich, old and young. He was an entertainer, but he was an artist as well. He learned the same songs that many others learned; yet he gave them his distinctive, individual touch. He was a man who loved the old songs all his life, particularly the ballads and other folksongs he had grown up with; and he will be remembered as one of the finest minstrels the Appalachian mountains have ever offered.

THOMAS CLARENCE ASHLEY CHRONOLOGY

1895	Thomas Clarence Ashley (named Clarence Earl Mc-Curry) is born in Bristol, Virginia, on 29 September; moves with family to Ashe County, North Carolina, then to Shouns, Tennessee.
1903	Receives first banjo.
1905	Mother remarries; leaves school to work at odd jobs.
1907	Receives first guitar.
1911	Leaves home to join Doc White Cloud's medicine show.
1914	Marries Hettie Osborne.
1914–1915	Sets out "busting" with George Banman Grayson and others.
1917	Works with Dwight and Dewey Bell as the West Virginia Hotfoots, with Cook Sisters, and with Greer Sisters; has his own radio shows.
1917 or 1918	Meets Hobart Smith.
1919	Daughter Eva is born.

1921   Son JD is born.

1925   Meets Dock Walsh.

1928   Records his first songs under pseudonyms Oscar Brown and Tom Hutchinson, also under Thomas C. Ashley; records later in the year with Carolina Tar Heels.

1929   Records with Carolina Tar Heels, also with Byrd Moore and His Hot Shots; records solo tunes, including "The Coo Coo Bird."

1930   Buys seven-acre farm; records more solos.

1931   Records with Haywood County Ramblers, also with Blue Ridge Mountain Entertainers.

1932   Works with Roy Acuff while performing with Doc Hauer's medicine show.

1933   Records with Gwen Foster.

1934   Works in the West Virginia coalfields; hauls goods by truck for the government.

1935   Touring is restricted by son JD's illness.

1941   Sells seven-acre farm and begins buying by sections an eighty-acre farm; travels with Charlie Monroe and the Kentucky Pardners; meets Lester Flatt, Tex Isley (with whom in later years he tours and records); plays bookings with Stanley Brothers.

1943   Ceases going on medicine-show circuit; trucks with his son JD; farms and works in lumber; injures finger.

1952   Three early Columbia recordings are reissued on Folkways anthology.

1953   Begins teaching grandson Tommy old songs; helps him with guitar and piano.

1960   Meets Ralph Rinzler.

1961   Records first LP; performs in Greenwich Village.

1962   Performs at Chicago Folk Festival, at Carnegie Hall; tours out west; makes second LP.

1963   In February performs at third annual University of Chicago Folk Festival; in May performs at first annual Monterey Folk Festival, also at UCLA; in July gives performance at Newport Folk Festival, recorded by Vanguard; and in November performs in Philadelphia.

1965   Plays in St. Paul, also in Minneapolis; wins ribbons at Union Grove.

1966   Has bookings in Boston, England, New York City, at
        Brandeis University; is featured at ETSU Folk Festi-
        val; makes third LP.
1967   Dies on 2 June at age seventy-one.

PART TWO

Sam McGee

BY CHARLES K. WOLFE

Music Notation by Annette L. Burton

It is October 1973, and Sam McGee, eighty-year-old veteran musician from WSM's Grand Ole Opry in Nashville, is traveling south by car from his home in Franklin, Tennessee, to Limestone County, Alabama. The new interstate highway I-65 ascends the Cumberland Plateau and begins a gentle slope into the flatlands of northern Alabama. From Sam's home to Athens, Alabama, is less than a hundred miles; to Birmingham, it is less than two hundred. The ease of interstate driving makes him reflect: "We used to come down here a lot when I was traveling with Uncle Dave Macon. Seems like we always had a lot of success with our music in Alabama; people down here are friendly, and we could usually make it back in for the weekends. It wasn't as easy going back in those days though; roads weren't too much either." A few miles into Alabama and it's time for a gas stop; it is early afternoon and the day is already warm. Sam is dressed in a conservative dark shirt and coat with a clipped tie. At the small service station he is recognized. The attendant, an older man of about fifty, notices the guitar cases in back of the station wagon and shakes Sam's hand. He remembers shows Sam did in the area in the 1930s and 1940s and recalls listening to him on the Opry. His wife comes out and mentions that she has a pile of old records she wants to show Sam. He expresses a polite interest, and soon she returns with a small stack of worn old 78s bearing the Vocalion label. They are records Sam made in the mid–1920s, and he looks through them pausing now and then with an embarrassed chuckle. "I want you to have them," says the woman. "No, you keep them," returns Sam; "I hear tell they're worth a lot." As the car pulls out of the station Sam comments that he would like to hear some of the old records sometime. "Didn't you keep any of them?" a companion asks. "No, I had some, but we somehow let 'em get away. I'd like to hear some of those old tunes again though; I think I can still play most of them." Sam is pleased at having been recognized because he has not toured the area for years.

Sam's destination is Athens College in Athens, Alabama, scene of the seventh annual convention of the Tennessee Valley Old Time Fiddlers Association. The TVOTFA is an informal group of assorted fiddlers, pickers, and singers who believe passionately in "authentic old-time traditional music" played acoustically by amateurs who have learned their skills from family and friends in their living rooms and on their porches. Most of the group's members come from Georgia, Alabama, and Tennessee; and they are generally united in disparaging what they call the "Nashville influence" on traditional music. The convention they hold has not yet become a tourist attraction. It is deliberately held in October — after the hectic season of summer folk festivals has ended — and appeals directly to the people of the mid-South. Sam is the special guest of honor this year, but even so he will not be paid for his appearance. He is coming primarily because he has an insatiable love for music and because the convention is going to play his brand of music, a type of music that only a few years ago Sam believed to be headed for extinction.

When Sam arrives Friday evening, the campus of the small college is dotted with groups of musicians jamming informally under the trees. The scene is typical of such conventions: soft drink stands, tables of records, bands playing around Volkswagen vans and campers, and omnipresent cassette recorders. Sam is met by Bill Harrison, an amiable, retired civil servant who founded the TVOTFA. As Sam's host for the convention, Bill introduces him to various musicians crowding around.

After supper, an organized jam session begins on the stage of the Athens College gym. Someone has built a stage that resembles the front porch of a rural house, and different groups take their turns playing ten- to fifteen-minute sets. A large crowd has gathered, for it has been announced that Alabama Governor George Wallace will attend tonight's concert; to the crowd's delight, he does arrive and is brought on stage for a few words. He talks about some of the old-time bands and musicians he remembers, specifically the Gully Jumpers (one of the first bands on the Opry) and Uncle Dave Macon. He is photographed strumming a guitar, and he distributes many pictures of himself. One of them goes to Sam McGee, who campaigned for Wallace in 1968. Sam himself then comes on and plays for the governor, who obviously enjoys the music.

The next day the various contests begin on stage at ten o'clock. Sam has arisen at six-thirty after having played until midnight the night before, and he walks restlessly around talking with friends and admirers. Many people are quite familiar with Sam's career, and they ask about other musicians he has been associated with: his brother Kirk, Fiddlin' Arthur Smith, Uncle Dave Macon, the Delmore Brothers, and Chubby Wise. One person asks Sam to show him how to make a certain run on "Railroad Blues," and Sam gets out his guitar and obliges, attracting a crowd of about fifty in the process, including many young guitar players who are fascinated with a guitar style that predates that of Doc Watson or Chet Atkins. Another fan asks Sam for the words to an old song called "Whistling Rufus"; "I didn't even know there were any words to that," remarks one onlooker, but Sam patiently recalls the lyrics to the song, which he recorded in 1927, as the fan writes them down. Someone else in the crowd comments: "I've never seen anyone that can remember the words to as many songs as Sam can."

By seven o'clock the evening crowd is gathering in the gym for the finals as well as for the various ceremonies and speeches. The fans attending the convention are unused to having a star performer on hand, and comments about Sam ripple through the crowd: "Say, did you know Sam McGee was here? He was outside playing a minute ago"; "Hey, I just jammed with Sam McGee." Thus when Sam is announced on stage for his guest performance, the applause is deafening: wave after wave floods over him as he sits in front of the microphone, almost dwarfed by his big Martin D-28 Dreadnought. When he starts "Buck

Sam in 1974 backstage at a concert with the Sons of the Pioneers.
Photo by Jack Gandy.

Sam, Al Tanner, Elmer Boswell, Jimmy (Sam's grandson) on stage.
Photo by Jack Gandy.

Elmer Boswell, Sam, and Jimmy performing in 1974. Photo by
Jack Gandy.

Clifton (Sam's son), Fuller Arnold, Sam, and Elmer Boswell.

Sam in 1974 with the first electric steel guitar played on the Opry.

Kirk and Sam in the early days of the Grand Ole Opry.

"Sam McGee of Tennessee" and "Uncle Dave Macon, World's Greatest Banjoist."

Sam (with guitar) posing alongside his father, Uncle John McGee.

Sam and Mary with two of their children (ca. 1932).

A publicity photo of Kirk, Sallie (Mrs. Edna Wilson), Sara (Mrs. Margaret Waters), and Sam.

Sam in 1928 playing his new Gibson banjo-guitar.

SAM MCGEE FROM TENNESSEE

Sam playing the cowbells.

Dancer's Choice," a tune he wrote in 1925, the crowd applauds again in recognition. Backed by guitarist Al Tanner, Sam does three more tunes, alternating vocals with instrumentals. He sings a song about changing times, called "When the Wagon Was New," and then starts picking "Wheels," a relatively modern song Sam has discovered, which he has made his own with his distinctive flat-top technique. In the crowd, a man in his forties comments to a companion: "Listen to that. He's getting an awful lot of guitar out of that big Martin." On the last chorus of "Wheels," Sam starts kicking up one immaculately booted foot in time to the music, an old trick he learned from Uncle Dave Macon in the 1920s. The audience is delighted and shouts encouragement. At the end of the number there is prolonged applause; then Sam and his old friend, disc jockey Carl Swafford, who is emcee for the night, swing into an old routine used by Uncle Dave Macon:

"Mr. Sam, what are you doing these days?"

"Who, me? Well, Mondays, Tuesdays, and Wednesdays, I don't do anything."

"You don't do anything? What about on Thursdays, Fridays, and Saturdays?"

"Oh, that's my busiest days."

"Oh, what do you do?"

"I'm getting ready to do nothing on Monday, Tuesday, and Wednesday."

"Hey!"

Laughter and more applause—no one in the audience seems to mind if he has heard the joke before. Finally Sam begins to play an old gospel hymn, "Whispering Hope." He takes it at a brisk tempo, throwing in an occasional funky note, but generally playing it straight. Sam works himself into the tune, getting comfortable, and it lasts for nearly five minutes. After his number, he leaves many of the audience on their feet and discreetly retires backstage to watch the beginning of the finals in folksinging, as a girl from Florida sings "The Lark" accompanying herself on the guitar.

The contest goes on into the night. By eleven o'clock it is chilly outside; and while none of the crowd has left, many of the picking jam sessions have broken up or moved inside to the basement and restrooms of the gym. But a few people are left standing around outside, and one of them is Sam McGee. A crowd of about thirty has backed him against the hood of a car, and he is singing. There are no cassette microphones in this crowd; but most of these people, men middle-aged or older, remember Sam from way back and have their favorites for Sam to sing. As he finishes a song called "The Burglar Bold," his crowd laughs with delight at the last line, and one of the men, dressed in an old flak jacket, asks Sam for the song he sings about the drunk man, "About the guy who comes home and finds his wife in bed — that's the funniest one you sing; I want my friends here to hear it." Sam chuckles: "You mean 'Cabbage Head.' Let's see." He starts singing:

> The first night I come home
> As drunk as I could be,
> I found a hat on the hatrack
> Where my hat ought to be.

And so, as the fiddling contest winds up inside the gym, Sam McGee entertains a group of Alabama workers — men who would never apply the adjective "folk" to any part of their lives — with a humorous ballad, the British origin of which can be traced back more than 200 years.

Sam McGee was born in Williamson County, a hilly agricultural area south of Nashville in Middle Tennessee. The McGee family, coming originally from northern Ireland at a date unknown in family history, have been in this county since well before the Civil War. Even though the oral traditions of the family do not extend much farther back than a hundred years, it was known that Sam's grandfather lived during the Civil War but did not fight in it; "he built rock fences down there on the Duck River for some big man, and that kept him out of the war." Franklin, the county seat and principal town of Williamson County, was the scene of a famous battle of the Civil War, a bloody and complicated fracas that finally yielded a tactical advantage for the Union. Since the McGee homestead was only about eleven miles from Franklin, Sam's father, John F. McGee, grew up with rather vivid recollections of the battlefield and the war's heritage that he passed on to his children. Sam's brother Kirk, for example, likes to tell of his father's finding an old musket on the battlefield and discharging it in a rainbarrel. Sam recalled his father's trying to use an old musket to kill some rats under the house. Sam's father spent most of his life in Williamson County (except for a short time when he moved his wife, Mary Elizabeth Truett, and his family to Texas), and many of Sam's brothers and sisters have remained there. Sam himself lived only eleven miles away from where his father built the McGee family home, which is still standing, and except for trips connected with his career as a musician, Sam seldom traveled out of his home county. As one would expect, Sam's ties with this community and the land were always strong, and they influenced both the formation and the development of his music.

Sam had been exposed to music since he was a small boy. From his mother's side of the family, he learned vocal music, ballads dating from the Civil War, and traditional religious songs and hymns; from his father's side, he learned traditional fiddle and instrumental music. His father, known locally as Uncle John McGee, had a brief taste of fame in early 1926 when he won a regional fiddling contest sponsored by Henry Ford. This regional championship qualified him to play in the state finals at Nashville; there he took the stage against Uncle Bunt Stephens, who was eventually to emerge as Ford's national champion, and Uncle Jimmy Thompson, the legendary fiddler who "started" the Grand Ole Opry.

Some of Sam's most vivid memories concerned his boyhood on the farm:

> I had four brothers and five sisters. The brothers were Alan, John, James Lighthall, myself, and Kirk; Alan was the oldest, and Kirk was the baby of the family. Both Alan and John went into farming; Alan played the fiddle, though, but he was more of a worker, he didn't put much time to it, practice too much—he could have been good as Kirk and I if he'd put any time to it. Of course, my father was an old-time fiddler, he liked music, and he liked to have his boys play. I had another older brother, Lighthall, he was a mandolin player. He died in World War I, died of bronchial pneumonia overseas. If he had lived, he would have played with me and Kirk—actually, he was probably better than we were.
>
> It was sure enough back in the country then. We lived back in the hills, up on the old Peytonville Road, in an old house, probably built in slave times. Had a big fireplace, a big stone hearth, fireplace that you could put a six-foot stick of wood in. I was raised to play

some kind of music all the time; I was raised in string music, you might say. Of course my daddy fiddled a lot, and I had two uncles who were musicians: Uncle Alan McGee, he played banjo and fiddle, and Uncle Willie McGee, who played fiddle. Then they had an uncle—my daddy's mother's brother—Uncle Bryce Poteet who came over and played fiddle a lot, and there was an old fiddler who lived with Uncle Bryce, named Uncle Joe Bennett, an old-time fiddler and a good one too. They'd all bunch in there and play before I was even big enough to play. Later on when we boys learned to play, why, we'd join in too. We had more music than anybody in the country, I guess—and they'd generally all try to play together. Sometimes it would happen that they'd take it separate, or maybe one or two of them; but sometimes there'd be five or six playing at once. And some would join in from around the neighborhood, sometimes thirty to forty people would be in there, listening, playing, dancing.

They'd go pretty well all night. Time didn't mean nothing to them, not like it is today, no time for this, no time for that, always in a hurry. They'd just keep fiddling up into the night, till one or two o'clock once they got started. I liked the music—even as a boy; as long as they'd play I'd be there. They would get together when it was too wet to get out and do anything like that, why, they'd get together and play. Maybe they'd come here tonight, and the next time they'd go to the other's house. Seems like people in that day and time had a better time than they do now. And there was always a lot of music making around Christmastime, though they'd play pretty much the same stuff as always. They didn't play carols or that kind of stuff very much. Just old country breakdowns and waltzes, two-steps, different things like that. My father couldn't read any music. My mother would sing a lot at Christmas, though. But my father played all kinds of breakdowns—by the dozen. "Mississippi Sawyer," "Arkansas Traveler," lots of them.

Those were the happy days of my life. I enjoyed it, whether I was big enough to play with them or not. After I got to be about ten years old, my daddy bought me a five-dollar banjo. I didn't know he was going to buy me this banjo until he went to Nashville. I don't know what a five-dollar banjo would be in this day and time, but back then it was a pretty good banjo. So I began to pick along with him pretty quick. He'd fiddle and I'd pick. I suspect he knew more tunes than any fiddler I knew anything about. The tunes—then I didn't think very much about them; but since he passed away, when I listen to a lot of these other fiddlers play, they don't play a lot of these old tunes that he played. He could do I bet 300 to 400 tunes. Fiddlers today—I've heard the best, I was up at the Grand Masters fiddling contest at Opryland [in 1973]—but of course they don't play that kind of tune. There's all kinds of the best fiddlers in the world supposed to be there, but I don't believe there's a man there that would have known, say, all those extra parts my father used to play in "Bonaparte's Retreat"; he had two or three parts in that that they've just dropped out of the modern version, like that one Pee Wee King played. A lot of those old tunes may just be lost. You know, I didn't think nothing about it back then; I felt that everybody was just going to keep on living like that — but I wish to goodness we'd had tape recorders like they do now, that we had some of the old tunes, not only the tunes but the *way* they played them. They didn't play them as fast as they do now; today they've ruined a lot of good music by playing it too fast. You know, you can get music so fast that it just isn't making much sense.

I played a lot with my father, played nearly everything with him except square dances. He was a church member, and he wouldn't mix it up like that; he was too strict; he didn't like to play for dances. He might play for somebody just to get out there and buck dance; but going out to play for square dances, just to make money, he wouldn't do it. My father himself was a good buck dancer; I wish some of the dancers that we see today could have seen him dance. He was a small man, and I reckon he'd maybe practiced all his life, when he was growing up, and he could really knock it off. To make a good buck dancer — first, you've got to have the right kind of a tune. He'll knock those notes with his feet, more different shapes of dancing, more different steps, knocking the steps but holding the time. Maybe dance off backwards, and then sideways. It takes a good one to do that; not anybody can do it; got to have a lot of experience. But I've seen 'em through the country just as good as I ever did on stage. Of course, there'd be more men do it than women; there were some women dancers, though. There was an old woman who lived over here — Della Hood, lived to be 100 years old — who liked to come over to our house because we always had music and all; she liked to dance, and she could knock these steps just like the men could.

My mother couldn't play any music, but she'd sing a lot, a lot of those old-time songs, some back to the Civil War. She talked about them, said they came from the time of the Civil War. She also sung a lot of Christian songs — the family was all pretty strong churchgoers — songs like "Wayfaring Stranger" and "Amazing Grace." I still sing some of these yet today. Today they'd be called gospel songs, I guess.

In 1899, when Sam was five, his brother Kirk was born; when Kirk was old enough to play music, he joined in the family's playing and singing sessions. Kirk began by playing the fiddle but then graduated to guitar, banjo, and even mandolin. Both boys were soon playing with their father. By the time they were in their teens, they were backing up other local fiddlers at square dances.

Sam made his first money as a musician by playing square dances with an old fiddler named Willie Williams. These old dances were quite informal and were often held in someone's home; the people of the community took turns hosting the events.

We didn't have many rugs on the floor like we do now, and they'd just dance on whatever kind of a floor it was. When they got ready to dance, they'd dance. I've seen 'em put sawdust and meal down on the floor to dance on—it made the feet slide easy, y' know. We'd have to play on these dances probably all night long—until just about day or maybe even day. We were paid—three figures would be called a set and they'd charge them, have a man to go around and take up money from all of them, ten cents a set. Well, how they'd work it on us, these callers would call a set so long; maybe they'd dance twenty minutes on one figure, and it would take three of them. We'd play one tune for twenty minutes, without stopping. You were doing good if you made a couple of dollars. That was really cleaning up. I never did get tired, playing one tune for twenty minutes; but the old fiddler would get pretty tired—he'd begin to just saw like, not make too many notes. They had a special caller, always; we'd have made more money if we had had our own caller that would call it out—we could have made those sets shorter. We had a good time, though; they'd treat you like you were a king. About twelve o'clock they'd always have a lot of stuff cooked up, and you could go in and eat or drink anything you wanted to; and the first thing you know, they were lined up and going again. Knocking dust. The next morning, after you'd played nearly all night, there'd be so much dust where they'd been in and out, bringing dirt in (on the shoes) and then carrying it all over the house, that stuff would rise; and they'd have us up on a platform in the corner, and that dust would come up—your eyes would look like two burnt holes in a blanket. But I liked it and had a good time. One time later on we had so many people dancing that they broke our house down—though the house wasn't that good then (you could feed the chickens through the cracks in the floor)—but they had so many in there they broke the sleepers down. Once we lived in a log house, didn't have much chinking and daubing; and it blowed the clock off the mantel with the door shut and the window down, the wind did. We'd wake up with the snow blowed in on us. I tell that down at WSM and they just die laughing at me, thinking it's some big lie; but it's solid truth.

Sam never did any real fiddling himself, however. As Sam said: "I can tell you the reason why. I can play anything I ever had my hands on just a little bit, strike tunes on it, but there's a difference in doing that and carrying a tune on. The thing that kept me off the fiddle was that my daddy and younger brother Kirk both played the fiddle, and there wasn't anybody to play accompaniment much, but me; so I just stuck to the banjo and guitar."

Modern scholars generally agree that the guitar was a relative latecomer to the rural South, not attaining much widespread popularity until the early 1920s. Sam substantiates this view: "The guitar was not a common instrument when I first started playing it; there was nobody playing it at all then, hardly. Really, it seemed like more Negroes playing it then than whites. As far as fiddling was concerned, a lot of it was done solo too, with maybe some banjo accompaniment. And as far as banjo picking by itself — well, there was some of it maybe in the cities; but around through the country, where sure-enough country music comes from, there wasn't too much of it, playing the banjo solo — and what there was, it seems like they didn't put much time to it."

After he had become fairly proficient on the banjo, Sam began to get interested in the guitar. For some time he had been hearing Negroes in the area play the guitar, and when his father left the farm to run a store in the nearby little community of Perry — a venture that was to last only about a year — Sam had a chance to listen even more closely to black musicians. But the man he credited with playing the guitar style that influenced him most was an old man named Tom Hood, who lived "over in the hills" near the McGee homestead.

He was really the first man — white man — that I ever played for any dances much or as second to fiddle. I heard him play and decided I liked the guitar best; so I thought I'd get away from the banjo and get me a guitar. I got my first one out of some pawnbroker's shop in Nashville. I was still living at home when I got my first guitar and soon learned to second to my dad on it. It wasn't but a short time before I could play anything on it I could play on the banjo, because I really had my mind on it and wanted to learn it. It was shortly after that, Tom Hood gave me a little old booklet that had a few guitar chords in it. There were just simple chords dotted out on paper, lines for strings and all, and Tom Hood had never got anything out of it himself; but that was the most help I really ever had on guitar playing — at that time. It showed different keys, and that was a lot of help because I'd never played with anybody that knew that. Back then you couldn't get any information from anybody because there wasn't any to get. Tom Hood taught me a lot; taught me songs too. One of his numbers was an old song called "Parce Nelson" — started off

> Parce Nelson was a bully;
> He bullied all his life.
> He bullied all over the wide world
> With a ten-cent Barlow knife.

I don't remember any more of it. I can't ever find anybody that knows anything about that song, and I ask everyone about it. It must be about 150 years old.

By 1920 Sam had perfected his flat-top guitar style, and it is to the important formative years of 1910–1920 that we must look for the musical sources of Sam's music. According to folklorist Mike Seeger, Sam's importance lies in the fact that "he gained access to the mass media at a time when Southern guitar playing was in its early formative state." Sam's guitar playing itself was perfected before the advent of extensive mass media, such as phonograph records and radio. Sam's is a case of a folk artist using mass media to disseminate a style that was developed earlier in a more traditional environment.

"My picking style, I didn't learn it from any one person. It just came to me that that would be the way to do it. I figured out which was the easiest to make my tune run in there smooth, and it just came natural for me to do it with three fingers. I used three fingers then and can still do it now, but I don't do it so much because I don't think I need but two fingers and the thumb."

The musical sources that Sam has suggested as influencing the formation of his style, though not his later development or repertory, can be grouped into five major categories: traditional fiddle and vocal music, the parlor guitar tradition, early phonograph records and cylinders, black musicians and blues, and piano music.

We have already noted that Sam had an early baptism of traditional fiddle and banjo music. His earliest professional activity was playing for square dances and informal gatherings in the McGee home. His sense of timing and rhythm was a prerequisite, as it is for any musician who plays primarily for dances; and his strong sense of melody was fostered by the traditional folksongs and hymns of his mother.

Phonograph records played only a limited role in the development of Sam's style. During the time that Sam was still at home, the family had no radio nor any sort of record player.

> I had heard music on records, though. A cousin of mine, he bought an Edison. That was the first record music I ever heard, on a round cylinder record. I remember listening to Uncle Josh and all that funny stuff he did. And they had some with old-time music on them, tunes like "Arkansas Traveler" and "Billy Cheatham" and that kind of stuff, "Eighth of January," just any number of these old-time things. Off the cylinder. Even had brass bands and things. There was some jazz. But that was the only record player I knew of anywhere. I guess they had 'em, but I was just a little country boy who didn't know what was going on in the world. And my cousin, he'd bring it over to our house; there wasn't enough chairs — we'd just sit on the floor anywhere and listen to that thing play. A little cylinder like a baking powder can, with music grooved round and round. Wasn't any doubt about it; it was fine. Somehow or another, there wasn't any static then; it wasn't any electrical instrument then. But there wasn't a whole lot I learned off records.

While the guitar was relatively new to the mid-South and mid-Tennessee area in the early 1920s, it was not entirely alien to other musical forms in nineteenth century America. By the middle of the nineteenth century, upper-middle-class American girls, emulating their European counterparts, had begun the custom of playing light, semiclassical guitar pieces for family, friends, and suitors. By the end of the century a body of popular set pieces was available for the literate guitarist trained in traditional European rhythm and harmony. Robert Fleder notes in his history of the old-time mountain guitar: "Parlor playing gradually filtered down to the lower middle classes, and the end of the 19th century saw, instead of music by the masters, a host of published compositions for the guitar like 'Siege of Sebastopol,' 'Wild Rose Medley,' and 'Midnight Fire Alarm.'" Although this exact body of compositions faded and did not go directly into any sort of tradition, "the tuning and picking techniques were retained and applied." One major parlor-picking technique which may have a direct bearing on the style of Sam McGee was the use of the thumb as a steady alternating bass. Fleder notes that "this technique facilitated guitar arrangements of ragtime pieces: the thumb keeps the beat in the bass while other fingers pick and syncopate the melody in the treble range."

Sam is not conscious of any parlor tradition *per se* in his life; by the time its influence reached Tennessee in the early twentieth century, the tradition was no longer a coherent and distinct entity. Part of this tradition was passed on to Sam in the little chord book that Tom Hood gave him. Another part may well have come from Dr. John Merrit, one of Sam's early mentors who taught him the tune that Sam was later to recast as "Franklin Blues." Sam's playing in "Franklin Blues" seems quite formal, even polite, and the number sounds as if it might have originated in just the type of popular parlor piece Fleder describes. Other numbers in the McGee repertory, such as "Dew Drop," "Little Texas Waltz," "Snowdrop," and "Drummer Boy," sound as if they were influenced by this picking tradition, although some of them are Sam's own compositions. But the parlor tradition is very hard to document, and some of the people who might have taught elements of it to Sam might themselves not have been aware of the source of their styles.

One of the most complex influences on Sam was Negro blues and dance music. When Sam was still quite young, his father left the farm for a year to run a store in Perry, Tennessee, about three miles south of Franklin. While there, both Sam and his brother Kirk were intrigued by the itinerant black musicians who would gather in their father's store to play. There was apparently a large black community near Perry, and the music of the street musicians fascinated Sam: "It would just ring in my head." One musician Sam remembered particularly was a banjoist and guitarist named Jim Sapp:

> Jim didn't play but one or two tunes, but I liked pretty much what he played, and I can play you his tune now, "Jim Sapp Rag," on the banjo. He played a sort of ragtime, and he did some blues; all his stuff nearly was blues, and he'd sing little something or other they could pat and dance by.
>
> Colored people were playing the guitar then more than anyone

else, at least in this area. But their music to me was—the songs sounded too much alike, all the tunes were too much alike. What I like: if you'd ever heard a tune, you'd know what I was trying to play the first time I ever tried to play it for you. Their music wasn't that way. And their timing; lots of players could make all kind of notes and everything, but their notes didn't run out just right; the timing wasn't right. I couldn't read music, didn't know a note in the world on paper, but it didn't sound right to my ear, sounded like it ought to come in there more even and regular. That's one reason I tried to have my own style.

Jon Pankake has pointed out that both Sam and his brother Kirk seem to have modified black blues tradition by borrowing the melodic content of Negro music and imposing on it a tighter and more logical musical form, to have solidified "the musical ideas of shifting improvisations into logical, repeatable, discrete patterns, i.e., 'pieces' that could be memorized and played exactly the same way in successive performances." This seems to be verified by Sam's reaction to black music as well as by the manner in which Sam "straightened out" the numbers he kept in his repertory that originated in black tradition.

Sam also learned certain important instrumental techniques from the black musicians around Perry; one of these was the use of the slide technique that was later refined into the steel guitar and dobro tradition.

They didn't have the regular slide steel bars they have to play these electric guitars with now. They'd just use a pocket knife or ever what they had. The biggest part of it, the first that I ever seen, maybe they'd have a piece of bottleneck on their finger, some kind of steel ring on their finger they could slide up and down with. These were Negroes, down here at a little place they called Perry, about three miles south of Franklin. My daddy moved down there one year. They'd come in there and play; there were lots of black people down in there. That's some of the first buck-and-wing dance too, you might say, that I'd ever seen much. I'd take a knife, or get me something with a hard surface, like a wrist pin from a car, you know, the cone-shaped bearing, like these things that holds your piston in, hole through it. That was a whole lot better, you see; this other way you could do several strings down at a time. You'd have to tune it, E tuning and A was the two best tunings. Some blacks would have it in regular tuning; some would have it more in the tuning of a banjo, or some in Spanish tuning. I tried to play a little that way myself, but never did make many records playing that way. Later I saw Darby and Tarlton play that way, and thought they were the best in the world — at that time, they were some of the best. No one on the Opry played that way; that was before they had that kind of music on the Opry.

A final influence, although not perhaps the most direct and most important, on the McGee style was piano music. The McGee household did not have a piano, but Sam recalls his early fascination with pianos and especially player pianos. "When I was just a small boy, I was in Nashville once with my daddy; and they had this self-playing piano out on the street then, in front of a piano company. You put your money in and it would play. Well, I just spent all of my time that I had right there. I enjoyed that thing, and it was beautiful numbers that it played. I could have stayed there and looked at and listened to that thing all night if they had let me." Sam had a chance to listen even more closely to piano music after he was married in 1914. "My sister-in-law, Hilma Pate, was a piano player. She would come to our home two or three times a year. We didn't have a piano, but we would go over to where somebody did. She would always bring up a lot of songs — sheet music — and she would sing and play, and she was good. She'd bring the songs that had come out in sheet music, and I couldn't read a note, but I would listen to her sing and play and then pick them up on guitar. This gave me a chance to learn songs that had been put in sheet music form." There were many songs in Sam's repertory that he learned from his sister-in-law, and his exposure to sheet music added yet another element of traditional European harmony and rhythm to already important blues and fiddling elements in his developing style. Sam is not the first old-time musician to incorporate early Tin Pan Alley songs into his tradition; and as we shall see, he was later to learn from oral tradition many songs that originated in sheet music publications.

In addition to these sources, Sam stressed the importance of his live contact with various traveling semiprofessional musicians. "Any kind of a little show or entertainment, for instance, somebody running for sheriff or something, if he'd have with him somebody to play, why I'd try to learn off of them." Moreover, he admitted that in his "early days" he had an uncanny ability to remember tunes. "If I could hear a tune twice back then, why it would just stay with me. If I liked the tune, I could hear the thing ringing in my head, just like it was playing nearly. I wished I was that way now. It's hard to learn tunes now." Sam's ability to do this of course complicates the entire matter of influences on stylistic formation. It means that his style could well have been influenced by something he heard only once or twice; it means that musical forms that we can document as having been close to him for a period of time might not necessarily have been the most influential. And Sam himself could not explain the complex process by which he amalgamated all of these diverse musical influences into his unique flat-top picking style, which was to dominate old-time guitar playing in the early years and remains one of the most potent forces in folk music even today.

As Sam moved into his late teens, neither he nor Kirk seriously considered making music full-time and attempting to earn a living from it. In 1914 Sam married Mary Elizabeth Pate, a vivacious young girl who liked music and remained his wife the rest of his life; in 1915 their first child, Mildred Louise, was born. With the added responsibility of wife and growing family, Sam became increasingly aware of his role as a provider and aware of the need to find dependable full-time work. In rural Tennessee of the early 1900s, music-making was hardly considered a full-time occupation, and thus it was not unusual that Sam started out life in farming, which was a more usual and secure occupation than performing.

My father was a farmer, and my first job was farmer before I became a blacksmith. The year I started in farming was a bad crop year, and I didn't make much, and I was awfully uneasy—afraid I couldn't meet my debts and all. So along in August, after the crops was laid by and everything, why, I set out to get any kind of a job I could get. But you couldn't get a job then; and if you did, you couldn't get any money for it. And I didn't have much education. But I came by this blacksmith's shop in Franklin, and they were working pretty well in there, looked like. I'd never shod a horse or anything, but I'd always felt I could do a little of anything somebody else did a heap of; so I went in to ask this fellow, Dorsey Grim, about a job. He says, "No. I can't hire you, but I'll tell you what I will do—I'll sell you a half interest in the shop." Well, he was a pretty-aged man, and he didn't work any at all, but he told me he was making good money at it, and I didn't know but what he was; so I listened to what he told. Then I said: "I don't have any money to pay you for half of this shop." He said, "You don't have to have it. You can pay it on time, or have you got a cow or two you can put with it?" All right, so I traded with him, and I was just about killing myself working there; there was a low roof with a tin top over it. You can imagine a man that's been out in the air all the time working there; there's a heap of difference between sun heat and fire heat, working under there where you couldn't get much air. But I was just playing with it, for everything I could do. We had two men hired, giving them four and a half a day—that was big money then, a dollar was big wages then—so I commenced peeling off shoes and trimming feet for them to shoe and, my, it was awfully hot; and I heard one of them whisper, "Him, he won't be here long." And I overheard this, and told him, "You're saying the truth now. I may not be here long, but when I go out of here I'll be dead as a hammer. I won't be able to pop my finger." So, I've outlived them; they've been dead now twenty years, and I'm still kicking. But I never did write any songs about blacksmithing. It was just hard work. Back then we were shoeing horses for $1.20 and furnishing the shoes and nails and everything. I had all those shoeing tools: horseshoe knives, draw knives, Hamilton rasp. I could build a whole wagon. I've still got a few of my tools out there now yet. The other day a friend brought over one of those old Sears and Roebuck catalogues that they've redone, you know, wanting to show me some old advertisements for records in them. But what I liked to look at best was the picture of these old blacksmithing tools, how much they were and all.

I left blacksmithing to go with Uncle Dave Macon, playing guitar with him; but even after that I still did some farming. I've never depended on one certain thing to make a living. I've felt this way: if I can make fifty cents with you today, I'll make that; and then if I can make five dollars tomorrow from somebody else, why I'll make that. I've always been that way, never depending on one certain thing. The way things look now, if I'd never done anything but played back when I was young, well, probably I could have more money than I've got now. But I don't need too much money anyway. What I crave now is plenty of good friends, crave that more than anything else in the world.

Throughout his entire career Sam was to follow this pattern of trying to "keep his hand in" a traditional occupation while playing music as much as he could. Sam confirmed that when he began playing, a professional career in country music was hardly possible: "There wasn't any demand for it much except in taverns and places like that, with a lot of roughnecks, where I never did want to play. Most of the musicians I knew as a boy were part-time, and that's all. It was just like a different world from now as far as the music business was concerned. A person, even if he played a little music, had to have a job that took nearly all of his time." Thus Sam was never completely comfortable in the role of a full-time professional musician; and although his early success showed friends and family in the community that music could be a viable profession, Sam always wanted to have a traditional occupation he could rely on if times were hard. Even after Sam was an established member of the Opry cast and recognized throughout the world, he still spent a lot of his time maintaining his 405-acre farm. He considered himself as much a farmer as a musician; and, not infrequently, fans driving out to pay homage to Sam were surprised to find him out cutting tobacco or working on his tractor. His life style reflected the fact that he was a transitional figure between the time that rural Southern traditional music was produced largely on an informal, amateur basis and the time that it became a major entertainment commodity in American culture.

During this early period Sam was continuing to play informally around the Middle Tennessee area; occasionally he played with his father and brother Kirk. An undated news clipping from the early 1920s describes a local fiddling contest at Hickman County High School where both Sam's father and Kirk competed in the fiddling competition. Yet the news story singled out Sam's playing as one of the highlights of the evening, and the account gives us an informative glimpse of Sam at the dawn of his performing career:

> A delightful feature of the program, not listed officially yet proving to be one of its strong points, was the clever work of Sam McGee of near Franklin, a versatile musician and comedian whose accompaniments and interpolated song numbers kept the audience clamoring for more. Somehow, this gifted young man produced unheard of music from the guitar; worked tirelessly in accompaniments for practically all contestants, and injected a comedy relief into the program with an infectious smile which won his audience and held them to the close of the program. Requests from throughout the audience kept McGee working during the delayed decision of the judges.

Sam's unique guitar style, his sense of comedy, and his love of the music are all reflected in this clipping; these traits were to characterize him for the next fifty years.

In 1925 Sam met for the first time the man who was perhaps the region's most seminal old-time musician, Uncle Dave Macon. As folklorists today learn more and more about Uncle Dave and his songs, it becomes increasingly clear that during the twenty-year association with Uncle Dave, Sam McGee was in touch with a major transmitter and shaper of folk traditions. In his choice of material, performing style, level of artistic self-consciousness, and vision of himself in respect to his community, Sam owes much to Uncle Dave. In the bio-discography of Uncle Dave Macon, prepared by the John Edwards Memorial Foundation, Ralph Rinzler describes him in these words: "Capturing the very spirit of rural America, Uncle Dave Macon — banjo picker, ebullient singer, raconteur, humanitarian — was the embodiment of wholesome fun tinged with mischievous humor, the product and symbol of vigorous country folk who work hard, live honestly, and believe in God and their nation. Uncle Dave's repertoire and style reflected his interests and heritage, and the breadth of his horizons laid the patterns for country music and the folk revival as we know them today."

Although he was born in 1870 in Warren County, Tennessee, near McMinnville, and had spent several of his most formative years in Nashville, Dave Macon had by 1900 settled near Readyville, Tennessee, about thirty miles east of Franklin. Macon's main vocation was his freight service, the Macon Midway Mule and Wagon Transportation Company, which hauled produce and merchandise between Woodbury and Murfreesboro; according to Sam, "he'd haul goods for those big stores in Murfreesboro, all kinds of freight; that was before they got these big trucks going, and he did all that with mules and wagons. He was a pretty strong man, a powerful man, when he was in his prime." Uncle Dave played the banjo and entertained mostly as a hobby until about 1918; by then his reputation had spread by word of mouth throughout the mid-state area, and he finally accepted some professional bookings for Loew's Theatres in Birmingham. By the time Sam McGee met him, Uncle Dave Macon had been playing professionally for two years and had become a well-known recording artist. Sam recalled their first meeting:

> I was running my blacksmith's shop out there in the country and I came into Franklin to get some material to work in the shop with

and I heard a banjo playing. Of course, I was always crazy about music and tried to locate where the music was coming from: there were several buildings between me, where I was buying my material, and where the music was going on. So I walked out on the sidewalk and I could tell it was at the courthouse: there was Uncle Dave, playing that banjo and throwing it around under his leg, cutting up and hollering and telling funny jokes and everything, passing the hat a little. I stayed there until he quit playing; I guess I'd stayed till dark if he'd kept playing and telling jokes, because it was really good. After he quit playing and all, I went on home, and I was telling my wife and everybody out in that part of the country about seeing him, about seeing Uncle Dave, about what a great entertainer he was, how I thought he was the greatest in the world. I told her, "I just seen the funniest old man I ever seen in my life."

So I didn't think I'd get to see him anymore, but in three or four weeks him and Fiddlin' Sid Harkreader came out through the country putting on entertainment. There were two little stores in the village where I was living [Perry] and they had in one of them this window card, what night they'd be there and what they played and everything, and they had a picture on that window card. That just set me wild then because there wasn't anything like that going on nowhere in the country; so everybody turned out. They had a bumper crowd, just all they could take care of, in a schoolhouse, a little school with two big rooms. I was sitting in the front row — I made sure to get me a front seat so I'd be sure to hear it and take it all in. So after they got through playing and everybody enjoying and having a big time — why, just as quick as they dismissed the crowd — I made a break to invite 'em to spend the night with me. And Uncle Dave says, "Yes, we'll be glad to. We haven't made any arrangements for any place to stay tonight."

I thought it was right interesting, what they had on their instrument cases. You see, I was just a little one-gallus farmer, raised up the hard way, a heap of work and just a little money; and I saw on Uncle Dave's banjo case: "Uncle Dave Macon, World's Greatest Banjoist." Well, that sounded awful big to me. And Harkreader, he says on his fiddle case: "Fiddlin' Sid Harkreader, World's Greatest Violinist." That struck me as kind of funny: I never heard it called very much but a fiddle. We didn't have no violin players around then — well, we thought Sid *was* the world's greatest violinist at the time.

Anyway, we went over to my house to spend the night and I had an old Martin guitar sitting over there in the corner and we were sitting in front of the fire talking and after a while Uncle Dave looked around and saw that guitar sitting over there and said, "I see you've got a guitar over there; do you play?" And I said, "Well, I play a little to entertain myself and a few of my friends when they come around." And he said, "Well, play me a number." So I got it and played him "Missouri Waltz," that was just popular about then. And he said, "Well, that is fine. That is beautiful." Uncle Dave told me lots of times since that I played for him that he had never heard an instrumental number just picked out on a guitar along with the rhythm at the same time. It sounded like there were two guitars, the way I played it there. He wanted to know if I'd consider going and playing some dates with him, and I told him yes, I'd be glad to in a couple of weeks, as soon as I got caught up. He said that he'd make us a couple of weeks of dates and see how we could do. So we played those two weeks up and bought us a car together and traveled around for eighteen or twenty years together.

Sam's first major professional appearance with Uncle Dave was at the Loew's Bijou Theatre in Birmingham in January 1925. Billed only as "Guitarin' Sam" ("He climbs all over a 'wicked' guitar"), he appeared on stage in a rural costume, and sitting on a plaster-of-paris stump, he played guitar solos while a vaudeville dancer named Bob Bradford danced the buck-and-wing. An inauspicious beginning, perhaps, but many major figures of old-time music, including Charlie Poole, John Carson, Tom Ashley, the Hill Billies, Crockett's Mountaineers, and H. M. Barnes' band (with Charley Bowman) shared such early vaudeville experience.

But to think that Sam and Uncle Dave played primarily vaudeville shows is to have a very distorted picture of their travels. Most of the time they were in much less formal and much more direct contact with the folk community. Sam's accounts of his travels with Uncle Dave confirmed this and revealed a great deal about Uncle Dave's own colorful and eccentric personality.

We went over most of the Southern states; didn't get up north much except in Illinois a time or two. We didn't take real long trips. We traveled by car a lot of the time, though we did some by train. Uncle Dave liked trains because he could see lots of people and talk to lots of people. He never stayed in his own seat on a train; after ten minutes — it didn't matter where he was going — he'd want to get up, go around and meet people. And he would; he'd meet any of them. I was bashful. And I always thought that he was going to run into somebody that didn't appreciate him sometime; he never did — he had a way that got by with everybody. He'd make up something to tell them that would be interesting to them. Had the biggest time.

And sometimes we'd get those instruments out and play for them, right on the train; it didn't make any difference to him.

A lot of times when we'd be staying overnight in a hotel, ready to do the show, I'd come and find him playing for a small crowd in the lobby; we had to watch it, for he'd give the whole show away — there wouldn't be anyone to come to show that night. Or we'd come into town to spend the night, and he'd say, "Let's go over here to this restaurant" (of course he was always in front; I didn't dare go in front), and he'd go talk to the management, and they'd tell him what they had and everything, and they'd invite him to come over and play a little — nice restaurants and everything — and he'd make as high as seventy-five to a hundred dollars there in a few minutes, when he'd get started to playing and they'd start pitching money in the hat. He always liked to tell about how there was one place so tough that he didn't even get his hat back.

Uncle Dave seldom made elaborate preparations for one of his trips with Sam.

He'd just take off, didn't give it a thought, not when we'd go back or anything. When the notion struck him which way he wanted to go, we'd go. But we did more traveling in the fall of the year and the wintertime. I didn't especially have to be home to plant the crops because you could always pick up men to plant the crops; not like it is now — you couldn't get anybody now. A lot of times we'd go out and play and maybe come in close to home where we could drive in. Maybe we wouldn't want to play every night; we'd drive in at maybe two o'clock in the morning, and I'd get up the next morning and make a hand in the field the next day. But Uncle Dave knew a lot of people, and he wrote lots of letters to people he knew would date him, and he got lots of bookings that way.

But if he wanted to go into a part of the country where he didn't know anybody or anything, why, he'd say, "Let's go up here to this big high school — this looks like it'd be a good place." Well, all right, he'd go in; the principal would come to the door; he'd talk to him, tell him: "This is Uncle Dave Macon, old banjo picker — from Tennessee." They'd talk a little bit — maybe it'd be close to recess — he'd say, "At recess, we'd like to come in and play the children a number or two." Well, that'd be fine, they'd be right in for it; I don't believe he ever had one turn him down. We'd go in, play a number or two; he was a great hand for comedy songs, for making people laugh, songs like "Chewing Gum." He'd be making maybe a week's dates around, a radius of 100 miles maybe — Uncle Dave had a little book, he'd put down the time we were to be there and all — and he'd tell 'em where we'd be, and they'd go tell their parents. That's all the advertising there was; there wasn't a stitch of advertising, not like you have now. No posters, no newspaper ads, unless it would be something they put up after we left, something like that. But that's the way he advertised; he said it was best. And I reckon it was. These kids—back at that time there wasn't too much entertaining going on, and when they saw something unusual, like he was, they'd tell everybody about it—the kids, they'd come back that night and make their parents come with them; so we'd have a big crowd that way.

We didn't have any certain way to play, didn't have any plan about playing in certain places or anything. Anywhere he thought we could play, why he'd go see about it—theaters, big schools, anything like that. He liked to play big schools because he could play just as long as he wanted to there—we'd play for two hours lots of time, just the two of us. We played some square dances, but not too many. About as uneasy as I was in all my life was one time we played back up there in East Tennessee, in the coal-mining section in there. It was back when there was so much trouble with those miners and government men and everything like that; it was awful bad. Well, we played up there at a place, and they wanted to have a square dance after the entertainment; so we agreed to play for them. And this sheriff said, "I want everybody to bring your guns up here and lay 'em on the table." And they did. You never saw the like of those big pistols—some of them pointed one way, some another. They laughed at me because I said, "Point them things the other way; I'm nervous anyway." But everything went off, as pretty as you please. It was dangerous then, during the troubles; but we could go anywhere because he was pretty well known and they knew what we were doing and that we didn't have anything to do with it on either side.

Sam's role was not merely to "second" Uncle Dave on guitar, for even in these early days Sam would play several guitar or banjo solos during a show.

Uncle Dave would tell them about "what a fine guitar player I have with me," what a fine boy I was, and all that; and he'd have me play a number. He'd play two or three on the banjo, and then he'd give me another big buildup. "Now folks I want you to listen to this boy who can really play the guitar," and I'd play a number, and it would go over good, and then he'd start back playing that banjo and me playing accompaniment. Well, after he'd wham, wham, wham for maybe thirty minutes, somebody in the audience would yell out, "Let McGee play another number." And sometimes he'd say, "I'm sorry, we're all out of time for tonight.

Many people acknowledge that Uncle Dave's banjo playing was only adequate and that his real effectiveness lay in his personality, and there were occasions when Macon seemed somewhat jealous of Sam's ever-increasing skill on the guitar and banjo. Whereas Sam could play quite well on any stringed instrument, Uncle Dave could only "second a little" on guitar. "Uncle Dave didn't teach me much as far as my own instrument was concerned, though I learned a lot watching him tell jokes and sing. For instance, he carried four banjos with him, one tuned in each key, like A, C, D, and G, you know. When maybe he could have done it with one banjo if he'd understood the difference in keys so he could have tuned it up like A, C, D, and G, and so on, so it'd suit the different tunes that he played. But that was the way he had learned to play." (While there are obvious advantages to having different instruments tuned for different songs in order to keep a show moving and avoiding awkward pauses for tuning, Sam did not feel this was the primary reason Uncle Dave carried his different banjos.)

One of Sam's favorite stories — one that he began to tell only after Uncle Dave's death — involves a championship banjo contest that both Sam and Uncle Dave entered in 1925 or 1926:

I didn't used to tell it, but it's the low-down truth. See, Uncle Dave was rated as one of the greatest banjo players, even up until he died. And he was the greatest entertainer, but there were a lot of them that could beat him playing. Once, about '25 or '26, we were playing dates down in Alabama, playing anywhere we could get dated up; and they were putting on an old-time fiddlers' contest down at Birmingham. The man that was putting it on heard that we were in that part of the country, and he came out to ask us, "Would you join the contest?" And we both said, "Yes, be glad to." Uncle Dave signed up as a banjo player and I signed up as a banjo player and guitar player, too. I hadn't been playing the banjo too much, since that was Uncle Dave's main instrument. But going down there to play when the time came, Uncle Dave says, "Well, Sammy, I'll make a deal with you." "What's that, Uncle Dave?" "If you give me half you win, I'll give you half I win." I says, "That's a *deal*," and we shook hands on it. Because I was sure that Uncle Dave, with his showmanship and his age and everything — as well as he was known, wouldn't anybody have much of a chance with him at that time. But it turned out altogether different. Got down there the night to play; and instead of playing on a stage wide open to the public, where they could all see, they played by numbers and played behind curtains, and nobody's name was ever actually called, and the audience couldn't see who was playing. If it hadn't been that way, I wouldn't have had a chance in the world. I happened to be number one, I went out and played before I got excited or anything. Went out and played two numbers on the banjo, "Old Black Joe" and "Swanee River." I couldn't tell much about it, but I thought I was playing it pretty good; they went on, maybe thirty banjo players. It was for the Championship of the South — the Skillet Lickers, all the big names were there. Well, I got the first on the banjo on that; and Uncle Dave, he didn't get anything. The prize wasn't very big, only twenty-five dollars; it was just winning it over that many people — I was awfully proud of that. But it took Uncle Dave down; coming back, he said, "Now don't tell that; that'd hurt me." And I never did tell many people about it until after he was dead.

In fact, Sam became a teller of tales when he began to talk about Uncle Dave. Both Sam and his brother Kirk, like many others who knew Macon, had a delightful repertory of "Uncle Dave stories," which themselves function as folklore about one of the great folksong preservers. Although most of Sam's anecdotes were undoubtedly more accurate than many other "Uncle Dave stories," some of them had been told and retold over the years until they have achieved an epic simplicity. Comparing versions of stories that Sam told with those he told as much as ten years earlier, one finds only minute changes in text, and they show that Sam's skill as a raconteur was second only to his skill as a musician.

Sam's career with Uncle Dave was by no means limited to traveling with him and playing live performances. This kind of activity certainly took most of his professional time, but the developing mass media of the 1920s were starting to reach into the South and to make available new opportunities for both Sam and Uncle Dave. The development of radio and the popularization of phonograph records offered folk musicians a chance to reach a much wider audience with much less effort. Instead of destroying folksong traditions, such mass media increased immeasurably their lines of transmission and influence. Radio and recordings had a considerable impact on Sam's career (both with Uncle Dave and by himself) and need to be examined rather closely.

Radio in Nashville began in the fall of 1925, first with a small station called WDAD and then a month later with the more powerful wsm. Both stations featured old-time music from the very first, and Sam accompanied Uncle Dave several times to the studios of wdad before wsm even went on the air. Soon after it went on the air, wsm hired George D. Hay, a nationally known announcer, as its station director, and Hay accelerated the trend to use old-time music on the station. (For a detailed account of these early years of the station and the Grand Ole Opry, see the author's *Grand Ole Opry: The Early Years, 1925–1935*.) During the first few months of 1926 Hay began organizing a stable roster of some twenty-five people to constitute the basic cast of a show he had begun in 1925 and was to call "The Barn Dance." Sam and Uncle Dave were among the first chosen.

> I didn't play that very first night, when it first started, but just as soon as the word circulated around about the Opry—the Barn Dance—everybody got excited about it. Uncle Dave and me were playing together that time, down in Alabama. Uncle Dave, he was the kind of fellow that would venture on, and I was always the other way, bashful and backward, and wouldn't venture out much. He says, "Let's go down and play on that Barn Dance." We were in an A Model car then, so we did; we drove up and went down and played on the Barn Dance. It wasn't any trouble to get on then because it was new and they didn't have the people they needed. So we got on; it was like striking a match, it was no trouble. Uncle Dave already had the name and the buildup, you see; and they wanted something like that.
>
> The first number we played—Uncle Dave played—was, I think, "Keep My Skillet Good and Greasy All the Time." Judge Hay was in charge of it then, but we hadn't heard it any—we didn't even have a radio at that time. When we played, I don't believe we were paid, even for the first two or three times I was on wsm. They said, "We don't know what this is going to do; if it gets on a paying basis, we'll pay!" And it was just a very short time before they commenced paying.

Sam recalled that after his first Saturday appearance on "The Barn Dance," Judge Hay wrote him a letter that Sam always considered somewhat prophetic. Hay wrote: "I hope you will come back again Saturday for the show, for I'm sure it will continue if you can." Aside from being prophetic, the statement reveals how closely Hay worked with the artists on the show in the early days; Hay had quite clearly defined notions as to what constituted folk music, and Sam McGee obviously fit into those notions.

Judge Hay has written that "for the first fifteen years on the air Uncle Dave was our biggest star," and through Sam's association with Uncle Dave he gained a great deal of exposure to an ever-increasing radio audience. People listening to Uncle Dave often also heard Sam McGee, and Sam's guitar stylings were widely disseminated and became quite influential. During the next three years "The Barn Dance" became the Opry and attained a remarkable popularity throughout the South and across the United States. The music from "The Barn Dance" was spread even further when, in November 1928, the Federal Radio Commission assigned wavelengths for all radio stations; this move helped prevent the jamming and overlapping of signals that had been developing with the proliferation of stations in the mid-1920s. WSM was allotted 5,000 watts of power; and this, along with its low wavelength assignment, put the station into the national radio class and allowed it to be heard regularly throughout the United States, Canada, Mexico, and even Cuba. (As early as January 1926 WSM's old-time music was drawing letters from as far away as Oregon.) A unique stylist like Sam, therefore, had the potential for influencing literally millions of people.

Sam quickly began to make a name for himself apart from his association with Uncle Dave. As early as the middle of 1927 his name begins to appear separately in the listings of the Opry performances. One of the earliest newspaper stories about the success of the Opry (*Knoxville News-Sentinel*, 7 July 1929) singles out "Sam Magee [*sic*] from Tennessee," who plays "a 'wicked' guitar," as one of the show's stars.

Like radio, the phonograph record demanded certain commercial concessions from the artist, but it offered distinct rewards. Historically, folksong students have tended to neglect the role of commercial recording in the transmission process, but recent research has shown that early commercial phonograph records are often intricately involved with oral and written folk traditions. By 1925 most of the major record companies had discovered that there was a flourishing market in the South for "old-time music" and "blues" records, and the companies began efforts to find and capitalize on authentic performers. Between

1925 and 1935 crews of talent scouts toured the Southern states seeking out musicians who were often only semiprofessional or amateur and who were generally closely attached to local communities. In some cases these performers were recorded on location by traveling crews using portable field equipment; in other cases, they were offered an expense-paid trip to New York or Chicago.

The resulting records, sold primarily to middle- and lower-class audiences throughout the Southern states, were undoubtedly profitable for the companies; but regardless of their use by folklorists, they were definitely produced for reasons that were neither idealistic nor altruistic. "Hillbilly" and blues records were produced in vast quantities before the depression severely curtailed their numbers. (The term *hillbilly*, though widely used today by scholars to refer to pre–World War II country music, was seldom, if ever, used by the musicians themselves in the 1920s. Most preferred to call their music "old-time music," and most record labels of the era boast "old time singing and playing.") A typical singer in 1928 might have been paid fifty dollars a side; this was for most artists a flat fee with no royalties on subsequent sales. Most folk artists who recorded during this time were never told how their records were selling, and many never realized to what extent their music — via records — influenced other musicians. And when we realize that throughout the late 1920s the major companies were releasing four or five new hillbilly records per week, we have some indication of the extent of the hillbilly boom of the 1920s. As one example, we might note that between 1925 and 1932 Columbia released 782 records in their 15000 "Old Familiar Tunes" series and that these records sold more than eleven million copies in seven years. This company alone—only one of seven major companies—accounted for the insertion of some twenty-two million recordings, songs with both texts and music, into the folk culture of the South. Through such quantities of records, it was possible for song texts, tunes, and instrumental techniques to be distributed from one end of the South to another.

But while we know that hillbilly records were popular in general, we do not have, and probably never will have, accurate sales figures for many individual artists or individual records. Recent research has dispelled the mistaken notion that many hillbilly records sold millions of copies prior to 1940; in 1926 the average Columbia record sold about 25,000 copies, and a sale of more than 200,000 was rare. Tom Ashley's important original recording of "The Coo Coo Bird" sold only about 3,000 copies. Indeed, it is quite possible that radio was more influential as a medium than records, but phonograph records have been preserved, whereas radio programs of the time have not; thus scholarship on early country music and its relation to tradition has been perhaps too heavily weighted on the side of records. However, records were important; they could be played over and over again until a song or instrumental technique was learned, whereas a selection on radio obviously could not. Records could be taken into geographical areas where radio reception was limited or impossible. Records could be traded, exchanged, borrowed, sold, and bought secondhand by a population whose financial circumstances prevented the massive and indiscriminate purchase of such records. Even the exact sales statistics of a record, therefore, would not register how many times it changed hands or how many listeners it reached.

Sam began his recording career in April 1926, when he and Uncle Dave journeyed to New York to record for the Vocalion division of the Brunswick-Balke-Collender Company. "The Sterchi Brothers, that big furniture store from Knoxville, Tennessee, they're the ones that sent us up there to record. They paid all expenses." The Sterchi Brothers were also distributors for Vocalion records in the mid-South, and they had paid for some of Macon's earlier trips to record; this time they obtained some fine recordings by Sam as well. Sam recorded thirteen songs with Uncle Dave and another five by himself. Using the same little Martin guitar he played the first night he met Macon, Sam backed the older man's singing and banjo playing; he even helped Macon sing on the famous recording of "Late Last Night When Willie Came Home," and thumped the back of his guitar to the high-spirited strains of "Way Down the Old Plank Road." The ornate gold and black scrolled labels of the records read: "Uncle Dave Macon/(Voice and banjo)/Guitar by Sam McGee."

Sam recorded by himself two samples of his singing, "If I Could Only Blot Out the Past" and "In a Cool Shady Nook," and three "hot" guitar solos, "Buck Dancer's Choice," "Franklin Blues," and "Knoxville Blues." He credits Jack Kapp, the recording engineer for the session (and later an executive with Decca), with persuading him to make his first solo records. "I didn't really go up there to make a record myself; I went with Uncle Dave to help him. I was sitting around a little while he was making changes for another tune, and I happened to be playing a little bit. And this Jack Kapp, he said, 'Why don't you make a record?' And I said, 'Well, I don't think I'm good enough.' And he said, 'Why, *I* like your playing; why don't you make one?' And I said, 'OK, I'll be glad to.'" The record Sam claimed (see discography) as his first, "If I Could Only Blot Out the Past," is a song he learned from his wife. "That song is way over a hundred years old; my wife sang it to me before we were married, and I got to playing it that way. She learned it from an old woman. I've never heard it by nobody, no time, nowhere. I thought it was a pretty song, and it was new in that nobody had played it that I knew anything about. That's why I recorded it."

The three instrumentals—all three of which are seminal numbers closely associated with Sam—are unique in that each of them is divided into two parts or movements, separated by comments from Uncle Dave, who was in the studio although he did not play. On both "Buck Dancer's Choice" and "Franklin Blues," Uncle Dave comes in after Sam plays the first movement and says (almost identically on both records): "Hallo, folks. This is Sam McGee, just from Tennessee, just a-gettin' right. Let 'er go!" This was quite likely one of the tag lines Uncle Dave customarily used to introduce Sam when the two were doing shows. "Buck Dancer's Choice," as the title suggests, was written by Sam as accompaniment to a buck dancer, possibly one that Sam used to play on the vaudeville stage. The basic tune is an eight-bar song in C which later became a favorite with black musicians, and, in the 1960s, a staple of the folk revival. "Franklin Blues" breaks into two sections; the first, slower section suggests a polite parlor piece of the late nineteenth century; the second, fast section ("Ding Dong!" shouts Uncle Dave) seems to be based on the chord progressions of "Railroad Bill." Sam recalled that he learned the tune from Dr. John Merrit of Franklin, at whose house Sam would stop on his way home from school. "I was bashful, but he wanted to hear me play; he'd even a lot of time come to the door and make me come in and play for him. He used

to say, 'That little devil can beat me playing my own tune.'"
"Knoxville Blues" begins with Uncle Dave saying: "Hallo, folks.
Talk about hot air and wind — we'll give you something real now,
right from Knoxville, Tennessee, from the Windsor Hotel. Let's
go." (In spite of the introduction, the number was recorded in
New York.) "Knoxville Blues" also consists of two separate
strains: a medium waltz and a raggy breakdown. The slower section Sam later identified as "Little Texas Waltz"; Little Texas
was the name of a section of Williamson County in which Sam
lived for a time. The fast section has been identified by guitar
historian Robert Fleder as a reworking of "Poor Boy Long Ways
From Home," a black piece often borrowed and adapted by
white musicians. Between the two sections, Uncle Dave tells
about an experience in New York: "Well, folks, I took a ride on
an underground car yesterday and the way folks run on there,
the only difference between them and stock is that a man just
needs a pole to punch 'em around with."

From 1926 to 1934 Sam recorded during five of Uncle Dave's
eight recording sessions: alone with Uncle Dave three times, with
his brother Kirk and Uncle Dave once, and with Uncle Dave,
Kirk, and local fiddler Mazy Todd (as the Fruit Jar Drinkers and
Dixie Sacred Singers) once. Although Sam generally established
his reputation as an instrumentalist, of the ten solo sides he recorded before 1935, six were vocals by Sam ("In a Cool Shady
Nook," "If I Could Only Blot Out the Past," "Easy Rider,"
"Chevrolet Car," "As Willie and Mary Strolled by the Seashore,"
and "The Ship without a Sail"). Of the twelve early sides he recorded with brother Kirk, all twelve feature vocals; but only
four feature vocals by Sam ("C-H-I-C-K-E-N Spells Chicken,"
"Rufus Blossom," "My Family Has Been a Crooked Set," "The
Tramp"). These ten numbers form an easily verifiable basis for
his early repertory and reveal that Sam, while developing his ac-
knowledged skills as an instrumentalist, was also developing as a
vocalist.

Recording with Uncle Dave was an experience in itself. Sam
and Uncle Dave were used to performing in schools and auditoriums that lacked any sort of amplifying equipment; they would
have to "give 'er all we had" in order to be heard. In the sensitive
recording studio, Uncle Dave had to be restrained at times from

getting too close to the microphone, and his boisterous foot stomping had to be cushioned with a pillow; perfect takes, therefore, were not always made the first time.

> Sometimes we'd have to do it two or three times. One time we were recording up there in New York; we were playing one of Uncle Dave's numbers, and he forgot some of the words—it was something he hardly ever did do, but he did that time. The fellow doing the recording was Jack Kapp, and Uncle Dave stopped in the middle and said, "Uh oh, Kapp. I ruined that one." Kapp laughed aloud about it and said, "I'm going to play it back over to you," and of course when it got to that part, "Uh oh, Kapp. I ruined that one," and Uncle Dave—man, he popped. Had the biggest time over that. But that's what'll happen. When you do your best playing is when you don't care about how many mistakes you make if you get to the last. I have more trouble about that than anything else: I get nervous sometimes.

While Sam was not exactly blasé about making records, the early records did not seem to alter seriously his relationship to his community or his concept of himself as a performing artist. He did not really "promote" the records in any sense: "When Uncle Dave and I were playing anywhere, he didn't try to plug records like they do now. That's done a lot today, on the Opry, other places; a little too much of it done, really. Say, I've got a late number here that's selling good, wanting to make a top number out of it; well, I got to plug that. And here you come with another one right behind me, just about the same thing nearly, maybe different words and all, kind of love songs and all —one right after the other. Maybe you're not interested in buying a record even if it is a top number. So me and Uncle Dave never did much of that really."

Sam's story about his first royalty check perhaps best illustrates how he viewed making records and his early professional musical career in general.

> My first records sold awfully good for that time, back then. Times was tough then, nobody had no money, no extra money floating around like it is today. A man today, if he doesn't work, he doesn't want to work; get a job anywhere, but back then you couldn't do it. And I didn't know a trade or anything. I had spoken to my older brother, John, about a fattening hog—he had some nice big barrows, you know, some weighing close to 500 pounds. He had these

big hogs, and I wanted one of them; so I'd spoken to him to save me one. He said all right he would. But I knew it'd be pretty close to get the money to pay for it—it would have been all right with him, I could have paid him when I got ready; but I like to pay for it as it goes. So for the first quarter sales on those records, the royalty came to $350—big money to me then. So I went down and said to him, "I want *two* of them fattening hogs." And he said, "What have you done, robbed a bank?" And I said, "No, that's the royalty on the records I made." He thought that was pretty good; he was a hard worker, a pretty well-to-do farmer, good manager, bunch of cattle, big crops, everything—he was on the job all the time. He had told me, "You'd be better off (I'd been playing somewhere, getting no money or very little money) if you'd throw that guitar up on the grapevine and burn it up." But he began to think different after this. I didn't mind working; but even working, still that music was about me, and I liked to hear it every once in a while.

Sometime about 1931 Sam broke with Uncle Dave. It was to be an important change for him, both personally and musically. The reasons behind the break—it was not a complete estrangement, for the two men continued to see one another and even to record together for a time—are complex. No small contributing factor was Uncle Dave's wanting his sons to perform with him; and by 1930 Dorris, the youngest Macon, had reached an age that permitted him to second on guitar for his father on many tours. But probably a more deep-seated reason was that Sam was continuing to develop as a musician and a singer, and felt confined in both of these roles with Macon. As we have seen, Sam felt that Macon dominated their stage shows and allowed Sam only occasional solo spots. Also, by 1930 the depression was making serious inroads into the music business. In December of 1930 Macon took Sam to Jackson, Mississippi, for one last session of duet recordings; here too the results were disappointing—only about half the recordings were released. A few months after that the actual break between Sam and Uncle Dave occurred:

We were just playing up in Virginia. I had already wrote home that I'd be back, and I never did write home or call home that I didn't try to call or come back or something, unless something had happened bad. So we met up with a bunch, having a big time, plenty to drink; that was on a Friday night, and they were wanting us to stay over and not come in home. So I told Uncle Dave, "I've might near got to go back home because I wrote home and told I would be there; and if I don't go back, they'll be uneasy about me, be having everybody on the lookout for me." Well, they outtalked Uncle Dave and got him to stay over, and I came on. We'd bought us a car together, an A Model Ford (man, we thought it was the stuff then; we'd been using an old T Model sedan, those with no glass windows in it), and we'd used it maybe a year or so. What happened, Uncle Dave didn't have to come back home if he didn't want to; he was pretty well fixed for money and everything else — he could be a free bully if he wanted to. So I took the car and came on home with it. So Uncle Dave comes home the first of the next week. So over to my house Uncle Dave comes, and he brought a mechanic and one of his sons to look over the car to see if I'd done anything to the car, since he'd seen it. He finally came in and told me what he came for. He said, "Well, since we are through playing together, we can't have this car together; one of us got to own it." And I said, "Uncle Dave, you be the judge and the jury. Whatever you say, I'll abide." And he said, "Well, I'll buy you out or you buy me out. I'll give so and so, or I'll take so and so." And I said, "All right, Uncle Dave. You just bought yourself a car." 'Cause I didn't have to have it; and I didn't care if I ever played another tune or not, because I wasn't afraid of working. I didn't enjoy being off from home all the time anyhow. I had my family by this time, young children and all. So it wasn't but a very short time before he began to look at it in a different way, and he began to write me about playing dates; but I would never go back with him anymore.

To a degree, Sam's job with Uncle Dave was taken over by his younger brother Kirk, who continued to travel with the older man off and on until Macon's death in 1952. By the same token, the McGees began to play together much more as brothers in the 1930s. In fact, the careers of Sam and Kirk during this time became inextricably intertwined, and for many of their fans they hardly had individual personalities. To some extent, it is difficult to isolate one brother and single him out for any kind of study, for too many of their tunes and styles have been developed in tandem: it is hard to say which brother contributed what. The story of Sam McGee at this stage must inevitably also become the story of Kirk McGee.

Sam referred to Kirk as "the baby" in the family, and certainly Sam dominated part of Kirk's musical heritage. While Sam was serving his "apprenticeship" with Uncle Dave in the 1920s, Kirk, who was five years younger than Sam, was beginning his career by traveling with a medicine show in Alabama. By 1927 Kirk was occasionally playing with Sam and Uncle Dave, as well as with fiddler Mazy Todd and his cousin Blythe Poteet. When Sam broke with Uncle Dave, Kirk was ready to step in, already knowing the tunes and routines by heart. Sam and Kirk had generally the same musical background, including learning from their father. Kirk learned to play the mandolin first, then the banjo; eventually he learned to play the fiddle, and Kirk during his time with Uncle Dave often played fiddle and paid much more attention than formerly to his father's playing. "Our father," Kirk recalls, "played slow but perfect. He had plenty of time to practice, just for his own benefit. He wanted to do it just right. He played just about half as fast as we do now."

Although Sam and Kirk have much in common, it is useful for our portrait of Sam to note some ways in which Kirk differs. Kirk learned from two sources that were different from Sam's: a banjo player named Felix Bennet and the old James D. Vaughn songbooks used in Kirk's school. "I learned a lot of those old hymns and gospel numbers from there, songs like 'Only a Step from the Grave.'" Related to this gospel music was a strong tradition at the turn of the century of unaccompanied quartet singing; it was apparently a rural counterpart to the barbershop quartet movement, and Kirk recalls that both he and Sam picked up a lot of their songs from a family in Franklin named Graves who sang in this style. As with the gospel music tradition, the McGees seem to have absorbed more of the songs than the actual performance style. Kirk also tends to emphasize the black influence more directly than did Sam; he not only acknowledges the importance of local black musicians, but also admits to listening closely to blues records by people like Gus Cannon, Papa Charlie Jackson, and Tampa Red.

Kirk's personality is quite different from Sam's, and this distinction is reflected in his music. He is not the technical innovator Sam was, and he is generally pragmatic about his music, more business-oriented. Kirk is a bit more serious than Sam and more self-conscious. Kirk likes to do rather formal laments or cautionary songs such as "Only a Step from the Grave" and "Master's Runaway," whereas Sam preferred light comedy songs such as "The Ship without a Sail," "Chevrolet Car," and "My Family Has Been a Crooked Set." It would probably be fair to say that Kirk takes his vocal chores a little more seriously than Sam, but he also tends to be more conservative about the way he appropriates his tradition. Often Kirk will sing a song he learned from another source in the same manner that he learned it; Sam was more inclined to put his own particular brand on a song and didn't hesitate to rearrange it to suit himself. (Which approach is closer to folk tradition is a matter for conjecture and has much to do with how one defines folk tradition.)

From about 1930 to the mid-1950s, Kirk and Sam made most of their public appearances together. Each became an almost inestimable influence on the other; nevertheless, each maintained his distinct musical personality, and each developed a distinct repertory of songs during this time. Even with the natural petty jealousies that come normally to two brothers who have been working in the same field for so many years, Sam was quick to praise Kirk's fiddling, and Kirk has never hesitated to acknowledge Sam's artistry on the guitar. Yet the two voices are hard to tell apart.

Before Sam moved completely into this new phase of his career, there was one last great recording session with Uncle Dave; it produced some of Sam's most influential music. Sam had not recorded since 1930, and more than twenty years would pass before the McGees recorded again. The session took place in 1934 at the Gennett Recording Studios in Richmond, Indiana. Kirk, who with his cousin Blythe Poteet had recorded earlier for Gennett, sent in a small seven-inch audition disc to the company; the result was an invitation to Sam, Kirk, and Uncle Dave to make the session. By 1934 the record market was picking up again, and some companies were starting to regain solvency. The group recorded fourteen sides, some individually, some as duos, some as trios; however, only six of these sides were ever issued. Among those issued are two by the McGees and Uncle Dave, "Thank God for Everything," and a rousing gospel-type number, "When the Train Comes Along." Both numbers were credited jointly to Sam and Kirk. It is significant, especially in measuring the McGees' emerging status as traditional performers, that they got equal billing with Uncle Dave on these records and that two of the six sides issued did not even have Uncle Dave on them. The two songs without Uncle Dave, "Brown's Ferry Blues" and "Railroad Blues," were to become closely associated with the brothers: "Brown's Ferry Blues," which became somewhat a classic among folk revivalists in the 1960s, was for many years attributed to the brothers. Neither brother, however, ever claimed authorship of the song; both remarked that the Delmore brothers had already been singing the song by 1934. (In fact the Delmores recorded it in 1933, and Brown's Ferry is very close to the Delmores' hometown of Athens, Alabama. It is quite likely, however, that the McGees had heard some of the blues stanzas of the song circulating orally long before the Delmores incorporated them in their song.)

"Railroad Blues" was a vocal and guitar solo by Sam, a song which became one of his most influential and enduring works. The lyrics of the song, transcribed here from the original 1934 recording, reflect both Sam's interest in blues lyric form and his tendency to personalize blues stanzas.

Went down to the depot, looked upon the board;
Went down to the depot, looked upon the board.
It read, "Good times here, but better down the road."

Well, you can't do me like you done poor Shine;
Well, you can't do me like you done poor Shine.
You took poor Shine's woman, but you can't take mine.
[Spoken over guitar] Here comes Deford Bailey now with his harmonica. Tom Long coming through Nashville with a load of pig iron.

3. Where was you, Mama, when the train left the shed?
Where was you, Mama, when the train left the shed?
I was standing in the front yard, wishing I was dead.

4. Two little monkeys, playing up in a tree,
Two little monkeys, playing up in a tree,
One says to the other, "Come on, let's make whoopee."

5. Met a little Gypsy in a fortune-telling place;
Met a little Gypsy in a fortune-telling place.
She read my mind and then she slapped my face.

The music for "Railroad Blues" is full of pulls on the guitar strings, bent notes, and choked chords. After the first sung stanza, Sam also plays a guitar break with which he sings in a high wordless falsetto—both guitar and voice in perfect unison, a technique often used by country blues singers (such as Robert Johnson and other Delta bluesmen) but seldom found among white singers. Part of Sam's playing here, however, also suggests piano ragtime, especially in his last guitar break of the instrumental verses, by repeating the break note for note three times (something a blues guitarist would probably not do) and spreading the break over two octaves, a range that is somewhat unusual for a guitar run. Insofar as the words are concerned, some stanzas (such as 3 and 4) seem adapted from fairly commonplace blues stanzas that Sam probably found in local tradition; in fact, stanza 4 sounds much like one used in "Brown's Ferry Blues." Yet there are some distinct elements in the song that personalize it for Sam: the reference in stanza 1 to the depression, the spoken asides after stanza 2 about Deford Bailey (the black harmonica player on the Opry whom Sam played with and knew quite well) and about Tom Long (an engineer), and the reference to "poor Shine" in stanza 2. (When asked who Shine was, Sam replied, "He was just any colored boy—he wasn't anybody I really knew.") Incorporating into the blues a reference to a generic black figure stamps it as a white product, as does the phrase "make whoopee" in stanza 4—an echo from the popular music of the twenties, perhaps specifically Gus Kahn's song "Makin' Whoopee" (1928). All in all, "Railroad Blues" is typical of Sam's best work; it is a song with fixed and repetitive passages, it contains distinct elements of humor, and it is a song taken partly from tradition yet personalized. It illustrates the method Sam used in dealing with his material throughout his career.

"Railroad Blues," if we can judge from the number of times the record was reissued, sold quite well throughout the 1930s, but apparently not well enough to attract further recording offers for either Sam or Kirk. By now the brothers were more consciously trying to succeed on their own, to emerge from Uncle Dave's looming shadow, and to find their own distinct musical identity. Throughout the late 1920s, in fact, they had regularly made appearances on their own and had even worked off and on in medicine shows. Sam recalled learning many comedy songs and even comedy routines in particular from these shows. "I'd go to these little shows where they'd have comedians and all singing songs; I learned lots of comedy songs that way. Medicine shows and tent shows, just any kind of show going on that way that might have music in it. Generally they'd have just one clown that did a lot of the comedy stuff." (The clown, or Toby, was a stylized figure common in such shows; another comic figure was the blackface Rastus such as the one Tom Ashley often played.)

Medicine shows were popular in Tennessee well into the 1930s and were a musical medium which both black and white folk musicians shared; these traveling shows undoubtedly played an important role in the black and white interchange of songs, jokes, and stories. Regarding one particular medicine show, Sam recalled:

> They'd generally have some kind of a little stage, or maybe it'd be right out on the ground. No seats, 'cause people would just stand up and listen. They'd always have a guy—a medicine man, typical medicine man who followed that for a living—he could almost sell you clear water, he was such a good talker. Kirk and me worked for one one time where we made the medicine at my house. It was gasoline and hartshorn and different things in it. We put the gasoline in bottles, bottled it up at my house: little vial about as tall and about as big as your thumb nearly. Well, you'd sell it for a dollar, a dollar and a half. Callary's Medicine Show was the name of it. On a typical show, we'd go out first and play a little music, get the crowd to come up; and then he'd talk to them. Sometimes he'd go out and tell them about what he had with him, the music and all. "Come on up; won't cost you a thing to look. Free, all free." When he got through, it wasn't free. So we caught up with him one night; he was taking dope. We had suspicioned it, but didn't know for sure; and we went to bed that night—we didn't go to sleep as quick as he thought we did—and he got up and got into that dope, and he was as wild as a bull for awhile. He was taking it all the time; so we told him, next day or two, that we had to quit. I didn't want to work for that kind of man, 'cause I didn't know what kind of a crazy notion he might take. One thing my mother and daddy always taught me: if you steal anything, steal away from bad company.

But by 1930 Sam was starting to play with another musician who was to have almost as great an influence on his career as Uncle Dave, Fiddlin' Arthur Smith. From about 1930 to about 1938, Sam, Kirk, and Arthur teamed up to form one of the most popular and influential string bands of the time, the Dixieliners. Even to this day, many fans associate Sam with Arthur Smith rather than Uncle Dave, and the impact the Dixieliners made on Southern traditional music can hardly be overestimated. Sam always felt that his relationship with Smith was more musically rewarding than his stint with Uncle Dave. Unlike Macon, Smith made few commercial concessions in his music; the shows of the Dixieliners were apparently fairly free from novelty and contained a high percentage of hard-core old-time instrumental and traditional music.

Sam and Arthur had much in common. Arthur was born in Humphreys County and lived only a county away from the McGees. Like the McGees, he came from a musical family, and family legend tells of his playing the fiddle at the age of four, standing the instrument up to play it since he was too small to hold it under his chin. As a young man, Arthur worked on the railroad, living in a railroad car and practicing his fiddle late into the night. By 1928 he was appearing with his cousin Homer on the newly named Grand Ole Opry. Sam and Kirk heard Arthur on the show and sought him out; they simply walked up to his door and introduced themselves. Sam recalled, "I met Arthur at WSM originally. He then lived at Dickson, Tennessee. He liked to play and I liked to play and we got together. He had a brother [*sic*] played with him for a while; his name was Homer Smith, a guitar player. I don't know why it was that Homer quit playing, but anyhow he did; I got to playing with Arthur in his place. We went into the Dixieliners and there for seven or eight years played on the Grand Ole Opry." Kirk soon joined, and the three found they shared a common repertory of traditional Middle Tennessee tunes; they were playing together even while Arthur held down his day job on the railroad. For a time Sam and Kirk picked up Arthur on Fridays, traveled weekends to play dates, and returned him for work Monday mornings. Soon the band, the name of which was taken from a train Arthur once worked on, caught on with the public, and Arthur quit railroading to play music full-time. Throughout the mid-1930s they continued to play and gradually evolved the practice of touring on weekdays and returning every Saturday night for the WSM broadcasts. The WSM Artist Service Bureau (formed in the early 1930s to help broadcasting artists get live bookings and enable the WSM musicians to make a full-time job of their music) promoted most of the Dixieliners' tours, and for its trouble took 15 percent of the gate. Managers usually received another 20 percent, and a similar amount often went to hire a hall or a schoolhouse for the performance. Nonetheless, the work was lucrative enough for the depression years, and the McGees had found in Smith a musical soul mate whose technical ability was in every way equal to their own. The work was also personally satisfying; Arthur Smith later said that the "McGees became like brothers to me."

Arthur Smith's playing with the McGees in the 1930s had an immense impact on amateur folk fiddling styles in the Southeast. Smith's popularity among fiddlers of the time was rivaled only by that of Georgia fiddler Clayton McMichen. It was McMichen and Smith more than anyone else who popularized the so-called long-bow technique in the Southeast. Before the late 1920s many fiddlers in the area, especially in the mountains, used a short "jiggy bow" style in their fiddling. This latter technique yielded a style that was highly rhythmic, driving, and a bit rough; it demanded more action from the bowing hand as opposed to the fingering. Conversely, the long-bow technique, traditionally associated with Texas fiddling styles, involved less drive but produced a smoother, clearer tone; each note was made distinctly, the bow seldom left the strings, and much of the work consisted in noting as opposed to bowing. In the 1930s McMichen and Smith were showing Southerners that fiddling was more complex an art than they had suspected. During this time Smith popularized many tunes that have since become staples at Southern fiddling contests, such as "Pig in the Pen," "Red Apple Rag," "Hollow Poplar," "House of David Blues," "Fiddler's Dream," "Mocking Bird," "Lost Train Blues," "Dickson County Blues," "Chittlin' Cooking Time in Cheatham County," and perhaps his most famous one, "More Pretty Girls Than One."

Although they usually performed with Arthur on his personal appearances, neither Sam nor Kirk ever recorded with him in those early days. (The many Bluebird records Smith made in the 1930s were usually recorded with the Delmore Brothers.) Sam was not to record with Arthur until the mid-1950s, when Mike Seeger recorded them for Folkway Records. It is unfortunate that the Dixieliners, who toured and broadcast so much together, never recorded in their prime, for one might well argue that for a time the Dixieliners could boast of having the most influential old-time guitar stylist (Sam) and the most influential fiddle stylist (Arthur) in the entire South. Jon Pankake has written of the collaborations of McGee and Smith: "The music . . . is a synthesis of several important American musical traditions. Although it is firmly based in a southeastern white folk music, the individual genius of the musicians and their unique opportunities to polish and sophisticate their music through cultural contacts denied the nonsophisticated or truly 'folk' musician has yielded a music of a different order than that usually documented by the folklorist." Ironically, from the standpoint of the 1980s, we can see that this very end product in itself has been a prime influence on many "nonsophisticated" or "folk" musicians of the Southeast. To many amateur musicians at fiddling contests and folk festivals today, Arthur Smith represents old-time traditional fiddling, and Sam old-time mountain guitar playing; they themselves in many ways became sources of traditional music.

Oddly enough, although he actually spent as much time with Arthur as he did with Uncle Dave, Sam did not have many special memories, opinions, or stories about that period in his life. Certainly Arthur's personality was no match for Uncle Dave's; Arthur was a tall, almost somber man who took his music quite seriously. In most of the shows, it was Sam who had to do the comedy, frequently drawing on his nonsense songs and a bag of showman's tricks picked up from Uncle Dave. "Arthur was a fine musician, but he wasn't a showman," Sam recalled; "he didn't hardly want to say anything on stage. He just whipped it out and played, but they sat up and listened." Sam stated, in fact, that Arthur did not entirely approve of some of his antics. For example, when the popular musicians needed to get through a crowd in a hurry, Sam would sometimes throw a "fit": he would scream, jerk, and make his eyes pop; then Kirk and Arthur would have to "restrain" him. "We got through the crowd, they parted for us quick enough, but Arthur sometimes thought it was a little foolish." Kirk tells another anecdote that illustrates this peculiar facet of McGee and Smith's relationship.

Once we were in East Tennessee, playing a school up there. There was a fellow, a miller; he came down — he wasn't going to be able to stay for the show. He says to me, "I just want to see Arthur Smith. I'm not going to see the show, but I just want to see Arthur Smith." And I pointed him out: "Why, that's him over there." And he said, "My goodness, what a big nose. No wonder that fellow can play the fiddle." And, you know, it kind of plagued Arthur. He didn't want anybody to notice his big nose; now it wasn't unreasonably big, but he did have a nice one. Well, I told him what the fellow said, and he worried about it for several days.

Smith, who died in 1972, was to remain a close friend and frequent musical companion to both Sam and Kirk in later years, but the Dixieliners themselves broke up about 1938. Smith went west to Hollywood to try his hand at playing the western music then popular; in addition, Sam, who was never overly fond of touring, had broken from Smith several times when tours ran too long. He was willing to break both with Uncle Dave and Arthur, it seemed, if the stability of his family life was threatened.

Thus for several years Sam and Kirk found their musical development more and more aligned with that of the Grand Ole Opry, and in the late 1930s they both played with many performers from the Opry. Sam played with Jack Anglin (later of Johnny and Jack) and taught him a version of "Railroad Blues." Sam and Kirk for a time also formed the musical portion of a rustic comedy act with Sara and Sallie, two of the first dialogue comediennes on the Opry stage. Both brothers also toured for a time with Bill Monroe after he joined the Opry cast in 1939. Sam and Kirk would generally do a thirty-minute music-and-comedy set at the end of Monroe's tent and ballpark shows, and Sam would feature his imitation of Uncle Dave Macon. Neither brother was overly impressed by the fact that Monroe was creating a new type of music, bluegrass. While Sam thought highly of Bill Monroe as a personal friend, he was not especially enthusiastic about bluegrass.

Although neither had trouble in the forties finding work as a musician, both Sam and Kirk became increasingly interested in producing their own kind of music more than in merchandising themselves as personalities. As the star system and commercialism continued to overtake the music they had helped make, the brothers began to wonder if there was to be a place in the new "country music" for the McGee brand of music. The music was moving uptown; and Nashville, as well as the Grand Ole Opry, was becoming increasingly complex. The old direct relationship between artist and audience that Sam experienced with Uncle Dave and enjoyed in his round of small schoolhouses and informally arranged concerts was becoming a thing of the past. Both Sam and Kirk sensed this change and determined to try to adapt as much as possible without compromising their artistic integrity, but the change was not easy for them. The glimpses one has of both brothers during the war reflect their dilemma as musicians: Sam, on the Opry in an NBC air-check in 1941, singing a comedy nonsense song, "Barefoot Boy with Boots On," not taking a single guitar break or playing one lick of his recognizable flat-top style; and Kirk, away from the music entirely, working for eighteen months, supervising German POWs in Indiana. There were jobs in music, to be sure, touring with various Opry groups; but the income from show business was not as reliable as it once had been, and Sam perceived that he was no longer in the vanguard of musical styles, as he had been for the prior twenty years.

Sam's musical home base, the Opry, was changing too. With the coming of Roy Acuff in the years immediately before the war, the Opry accelerated its shift away from the instrumental string band tradition that had made the Opry a household word and moved toward the newer music that was based on the vocal country lament. In the early 1940s, many of the Opry old-timers watched with disbelief as western swing star Bob Wills unloaded his white bus full of saxes, trumpets, music stands, and drums on the sacred Opry stage. At the same time Pee Wee King's Golden West Cowboys began regularly to feature an electric steel guitar. After the war, George Hay, the "Solemn Old Judge" who had on occasion forcibly held the Opry on a traditional course, began to relinquish control of the program. By the early 1950s, his successor, Ott Devine, was attempting to push the show in the direction of mainstream music. Transcriptions of the Opry made during this time reveal a rather sobering assortment of musical pabulum: syrupy-smooth vocals, barbershop quartets, honky-tonk sing-alongs, hokum harmonica solos, fiddles playing polkas, and an announcer always careful to specify that this was "real American folk music" or "music in genuine folk style." Many of Hay's contemporaries—the originators of the show's genuine folk content—left or passed away. Deford Bailey left in the 1940s. Uncle Dave Macon himself died in 1952 (Kirk was one of the pallbearers), and the great old colorful Opry bands—the Clodhoppers, the Gully Jumpers, the Possum Hunters, the Fruit Jar Drinkers—began to be condensed, combined, and phased out. Vocalists like Red Foley and Hank Williams set the pace for the Opry music in the early fifties.

In order to survive at all, the McGees had to be increasingly adaptable, both in their music and in their lives. Musically, Sam added newer tunes to his repertory, songs reflecting western swing ("South," "San Antonio Rose," "Under the Double Eagle," "Steel Guitar Rag") and the newer vocal tradition ("Just Because," "Alabama Jubilee"). And it was Sam who had tried to bring one of the first electric guitars into the Opry during the late 1930s:

> Fellow by the name of McLemore come here, come there; he had this electric steel guitar. I heard him play the thing and I thought it was pretty — I'd never heard one before — so I bought if off of him; I was going to learn to play it, I thought. I got by with it for two Saturday nights; and on the third Saturday night I was ready to play on our half hour, and Judge Hay came out and tapped me on the shoulder, said, "Sam, I'd rather you not play that on the Grand Ole Opry; we want to hold it down to earth." I said, "All right, thank you, Judge"; and I never did bring it back no more.

The novelty of the electric sound soon wore off for Sam; and even when the Opry became electrified, he kept to traditional instrumentation. (However, he retained the little electric National as well as two newer electric Gibsons, which he played on rare occasions.)

After the war both Sam and Kirk pursued other vocations in addition to their music. Sam had always maintained a farm, and during 1945–1955 he spent more and more time developing it. Kirk entered the real estate business, first in Nashville, then in Brentwood, and finally in his native Franklin. Sam and Kirk began in the 1950s to establish a pattern of working during the week at their regular jobs and playing music on weekends, usually for the Opry and occasionally at dances and concerts. Their performances became so much less frequent that one account of the brothers written in the late 1950s mentions both of them as being "retired from the music business." Sam had always been insecure about depending on music as his sole source of income: "I've always done a little farming, only more so recently. I've never depended on any one certain thing to make a living. I guess, looking back now, that I would have been better if I had put it all in music." Kirk, for his part, found considerable satisfaction in the real estate business; it agreed with his temperament and allowed him to exercise his considerable knowledge of local history, lore, and customs: "I knew personally the history of a lot of the land around here, who lived there and who he was."

Music remained a vital part of the McGees' lives; but in spite of their natural adaptability and willingness to innovate within tradition, both brothers found themselves encountering problems they had never imagined. Like most of the semiprofessional musicians from the early days of music, they preferred staying home with their families to extensive touring. Unlike some, both McGees had always been willing to make sacrifices in their careers for the sake of their families. Now, with Sam spending more time farming and Kirk working in real estate, they had even less desire to tour. About 1955 these circumstances, along with the Opry's attempt to move toward mainstream music, brought about a confrontation between the brothers and the new Opry personnel. Sam, as usual, was content to leave business matters up to Kirk. As Kirk tells the story:

> They decided they would stop us from singing, and we had the biggest round you ever heard. Vito Pellettieri said to me one day, "Now Kirk, you and Sam come on down here and get your money. Just play in with anybody, but you won't get any more recognition. Your name won't be called." And I said, "Why, what's happening?" And he said, "Well, you won't go on the road." And I said, "That's right, I won't go. I was on the road twenty years trying to make a living of it. But I won't take that for an answer; who decides this?" And he said, "There's a committee of seven of us, including Jim Denny, Jack Stapp, Jack DeWitt, and Ott Devine." So next week Sam and I went to see Jack Stapp, and he said, "Well, you boys won't go on the road no more, and these new boys needs the time; you're taking up their time." And I said, "I want to tell you something. I helped create this thing. It's part of my creation. I came down here on many a cold night in a Model T Ford with ragged side curtains, with no heater, in the dead of winter, and the Craigs [the owners of National Life and of the Opry] told me, 'If this thing ever got on a paying basis, you and Sam will have a home.'"

Kirk eventually went up to see Mr. Craig himself, and the order to shelve Kirk and Sam was soon rescinded. Kirk reports Mr. Craig's saying, "If I catch them mistreating any of you old boys, I'll fire the whole works of them." Even though Sam and Kirk had won a victory of sorts, the incident left both brothers unsettled.

If the confrontation with the Opry personnel was the nadir of their career, their zenith was just around the corner. The folk revival began in the late fifties; and along with enriching popularizers like the Kingston Trio, the movement succeeded in refocusing attention on a number of genuine folk performers. A new, young, mostly urban audience was developing, an audience who would see the McGees not merely as competent back-up musicians or old fogies who refused to step out of the way for would-be Eddy Arnolds, but as rare, vibrant links with a rich musical past.

The rediscovery of the McGees can probably be traced to a series of shows they played in July 1956 at New River Ranch in Maryland. Although they appeared as sidemen for Grandpa Jones, a group of young enthusiasts (among them Tom Paley) recognized them and prevailed on them to do Kirk's classic "Milk Cow Blues" and Sam's "Railroad Blues." A year later, in November 1957, Mike Seeger visited the brothers in Nashville and asked them to record a Folkways album; the brothers agreed but suggested that their old fiddling partner Arthur Smith be included as well. This album, reuniting the Dixieliners and providing the first recordings of them, was successful enough that a second Folkways album was later released. Both records, along with the enthusiasm of people like Mike Seeger and *Sing Out!* writer Jon Pankake, helped the brothers to discover their new folk audience and to begin a series of folk festival appearances.

Soon the Newport Folk Foundation sponsored the McGees (with Smith) in a series of concerts in New York, Boston, and Philadelphia. After hearing them in this series, *New York Times* critic Robert Shelton remarked, "I heard more playing by the McGees in one New York concert than I had heard in half a dozen 'Grand Ole Opry' shows." Yet getting the McGees to strike out for new audiences had not been easy, and some early offers to go north were turned down. "I didn't want to go, and I wouldn't go," said Sam; "and I guess I kept Kirk from going." And Kirk adds: "He didn't think they'd like our music, but I finally convinced him that the people knew what they were talking about." Sam was finally convinced after the Newport tour was a success: "The folks were real nice up there; they liked our music, and we had a real good time." So the McGees had a new audience for their music, and this was a sort of revelation; but an even greater one was that the audience was interested in them as

the McGee Brothers *per se*. The sense of their own musical identity, which had been somewhat eclipsed in earlier years, was now
brought home to them with stunning swiftness. A story Kirk tells
illustrates this.

> They asked us once to come and play the University of Chicago; and
> I thought there'd be twenty people on the show, it was so big and all.
> So the man came and picked us up at the airport, name was Burline,
> and I said, "Mr. Burline, I'd like to see the rest of the show, so we'd
> understand each other." And he said, "No, just you and Sam's all
> the show." So I said, "I guess *we* understand each other all right."
> With that big audience and that big place, I kinda dreaded to get
> started. But there was a man in the audience that we'd already
> played with before, with Jim and Jesse, a man named Greenburg;
> and I said, "Come on up here brother Greenburg and play with us."
> So he did, and it helped us do the whole show by ourselves.

Later the McGees grew more used to the idea of being featured
performers and playing to audiences that appreciated "the Mc-
Gee lick." When asked when he started really to become aware
of the McGee brothers as distinct musical stylists, Kirk says:
"We never really noticed it until here in late years, maybe ten
years back" (around 1963).

Sam, for his part, enjoyed himself immensely at folk festivals.
With his insatiable appetite for playing and hearing music, Sam
found the loose, unstructured jam-session atmosphere of festivals more congenial than the somewhat formal, time-restricted
programming of the Opry. Sam enjoyed these outings so much,
in fact, that he frequently made solo guest appearances at various festivals, such as one at the University of Oklahoma and the
American Folklife Festival in Washington.

The McGees' popularity as folk artists helped enhance their
position on the Opry. They played only one or two specialties on
a typical Opry night, but they often played with the Crook
Brothers and Fruit Jar Drinkers and could be frequently heard
in the square dance segments—also, picking sessions in their
dressing rooms backstage attracted substantial numbers of Opry
fans who felt more at home with their type of music. In addition,
the nationwide popularity of bluegrass contributed to easing
work relations with the Opry management. Yet the Nashville
record industry did not see fit to record the McGees and present
them to the traditional country market. The Folkways LPs and a

later album that Sam made solo for Arhoolie were more accessible to the McGees' Northern audience than their Southern one. Starday did record the brothers on an LP with the Crook Brothers; but nearly all the numbers were vocals, and the music had few distinctive McGee touches. The brothers finally resorted to a method that was gaining wide acceptance among other musicians: they decided to produce their own records. Fuller Arnold, a lifelong friend of the brothers and a Franklin banker, initiated the project. "I wanted to see them properly represented on records," he recalls; "and I was afraid time was running out. Sam was pushing eighty and I didn't know how long it would be before arthritis got his fingers. I felt we had to do something." As a result, MBA Records was born, with Sam, Fuller Arnold, and another McGee fan, Elmer Boswell, as major forces. Fuller constructed an excellent little studio in his garage and began to invite Sam and Kirk over for Wednesday night picking sessions. The first album, *Pillars of the Grand Ole Opry*, featured Sam and Kirk doing the numbers they themselves wanted to do; a second album, *Flat-Top Pickin' Sam McGee*, was devoted to Sam's guitar virtuosity. Sam worked hard in Fuller's studio, taping old songs and tunes by the dozens from his immense repertory. Fuller has more than a hundred hours of Sam's music, amassed as a labor of love and for documentary purposes as well as for future albums.

Not only did the McGees continue to evolve as musicians, but they became more confident of their own musical roles. By the 1970s they were willing to see themselves in perspective and to comment on the current musical climate. About bluegrass Sam said: "Just plain old country music played too fast; *bluegrass, crabgrass,* it's all the same to me." Kirk listens to the "superstyle" that fiddling contests today have developed and complains that the music is "so fancy that only another fiddler can appreciate it. It would take a three-legged man to dance to it." Sam was not seriously interested in rock but noted that "it's good to dance to, or it wouldn't have gone so far." Sam played a pop tune if it suited him, tunes like his own special version of Nancy Sinatra's "These Boots Are Made for Walking." He was also quick to praise the playing of Opry mainstays like Howdy Forrester and guitarist Billy Grammer. But he did not like all he saw on the modern Opry stage. "A lot of people ask how the Opry has changed from the 1930s to the present. Well, there's just as much difference as night and day, music and everything. There were no electrical instruments, no drums — oh, they had a piano — but none of this other while Judge Hay was here. He would have none of it. And the Opry would be different today if he were still alive. It would be more down to earth if he lived now." Another thing Kirk notices is the multiplicity of acts at the Opry: "There are so many new ones, it seems, we don't hardly know their faces. About our best friends are Roy Acuff and Bill Monroe and the Fruit Jar Drinkers and the Crook band and some of the other old-timers." Yet about the significance of the Opry and its responsibilities, the brothers' opinions haven't changed: "I've always thought it was the finest thing in the world," said Sam; "I think the new Opryland is great. I hate to see the old Ryman torn down and all, but we're living in a different day, and we've got more people to take care of."

Yet if Sam was not a typical modern-day Opry star, neither did he (or Kirk) fit the mold into which the folk revival placed him. Sam was never a musical purist living in the past; for example, he couldn't see why a fan would get excited about one of his old records made in the 1920s or 1930s when, as he often said, "I can do the same tune now for you in person." In 1973 Sam was approached with the idea that a major record company might reissue some of his 1920s sides from Vocalion masters; Sam was pleased but said, "If they're willing to put out a record by me — if the vinyl is available and all — I think it would be best to put out a new one and all." Both brothers have tended to be eclectic in their music, not worrying whether or not their sources were "traditional" or the songs "old-timey." Sam's 1973 repertory consisted of songs drawn from sources as diverse as Uncle Dave, Arthur Smith, western swing, Hank Williams, Ernest Tubb, other Opry performers (past and present), Burl Ives, modern "countrypolitan sounds" (manifested, for example, in "Yackety Sax" and "Wheels"), radio, television, and even the folk revival itself.

Sam was always receptive to musical innovation and willing to try new instruments and techniques. In short, he took his music where he found it, regardless of source or circumstances. One morning when he was flat-picking a pop song from the 1920s, "Tip Toe through the Tulips" (also popularized by Tiny Tim in the 1960s), he was asked from which old-time musician he had learned it. "Oh," he laughed, "the TV set was on this morning, and I happened to notice this here Captain Kangaroo was on, and they were singing this song on there, and I hadn't heard it for years, but I liked it and started playing on it." Sam was also willing to experiment with different instruments and different or unorthodox sounds. He had a Mastertone banjo-guitar that he bought in 1926, and he was one of the few traditional musicians to take that strange instrument seriously. "Wreck of the Tennessee Gravy Train," "Brown's Ferry Blues," and some other pieces by him are perhaps the only instances of this instrument's use in old-time recordings. Sam's close friend Fuller Arnold said of him: "Why, he'll pick up anything that's got strings and try to play it. One time in Nashville he even got hold of a tipple and learned to play it. He's not half bad on the mandolin and he can even fiddle a little if he wants to. And then there's those cowbells." Sam had a set of tuned cowbells that he played for years, even on the Opry: "I had to stop that, though; I lost one of my bells, or somebody borrowed it, and I need to have all of them to play any tunes at all." ("Don't get him started on the bells," Mrs. McGee would caution.) Sam's attempt to bring the first electric guitar on the Opry stage was by no means out of character. Also he would daringly play a number on a particular instrument normally not associated with that instrument; for instance, he would pick on the guitar old fiddle breakdowns like "Bonaparte's Retreat," or play on the five-string banjo numbers such as "San Antonio Rose," generally played on fiddle or guitar.

What is more important, this eclecticism had always been one of McGee's hallmarks. Whether it is a cause or an effect of Sam's having survived fifty-five years as a working musician is unclear. However, it can be strongly argued that Sam preserved his musical identity not so much through his choice of songs as through his manner of performing them; and from this point of view Sam's identification with folk music itself relates perhaps more to matters of technique than repertory. Any of Sam's songs, whether its source was Uncle Dave Macon, Bob Wills, Hank Williams, or section hand Jim Sapp, was played in McGee's stylized manner, in an old-time mountain flat-top picking style involving mostly simple first-position chords for the left hand and an alternating bass style for the right. Modern songs such as "Wheels" Sam` stylized by deliberately injecting archaisms;

"Wheels" was normally played by modern guitarists with a sharp, electric pizzicato effect, but Sam played it with a smooth, open flowing sound, full of long, sinewy runs typical of his classic style. By putting the burden of tradition on form rather than content, Sam found an ideal way to survive commercially and yet maintain some artistic integrity. A visit to any modern Southern fiddling contest or bluegrass festival will reveal that Sam was not unique in his notion of tradition; fiddlers adapt modern pop tunes to old forms, and bands play modern rock or country songs in vintage 1946 Flatt and Scruggs bluegrass arrangements. Because of this, a simplified look at repertory does not always give an accurate picture of Sam's music. Furthermore, through his many years as a working semiprofessional musician, Sam was exposed to a much wider range of songs than a purely traditional singer would have been. Sam did not always have absolute freedom to pick and choose his songs; he had at times to please his audience or his musical boss (such as Uncle Dave).

Al Tanner, a frequent partner of Sam's in his last years, once pointed out that being a "folk musician" was not a matter of "skill on one or two numbers—any number of amateur pickers can practice up on one or two showcase numbers. I call Sam a genuine folk musician because he can play 200 or so numbers, all fairly well." For the record, Sam's working repertory—the songs he most often sang in concerts, on the Opry, and in informal surroundings—included about one hundred songs for the last few years of his career (1971–1975). These were by no means all of the songs he knew, however; some songs that he once performed almost every day dropped totally out of his modern repertory; others that had been cast aside years before were reinstituted after folklorists began expressing an interest in Sam's early career. Sam was aware that he also played to different audiences and that different audiences preferred different types of song. The "country and western" audience that attended a typical Opry show, for instance, responded well to numbers like "San Antonio Rose," "Yackety Sax," or "Just Because"; the fiddling contest audience liked what Sam called "them old, old numbers, going way back there," and for them he would perform pieces such as "Needlecase," "Amos Johnson Rag," and "Rufus Blossom." Sam was also aware of a "folk" audience when he performed at folk festivals, and there were some songs that he performed only in informal surroundings among friends. Sam himself was curious about the total number of songs he knew: "Once I started me a little book around here, vowed to write down in it every song I knew—whenever I thought of it. I guess I finally lost it. I'll reckon it had around 200 songs in it."

Although one could classify Sam's songs according to their sources (that is, from whom Sam learned them), Sam himself generally classified them according to his notion of type, and he tried always to balance his programs with a mixture. Labels Sam used to describe his songs include: blues, sentimental songs, rags, sacred songs, comedy songs, and guitar pieces. These categories often cut across folklorists' cherished boundaries between popular and traditional material. Sam's notion of comedy songs included a genuine Anglo-American ballad such as "Cabbage Head" ("Three Nights' Experience," Child 274) as easily as the old popular "Rufus Blossom" (written in 1899 by Kerry Mills) or the modern country song, "The Man Who Comes Around." Guitar pieces included archaic nineteenth century black country jigs as well as contemporary pieces such as a version influenced by Billy Grammer of the love theme from *Doctor Zhivago*. Sentimental songs included items as diverse as the nineteenth century parlor song "If I Could Only Blot Out the Past," the eighteenth century ballad (derived from a British broadside) "As Willie and Mary Strolled by the Seashore," and the country hit recorded by the Delmore Brothers in 1937, "Southern Moon."

While it is impossible to survey in detail Sam's entire working repertory in a study such as this, some indication of its depth and complexity can be seen by looking at representative songs with which Sam has been associated for years and that indicate the various types he performed.

If Sam had ever chosen a "theme song," it would have most likely been "Buck Dancer's Choice," his most famous instrumental piece. We have already seen how Sam originally wrote and recorded the piece in 1926. On that initial recording, Sam played the tune in C (his guitar was capoed to the seventh fret) and generated three separate strains. (This original 1926 Vocalion recording has been transcribed by Stephen Cicchetti in his *Old-Time Country Guitar*.) Later Sam recalled that he had originally added a vamp to the piece as well as a section in *stop time,* where in Sam's words, "the buck dancer wants you to stop and he does the rest with his feet" (cf. his 1971 recording of the number on Arhoolie). Sam was never sure which sections he "picked up" and which he originated. The main melody has ragtime qualities yet sounds enough like a traditional fiddle tune to make it appropriate to accompany the flat-footed style of buck dancing common in the Tennessee-Alabama region. The tune has become a standard exercise for young guitarists trying to learn mountain styles, and it has spread to several widely different sectors of the current folk and blues scene. It has been recorded as blues-like rag by popular black guitarist Taj Mahal and as an autoharp solo by folklorist and folk musician Mike Seeger. It has lent its name to a Canadian folk music magazine (*Buck Dancer's Choice*), a modern western swing band (Red Steagall and the Buckdancer's Choice), and to a prize-winning book of poems by a major American poet, James Dickey (*Buckdancer's Choice*). To all of this, Sam merely said: "I just made it for a buck-dance tune when I started out in vaudeville; in fact, sometimes I didn't even call it 'Buck Dancer's Choice,' I just called it 'Buck-and-Wing.'"

Sam was generally not as innovative on banjo as guitar; he preserved intact older banjo styles and numbers like "Rainbow" and "Needlecase." But on the guitar, he often altered and combined traditional numbers to suit his own taste. "Sometimes I'd move part of one tune over to another one, to make it sound a little fuller or make a little more to it." Many of his instrumental numbers, including "Knoxville Blues," "Franklin Blues," and "Sam McGee Stomp," are such combinations. Other numbers Sam adapted directly from fiddle tunes: "Blackberry Blossom," "Leather Britches," and "Bonaparte's Retreat."

Sam attributed much of the quality of his instrumental music to his own appreciation for fine musical instruments. "I always tell anyone that's wanting to learn my style of guitar, the first thing is to get the very best instrument you can afford. You need to know what you really sound like from the very first — that's the best encouragement there is." Sam's first guitar, which he got before 1920, was a little Stella. After he began traveling some and making more music, Sam acquired his "little Martin"; he bought it new from the H.A. French Music store in Nashville for the sum of eighty-five dollars. (The serial number of this guitar,

29983, indicates it was manufactured in 1927.) This guitar Sam used in much of his early career and to make many of his early records. One of its most famous characteristics is the initials *SM* on its front: "A sign painter up here at Carthage put my initials on her for me." In later years, this little guitar was mistakenly left out in the rain, and the neck bowed, making it difficult to finger; Sam could still play on it if he had to, but preferred his big Martin D-28 Dreadnought. (This guitar bears the serial number 78644 and was apparently manufactured in 1940.) Sam refused to price it, although he was offered as much as $3,000 for it.

> When I first started playing this on the air, a lot of people wrote in, a lot of my mail, just to ask what kind of guitar I was playing. I got this one for $140. The L.C. Tiller Company, piano company on Eighth Avenue there in Nashville, didn't make a specialty in selling guitars, but they got this guitar and had it in the show window. Zeke Clements—he first found it—strolling around Nashville, he come upon this guitar. Came back down to wsm telling all of us, "That's the best one I ever had in my hands." Says, "Ask too damn much for it." I said, "What'd they ask for it," and Zeke said, "$145." I said, "You ain't going to buy it?" "Heck no, that's too much for a guitar." So I made a beeline up there and brought it back with me. One time somebody took it out of my car down there by the Opry house. I put out the word to those pawn shops down there, I wanted it back in one day and no questions asked, but after that it was heck to pay. So that next day, I got a call from one of the pawn shops, says, "Mr. Sam, I got your guitar down here," and I never had any trouble with anyone taking it after that.

Sam got his other prized instrument, his banjo-guitar, in Alabama about 1926. "I was down there with Uncle Dave on a trip; and this fellow, this dealer, name of Joe Sapp, he had these new Gibson instruments in. Now Uncle Dave's old banjo was a Gibson, I think, but it didn't have any resonator and the tuning pegs were made cheap and wouldn't hold. So Uncle Dave, he got a new Mastertone five-string banjo, and I got this Gibson Mastertone banjo-guitar. I liked the sound of it, and still do, over a regular five-string banjo. People say these things are hard to play, but I've never had any trouble. It was right after we got these banjos that we had our pictures made."

Over the years Sam collected a virtual museum of old instruments of all sorts, and he saw them as an important part of his music. They were also links with tradition; he had, for example, his father's old fiddle and the banjo belonging to Opry pioneer Theron Hale.

Comedy songs always played a large part in Sam's career, partly because of his apprenticeship under Uncle Dave. "Uncle Dave was a great hand for comedy songs. Something to make the people laugh. And I'm something of that way myself." In fact, Sam's flair for comedy extended not only to songs, but also to jokes, mugging, trick playing, and imitations (he did fine ones of Macon, Ernest Tubb, and Roy Acuff). One of the favorite stories that Sam told about himself centered on his skill with comedy. Once in the early 1970s he played for some old people in a nursing home in North Carolina. "There was this one lady over there, she hadn't smiled in six years. This man who sent for me, he had been a-doctoring on her. And I began to sing some of those old comedy songs and she sorta smiled. And he says, 'Now that's what I been trying to get her to do in the last six years.' And I said, 'Doc, you wasn't giving her the right medicine.'"

Sam did several types of comedy songs. One was the nonsense song, such as "Barefoot Boy with Boots On" or "The Ship without a Sail," in which he played on verbal paradoxes. Another was the song centering on a comedy of situation, such as Sam's version of "The Very Unfortunate Man" (which he calls "Burglar Bold"), about a burglar who, caught in an old maid's room, watches her remove her false hair, glass eye, and wooden leg. "I Don't Reckon It'll Happen Again," "My Family Has Been a Crooked Set," and "Shut the Door, They're Coming in the Window" are similar songs. One of his favorite comedy songs is "Uncle Doody," "a song about an old man kinda like myself." Sam learned "Uncle Doody" from the Kentucky trio, the Coon Creek Girls, at a festival in Montreal in 1970 (fragments of earlier versions appear in Sharp's *Folk Songs of the Southern Appalachians*). Sam almost always included this song in his concerts after he learned it, although he never formally recorded it.

"Rufus Blossom," or "Whistling Rufus," as it is more commonly known, is what Sam called a "coon" song. Such songs, with their highly stereotyped portrayals of blacks, were very popular in the late nineteenth and early twentieth centuries in vaudeville and burlesque. Coon songs are highly objectionable to today's audiences, however, and Sam was aware of this; he seldom performed them in public. "Whistling Rufus" was an exception that Sam was able to keep in his repertory by changing "nigger" to "man." The image of the fantastic black guitar player described in the song is intriguing to those aware of Sam's own black mentors such as Jim Sapp, but Sam never made any specific connection between the song and any black musicians he had known. Other similar coon songs in Sam's repertory included "C-H-I-C-K-E-N" (a 1902 ragtime song) and "Booker T. Washington"; the latter is a satiric account of Washington's 1901 meeting at the White House with Teddy Roosevelt, and Sam learned it, oddly enough, from a 1927 recording by Gus Cannon, a black musician from Memphis.

Much has been made of the importance of blues in Sam's music, and certainly "Railroad Blues," discussed earlier, is one of his most popular pieces. But Sam generally saw blues lyrics in a lighthearted vein; his brother Kirk was far more serious about blues as a genre, and it was Kirk who intensely listened to local blues singers and to the phonograph records of artists like Papa Charlie Jackson and Kokomo Arnold. Many of his blues songs Sam learned not from black sources but from white sources in the 1930s, when singers like Jimmie Rodgers, Cliff Carlisle, Jimmie Davis, and Billy Cox popularized *white blues.* Sam learned a lot of these popular blues from Slim Smith, a fellow Opry member from Kentucky; Smith taught Sam "Black Sheep Blues," "Penitentiary Blues," and even some parts of "Railroad Blues." Other blues in Sam's repertory came from Opry artists like the Delmore Brothers ("Brown's Ferry Blues"), Roy Acuff ("Freight Train Blues"), Burt Hutcherson ("House of David Blues"), Arthur Smith ("Chittlin' Cookin' Time in Cheatham County," a version of "St. James Infirmary"), and Clayton McMichen ("Farewell Blues"). "Any kind of blues was all right on the old Opry," recalled Sam. "It was down-to-earth music, just like the rest. Only some of it, I didn't fall for, on account of there wasn't enough changes. A good sound, but it didn't put enough into it to make it a good long tune, y' know. Maybe you'd get tired of playing it before you'd play it two or three minutes." One song Sam might well have learned directly from black tradition was his version of "Easy Rider"; many of the couplets here are found in numerous other songs, and many are found in versions of the bluegrass standard "Salty Dog Blues." But in general, any substantial black influence on Sam's music probably was evident more in his style, with its pulls and bent notes, than in his repertory.

Sam's notion of "rags" included examples of the so-called classic ragtime of Scott Joplin and others, such as "Maple Leaf Rag" and "St. Louis Tickle"; examples of rural ragtime, probably learned from black musicians near Perry, such as "Jim Sapp Rag," "Amos Johnson Rag," and "Pig Ankle Rag" (the last was recorded by the black Memphis Jug Band); and examples of modern country and bluegrass rags, such as Maybelle Carter's "Victory Rag" and the bluegrass standard "Black Mountain Rag." When asked to define a rag, Sam explained, "It's not quite as fast as breakdown music, y' see. Not to be played too fast — just a tempo gait." (Scott Joplin often made the same point, occasionally writing on his compositions, "It is never right to play Ragtime fast.") Sam often divided his instrumental pieces into four or five different strains, much like traditional ragtime. His guitar solos certainly owe as much to ragtime as to blues.

Most of Sam's religious songs were rather well-known gospel hymns dating from the late nineteenth century and still popular throughout the South today: "Whispering Hope," "Amazing Grace," "Wayfaring Stranger," "What a Friend We Have in Jesus," "How Great Thou Art." One rather unusual one was "S-A-V-E-D," a sprightly piece that is apparently a folk parody of an earlier Salvation Army song. Sam played the piece often, although seldom in the slot at the end of his programs that he usually reserved for a hymn; the song attacks the hypocrisy of sanctimonious churchgoers who wear their religion on their sleeves. Throughout his life, Sam customarily played his guitar and banjo in churches and at revivals. By the 1970s, when Sam was beginning to lose a little of his speed and dexterity on the guitar, he began to play guitar solos of hymns in concerts and on the Opry stage. (He said that Billy Grammer had inspired him to do this.) He would take the hymns at a fairly brisk tempo and embellish them with his stylistic hallmarks: long, flowing melodic lines, an occasional bent note, a strong right-hand bass. The Opry audience responded enthusiastically, and in 1975 Sam finally recorded an album of hymns for Davis Unlimited Records, a small company based in nearby Clarksville. They were to be his last recordings.

In May 1973 the local radio station in Franklin devoted most of a day's programs to honoring Sam's seventy-ninth birthday; people from across the state phoned in their regards. Members of the Farm Bureau, to which Sam belonged, called in; so did fellow tobacco farmers from Middle Tennessee; and officials from a nearby Veterans Administration hospital called to thank Sam for his extensive volunteer work. Sam was asked if he felt his playing music had made a difference in the way the people in the community looked on him. "Nothing only one way I know of: more people know me than would have if I had never played any music. But as far as changing my life, the attitudes toward me, I don't think it changed that way. I've got plenty of good friends, some good land, got three good sons and good grandchildren; I guess maybe my music helped with some of that."

A few months later, in March 1974, Sam helped his beloved Opry move from the Ryman Auditorium, its old headquarters of more than thirty years, to an entertainment park a few miles east of Nashville. The first show in the modern Opry house was attended by all manner of dignitaries, including President Richard Nixon; Sam, before it started, was in a reflective mood.

> We've come a long way with the show. There's people here now, I tell 'em how it was back in the early days, they don't even believe me. But I was there. This is the finest thing to happen to the Opry: wish all of 'em could be here to see it. There's only seven or eight of us original members left now; we had no idea when we started the Grand Ole Opry that it would make such a go of it, but it has. There were times when I felt like pulling out, just quitting. I felt for a while there that when our music was over, when we were gone, why, that'd be the end of it. But it seems here lately that people are getting interested in our music again. And this Opry house, it's fine. It's a place to show off. You know, you can't sell barbeque without setting it out and saying, "That's barbeque, folks."

As the oldest member of the Opry, Sam was in the first group to perform on the elaborate new stage, and for their opening number, Sam and Kirk played "San Antonio Rose." The audience loved it, and the number was singled out by a writer for the prestigious *New Yorker* as the highlight of the show. "It was the acoustic moment of the show, when the skies cleared and the weeping steels were silent and out of the clear blue came a little ole guitar duet. Stunning and simple." A few days after the show, Sam was asked about the number. "Well, I thought I sounded a little stiff on it. You see, the Monday before the show I got these two right-hand fingers caught in the power lift of a tractor. I got 'em out, but I thought to myself, 'Boy, that's it.' But I kept on working them, wouldn't let 'em stiffen on me. If I had let them, I wouldn't have been able to play. I kept working them, and the night came, and I was able to make a pretty good do of it. I'm glad the people liked it."

On 21 August 1975, Sam was out in his field baling hay. His tractor had been acting up, and after he came back from lunch, he tried to start it by hotwiring it. He apparently forgot, however, that the tractor was in gear, and when the machine started it ran over him. Sam died in the Franklin hospital a few hours later. An overflow crowd attended funeral services in Franklin, and a small choir from the Cool Springs Primitive Baptist Church sang some of Sam's favorite hymns.

In October 1975 young Jimmy McGee took his grandfather's customary place at the Athens fiddling convention. He helped to present the first annual Sam McGee Memorial Award, a trophy given by the fiddling association to the musician best typifying the spirit of old-time music. Then, using one of Sam's old Martin guitars, Jimmy played "Buck Dancer's Choice."

BUCK DANCER'S CHOICE

UNCLE DOODY

♩=184

Well - a, old Un - cle Doo - dy in the shade of the tree Played on the

fid - dle in the key of C. Sheep's in the mead - er and the cow's in the

co'n, But old Un - cle Doo - dy don't give a dog - gone. Fid - dle

on, Un - cle Doo - dy, fid - dle on, fid - dle on, Fid - dle on, Un - cle

Doo - dy, fid - dle on, Fid - dle on, Un - cle Doo - dy, fid - dle on, fid - dle on;

Keep on a - fid - dlin' till the old man's gone, Keep on a - fid - dlin' till the

old man's gone.

1. Wella, old Uncle Doody in the shade of the tree
Played on the fiddle in the key of C.
Sheep's in the meader and the cow's in the co'n.
But old Uncle Doody don't give a doggone.

Fiddle on, Uncle Doody, fiddle on, fiddle on,
Fiddle on, Uncle Doody, fiddle on,
Fiddle on, Uncle Doody, fiddle on, fiddle on;
Keep on a-fiddlin' till the old man's gone,
Keep on a-fiddlin' till the old man's gone.

2. "Wella, hi, Uncle Doody; how you feelin' today?"
Spoken: "Not very well, I'm bound for to say.

Got no use for the shovel and the hoe;
All I need is a fiddle and bow."

3. Wella, old Aunt Viney hollered loud as she could,
Spoken: "Hey, Uncle Doody, fetch me a load of wood!"
Kept on a-fiddlin', didn't turn his head;
He never heard a single word the old gal said.

4. Wella, old Uncle Doody, when the crop was bein' made,
Grabbed his old fiddle and he ran into the shade.
The horseweeds, the cockleburrs, the fiddle and the frost—
Spoken: Just ought to see the co'n that Uncle Doody lost.

EASY RIDER

♩= 288

Stand-in' on the cor-ner with a dol-lar in my hand Just look-in' for the wom-an ain't got no man; Oh, eas-y rid - er, don't you know my name?

st. 5 ref.: "You ain't noth - in' but my salt - y dog."

1. Standin' on the corner with a dollar in my hand
Just lookin' for the woman ain't got no man;
Oh, easy rider, don't you know my name?

2. Down on the river sittin' on a log,
Singin' the song called "Salty Dog";
Oh, easy rider, don't you know my name?

3. Ain't but one thing bothers my mind:
   The world's full of women and none of 'em
      mine;
   Oh, easy rider, don't you know my name?

4. Come get your wienie 'cause it's always
      hot,
   Wienie in the middle and the mustard on
      top;
   Oh, easy rider, don't you know my name?

5. Two little children lyin' in the bed,
   The one turned over to the other and said,
   "You ain't nothin' but my salty dog."

6. Two little children playin' in the sand,
   Run and tell your mama, "Here's the Nu-
      grape man";
   Oh, easy rider, don't you know my name?

7. God made the woman and He made her
      mighty funny,
   Juice around her mouth just as sweet as
      any honey;
   Oh, easy rider, don't you know my name?

8. Just like a needle in a pile of sand,
   Tryin' to find a woman ain't got no man;
   Oh, easy rider, don't you know my name?

WHISTLING RUFUS or RUFUS BLOSSOM

♩ = 200

Way down yon-der lived a shy old pos-sum. High in the syc-a-more tree:

Lived an old man named Ru-fus Blos-som. Was black as a nig-ger could be.

Ru-fus had a head like a big sledge - ham-mer And a mouth like a ter-ri-ble

scar: Well, noth-ing could touch him in the state of Al-a-bam-a When he

picked on his old gui-tar. Don't you make it no blun-der: You

could-n't lose him. It's a per-fect won-der: We had to choose him.

Fine mu-si-cian. Had the high po-si-tion. Was Whist-lin' Ru-fus. The

one bad man.

1. Way down yonder lived a shy old possum,
   High in the sycamore tree;
   Lived an old man named Rufus Blossom,
   Was black as a nigger could be.
   Rufus had a head like a big sledgehammer
   And a mouth like a terrible scar;
   Well, nothing could touch him in the state
      of Alabama
   When he picked on his old guitar.

   Don't you make it no blunder;
   You couldn't lose him.
   It's a perfect wonder;
   We had to choose him.
   Fine musician,

   Had the high position,
   Was whistlin' Rufus,
   The one bad man.

2. While he'd travel to the ball or the party,
   Rained the weather so fine.
   When he arrived, he was welcome at the
      party;
   Out come chicken and-a wine.
   When he was through with the wine and
      the chicken,
   He whistled and he played so grand;
   You'd thought it was angels on their harp
      was a-pickin',
   And they called him the one bad man.

AS WILLIE AND MARY STROLLED BY THE SEASHORE

♩ = 208

As Wil - lie and Mar - y strolled by the sea - shore —— Their last fare - well to take. Says Mar - y to Wil - lie, "If you nev - er re - turn, I'm sure my poor heart will break."

1. As Willie and Mary strolled by the seashore
   Their last farewell to take,
   Says Mary to Willie, "If you never return,
   I'm sure my poor heart will break."

2. "Don't mourn for a little absence, Mary,"
      cried he
   As he pressed the dear girl to his side.

   "If I live and ever return
   I make little Mary my bride."

3. Three years had passed when the news
      came at last.
   She stood in her own cottage door;
   A beggar passed by with a patch on his eye
   His jacket all ragged and torn.

. "Your company is sweet, little Mary,"
    cried he;
"A message for you I've beside:
The one that you love will never return
To make little Mary his bride."

. "Oh, sir," cried she, "how can that be?
My love for him's never been told.
He's welcome to me in his poverty
As though he was covered in gold."

6. Then the beggar drew the patch from his eye
And lay off his jacket beside;
With cheeks red as roses and bloomin'
    with youth,
It was Willie who stood by her side.

7. "Forgive little Willie, little Mary," cried he;
"It's only your love I have tried.
Now off to the church and let us go;
I make little Mary my bride."

WHEN THE WAGON WAS NEW

= 152

There's an old rus-ty wag-on that's left to rot a-way; It's the
one the fam-ily rode in, back in the good old days.
Peo-ple all loved their neigh-bor; ev-ery-bod-y was so free; And
rid-in' in the brand-new wag-on was some-thin' to see.
I can see my dad-dy, sit-tin' on the wag-on seat,
Ma-ma in an old sun-bon-net, she looked so nice and neat,
Chil-dren all in the wag-on, Grand-ma and Grand-pa too; Oh, we
used to go to church on Sun-day when the wag-on was new.

1. There's an old rusty wagon that's left to rot away;
It's the one the family rode in, back in the good old days.
People all loved their neighbor; everybody was so free;
And ridin' in the brand-new wagon was somethin' to see.

I can see my daddy, sittin' on the wagon seat,
Mama in an old sunbonnet, she looked so nice and neat,
Children all in the wagon, Grandma and Grandpa too;
Oh, we used to go to church on Sunday when the wagon was new.

2. Red wheels were on the wagon, and the body it was green;
But we were all as happy as riding in a limousine.
People used to gather round from all over the mountainside,
Take a look at the brand-new wagon and all take a ride.

3. The automobiles are here now, and the wagon days are through;
The airplanes are a-hummin'; good neighbors are so few.
Everybody's in a hurry; it's the money that takes you through;
But we didn't need much money when the wagon was new.

SAM McGEE CHRONOLOGY

1894   Sam Fleming McGee is born 1 May in Williamson County, Tennessee.

1899   Brother Kirk is born in November.

1910–   Begins to play guitar, developing his style by listening
1920   to various black and white musicians in rural Williamson County.

1914   Marries Mary Elizabeth Pate.

1915   First child, Mildred Louise, is born.

1922   Begins blacksmithing in Franklin, Tennessee.

1925   Meets Uncle Dave Macon and begins touring with him.

1926   Starts appearing on WSM Barn Dance (renamed in 1927 the Grand Ole Opry); in April makes first records, in New York, for Vocalion, including "Buck Dancer's Choice," "Franklin Blues," and "Knoxville Blues" — all closely associated with him throughout his life.

1927   Makes first recording with brother Kirk under the name McGee Brothers, for Vocalion in New York.

1931   Breaks with Uncle Dave Macon; with brother Kirk joins Arthur Smith to form Dixieliners, one of the most popular old-time bands of the 1930s.

1934   Records "Railroad Blues" in last recording session for more than twenty years.

1938 After breakup of the Dixieliners, continues to work as a duet with Kirk, often teaming with the Opry comedy act of Sara and Sallie.

1939 With Kirk begins to tour with bluegrass founder Bill Monroe and continues to work intermittently with Monroe for next ten years.

1941 Continues on the Opry as a solo act when Kirk temporarily leaves music for work related to the war.

1945– Continues to work regularly on the Opry with Kirk (ex-
1955 cept for a brief stint at WNOX in Knoxville) and to develop his farm on Peytonville Road near Franklin.

1955 Kirk confronts Opry management about touring (resolution is in favor of the McGees).

1956 Plays a concert with Kirk in July at New River Ranch, Maryland, and begins to attract a folk-revival audience.

1957 Records for Folkways with Kirk and Arthur Smith; with reunited Dixieliners begins a series of tours in the North, sponsored by the Newport Folk Foundation.

1960– Continues to work on Opry, doing solo spots and duets
1970 with Kirk, as well as playing with other old-time bands; performs at folk festivals across the country.

1970 Records first solo LP album, for Arhoolie.

1971 Forms MBA Record Company in Franklin with Kirk and a couple of friends.

1974 Appears on first show in new Opry house; draws much praise.

1975 Dies 21 August in a farming accident at age eighty-one.

PART THREE

Bukka White

BY F. JACK HURLEY AND DAVID EVANS

Music Notation by David Evans

Memphis loves to proclaim itself the "home of the blues," where Beale Street once rang to the sounds of the street singers' guitars and W.C. Handy's horn spat sweet and lazy phrases from the upper floors of Pee Wee's. Every year at Cotton Carnival time the tradition is brought out from the municipal back shelf and dusted off for a ceremonial airing. Usually one of the old bands and a bluesman or two are "rediscovered" to play for the innocent amusement of the affluent; and for a few days Memphians bask in the illusion that something unique happened here, that somehow Memphis provided the magic combination of river and stern-wheelers, of colonels, field hands, and floozies out of which emerged the only form America has contributed to the world's music, the blues.

The illusion does no real harm and may even be a good thing from the viewpoint of the chamber of commerce, but one should not confuse the illusion with the reality. Of course, there was a time when the musical form generally known as the blues was common in Memphis, and the music was probably popular here earlier than it was in Kansas City or Chicago (although probably no earlier than it was in Dallas or Atlanta). But blues music probably did not originate in Memphis; and when it did arrive, it was not made to feel particularly welcome by the white power structure. The community's leaders learned early to conceal their own subtle economic exploitations of the region by loudly attacking the more obvious forms of vice around which blues music flourished. It is no coincidence that Handy wrote "Mr. Crump Don't 'Low No Easy Riders Here" in 1909, satirizing the "easy boss" attitude toward sin, but then left town for good after a decade of experience with Crump's oppressive administration. Blues music came to Memphis as the black people who carried it in their heads came to Memphis. They came for one basic reason, economic opportunity. The country-style music flourished in the city for a time, under stress, and died when the changing tastes of the black community rendered it obsolete.

No one today can say with precision where or when the blues began. Certainly the vocal lines relate to the work songs and field hollers of slavery days. But blues vocals require an instrumental accompaniment and response. The new availability of mail-order guitars around the turn of this century made a difference, for the blues also requires an instrument that can sustain its bass tones (as the banjo cannot) and allows the strings to be pulled, thus "bending" the note. Migratory workers took their songs and guitar playing with them as they traveled from one plantation, work camp, or town to another. The traveling shows, the medicine shows and minstrel companies, also helped to spread the new music as they entertained the folks in the small towns of the South.

Wherever the music came from, it came to Memphis. For a generation, from about World War I to World War II, the music existed on several levels in the Bluff City. There were street singers and pickup performers playing to primarily black audiences; these musicians were seldom able to earn more than a marginal living with their music and often held other low-paying jobs. There were sophisticated musicians like W. C. Handy who made modest fortunes by scrubbing and sanitizing the blues for mostly white audiences and who moved away to cities like New York to enjoy their wealth. Between these extremes there were many shades of professionalism. Many musicians played to any audiences they could find, black or white. Some of the best — Gus Cannon, Will Shade, Furry Lewis, Jim Jackson, and Frank Stokes — had modest successes in the early recording industry, making records for the "race" labels. Their names are well known to blues listeners today; others left no recorded evidence of their skill and sank into oblivion.

The blues musicians who made up the "Memphis blues scene" during the 1920s and 1930s came for the most part from the area immediately around the city. Gus Cannon from Red Banks, Mississippi, formed his famous Jug Stompers band with Noah Lewis and Ashley Thompson, both of whom were from Ripley, Tennessee. The little-known "Hambone" Willie Newborn, who recorded "Shelby County Workhouse Blues," was also from Ripley. Joe Dobbins, a fine unrecorded barrelhouse piano player, came from Brinkley, Arkansas. The Mississippi Delta was particularly productive of blues musicians. This was the home ground of legendary bluesmen Charlie Patton and Son House. Both came to Memphis from time to time, although neither recorded there. John Hurt, one of the most sensitive Delta musicians, recorded in Memphis in 1928. Walter "Furry" Lewis came to Memphis from Greenwood, Mississippi, and remained. By 1927 he was recording incomparable blues with slide bottleneck guitar. He had a fine voice, and his version of the folksong "John Henry" remains among the best on record today. The list could be continued to form a book in itself, but the point is made. The primary role of the city of Memphis was as a gathering place for musical talent. For young black musicians in western Tennessee, Arkansas, and Mississippi, Memphis was one of the primary places one could go to hear and be heard, and possibly even to record.

One of those whose experience typifies that of early bluesmen generally was Booker T. Washington White. A product of the Mississippi hill country and Delta culture, Booker, or Bukka, as he is usually known, was born on 12 November 1909 on a small farm near Houston, Mississippi. His father, John White, was a railroad fireman whose work frequently kept him away from home. His mother, Lula White, was the daughter of a fundamentalist preacher who owned more than four hundred acres of farmland and managed to keep four churches under his control. Lula was a God-fearing woman who produced five healthy children. She and her father, Punk Davisson, raised Bukka and his brothers and sisters. Bukka recalled his upbringing in a series of loosely structured vignettes, difficult to date precisely but indicative of the general milieu that produced the final musician.

Bukka White at his "office" on Mosby Street in Memphis. Photo by
F. Jack Hurley.

At age sixty-five, Bukka contemplates the passing scene from his "office" on Mosby Street in Memphis. Photo by F. Jack Hurley.

Bukka plays his steel-bodied National guitar for a folklore class.
Photo by F. Jack Hurley.

Bukka's hands. Photo by F. Jack Hurley.

Bukka's hands, bar style of playing blues. Photo by F. Jack Hurley.

Bukka's hands (the short section of conduit pipe has taken the place of the more traditional bottleneck). Photo by F. Jack Hurley.

Bukka White at home. Photo by F. Jack Hurley.

Bukka plays for a folklore class from Southwestern at Memphis in the home of the late Professor John Quincy Wolf (1968). Photo by F. Jack Hurley.

Bukka on stage and in his element at the Memphis Blues Festival, 1967. Photo by F. Jack Hurley.

There was music in the White family. The mother sang hymns as she did the work around the house. Bukka and the other children heard these and sometimes joined in. They also went to his grandfather's church and joined in the music there. Bukka's uncle Jesse Davis was a good blues guitarist. As a major musical influence, however, Bukka's father, John White, comes first. John was a natural musician who could play almost anything. Bukka remembers him as being primarily a fiddler, but he also played mandolin, guitar, piano, drums, and, later, saxophone. He could read music as well. With a friend named Luke Smith, who played guitar and harp (harmonica), John White was in constant demand around Houston, Mississippi, to play for dances and parties. Sometimes they played for white people who paid a little; often it was for blacks who might or might not contribute a few pennies at the end of the evening. His father's playing is a very early memory for Bukka White.

> Frolics! We're going to have a frolic tonight! Who playin'? Luke Smith and John White! And, brothers, I'm going to tell you the truth, you could hear they feet way across the field to them old log houses. And the guy named Billy Cocker was calling the set. God knows from here to heaven, that little brown-skinned man could call it so it'd make you cry. When he'd stomp his foot and say, "Choose your left," they's fall in there like horses. I'd have on my little knee pants and I'd have my arm on Daddy's shoulder and you could hear that guitar and fiddle from here to Main Street, look like.

The music that Bukka recalled his father playing is right for the period. It was an amalgam of white folk tunes such as "Buffalo Girls" and "Turkey in the Straw" with a few early bluesy tunes such as "I'm Alabama Bound," "Stagolee," and "Shoo Shoo Mama." These constitute some of Bukka's earliest clear memories, and their influence on his later life was strong. His daddy made music! His daddy was somebody! There were not many avenues open to a young black man in Mississippi who wanted to have some status. Music was one of the few, and Bukka learned to appreciate it early.

Bukka's father gave him a guitar for his ninth birthday, put it in standard tuning, and turned the boy loose on it. It wasn't long before Bukka was entertaining his friends with the blues songs he had learned. Inspired by an elderly local guitarist named Sam Peterson, he soon picked up the technique of playing sliding

tones and was advised by his father's friend Luke to switch from
a pocketknife held in the left hand to a short piece of bottleneck
worn over the little finger. (The advantage of the bottleneck is
that it frees the other fingers of the left hand to fret the strings
and hence allows the player much greater versatility.) Later in
his career Bukka switched from a glass bottleneck to a piece of
metal tubing.

The effect of the bottleneck was both driving and subtle.
Many musicians in Mississippi at this time were using the bottleneck, but few used it any better than Bukka. Some even made
the slider improperly, as Bukka explained:

> Boys' fingers used to bleed because they didn't know how to cut the
> neck off. Well see, they just try to take a hammer or something — got
> that jagged part sticking their fingers, you know. You supposed to
> wet you a string in coal oil and wrap it around the bottleneck and
> strike a match to it and let it get hot. Let the string burn off, then tap
> it. It'd break off just like that.

Most of the guitar players that Bukka knew played in open
tunings. The first open tuning system that he remembered learning for the guitar was open G (d B G D G' D'); soon he picked up
open D (d A F# D A' D') from a white boy named Victor Smith.
Some of his early songs were played in standard tuning (e B G D
A' E'), which he played in three different keys, probably the result of his father's influence. As Bukka learned music, his interest grew. He loved to sit down for hours playing his guitar or listening to the older, more experienced musicians in the area. This
sort of pleasure was infrequent, however, for the basic work of
Bukka and all his people was time-consuming cotton farming.

From all indications, Bukka's early family life should have
been close and stable, but it was not. Bukka didn't seem to be
able to identify those elements that were wrong, but whatever
they were, he began to drift out of the family circle at a very early
age. During his early school years he lived with an uncle, Alec
Johnson, at Grenada, Mississippi. Johnson owned a farm, "as
good a land as a bird ever flew over," and there was plenty of
work for Bukka and his cousins. He also owned a pump organ,
which Bukka quickly learned to play. Best of all, Grenada was
on the Delta, in the heart of the blues country. Here Bukka
would have a chance to hear the best musicians in the area. He

remembers a little guitar player named Jap Pulliam and two cousins, Tom and Edmond Hatchett, who also played guitar blues. Most of all, however, Bukka remembers Charlie Patton. In an interview quoted in *The Bluesmen* with John Fahey and Ed Denson in 1964, Bukka remembers his early impressions of the legendary bluesman:

> I always wanted to be like old Charlie Patton, long time ago when I was a kid out here, and play them numbers about "Hitch up my buggy and saddle up my black mare"; and I used to pick cotton and come around in Clarksdale there to them cafés and things, eating cheese and cracker—none of the other boys, they didn't have any idea what I was thinking about—I'd say, I wants to come to be a great man like Charlie Patton. [p. 34]

Like Bukka's father, Charlie Patton had status in the community because he played music. The lesson was not lost on the foot-loose Delta boy.

Bukka got hold of an old guitar and began to practice. His uncle disliked the constant noise (perhaps also the time taken from farm work) and finally broke the instrument. Bukka looked hard, found a second, even worse instrument, and kept on playing. His second guitar did not even have tuning pegs. Since the machine heads were worn out, he could only turn them and tighten the strings to roughly the right pitch by using a pair of pliers that he carried in his pocket. In order to improve the tuning, he would capo up three frets and force chips of wood under the strings behind the capo. This, he remembers, would bring the strings up to pitch; but if he played too hard, the chips would fly out and go whizzing across the room.

The growing of cotton on the Mississippi Delta was a simple, unremitting, brutal process, and much depended upon chance. In the spring the ground was broken, man and mule working together as one straining team for hours on end. After planting, there were a few weeks of rest; then came the constant chopping and "running the middles" of the rows with a light plow to keep the weeds from choking the young plants. This labor was not terribly hard, but it was steady and broiling hot. Finally, at the end of the season came the harvest time, the picking time. Men, women, and children worked from first light to full dark, "from can to can't" in order to get the precious crop out of the fields. If the work had gone well and the weather had been benevolent, "settling up time" might see the farmer with a few dollars left over for miniscule luxuries after debts at the store were paid. There might be a few treats for the children or a new dress for the wife, seldom much more. Bukka learned the cycles of Delta life well, but he never learned to relish them. There must, he thought, be a better way.

While he was still a youngster, Bukka began to play for local parties and dances. Usually no money was paid for these jobs; someone simply asked him to play and he played. If he was given a nice meal, he felt compensated:

> I was living around them little places, you know. They'd give me a rabbit sandwich, you know. Chicken, rabbit — make sausage out of it. I played for a rabbit sandwich, piece of egg pie or tater pie and all the water I could drink. One night I played all night and the man give me a tin of sardines and some crackers and two dollars and a half. I thought I owned the world!

To Bukka, his early life was not all bad by any means. He did not remember feeling particularly exploited during this period. When asked about racial attitudes in rural Mississippi during his childhood, his reaction was to defend his home state and the people of both races in it. "Back in them days you could go down and hear the best music! The colored and the white be playing together. There wasn't no trouble, nothing happening. Everybody was cool." Bukka recalled even having white friends as a boy. "I'd go home with them and stay all night and next time they'd come home with me. They just loved my auntie's cooking. Now you take that white boy, Victor Smith. Him and me used to play together all the time. He's the biggest lawyer in New York now."

Of course, one should keep in mind that Bukka was remembering his early childhood when he made these statements. The deep South has always been tolerant of interracial contacts between prepubescent children. As Bukka grew older, however, he found himself at times the target of the same discrimination that all Southern blacks experienced. But for Bukka, such experiences never seem to have been embittering, for above all Bukka concentrated on survival.

As a boy Bukka must have been fairly tough or at least self-assured and resilient. If his memories are at all to be trusted, he moved around a great deal, had his own friends, and spent long periods of time away from home. In two separate interviews years apart, Bukka recounted going to St. Louis by himself at the age of nine. Even though Bukka's concept of years was often hazy and internal evidence in the story seems to indicate that he was twelve or thirteen, the story gives a general indication of the sort of life young Bukka led:

> Well, I didn't intend to go to St. Louis. I had no idea of going up there. See, we were playing with a freight train. Me and my brother and Ed Hardin and James Mim, we was boys, you know, and we had been runnin' middles down the furrow. And it was summertime, in August, and we just stopped the mule there, and there was a wire fence between there and the railroad, and we were just playing like boys do; so we jumped on a freight that was stopped along there. Well, Henry had my guitar. See, we'd work like the devil for hours; then we would play the guitar.
>
> Well, the train started moving, and all of them got off but me. I want to get off, but the train was going faster than I thought it was going. And Henry seen I wasn't going to get off. He run up with the train and said, "Look like you ain't going to get off. If you don't get off, well, here, you'll have your guitar." And he threw me that old guitar.
>
> So I got to St. Louis the next morning about eight o'clock, soda cap on, knee pants and barefooted. And every time I be in St. Louis to this day I look at that old railroad bridge and think how I felt that morning. Nobody knew what be on my mind but the good Lord.

Bukka's precise age at the time of the incident is relatively unimportant. What is important is that he was a very young Delta Negro who, although he had never been in a big city before, rebounded when a sheltered boy might have given up. There were a few tears; but within a few hours after Bukka arrived in St. Louis, he found a job cleaning and doing general work around a roadhouse on the West Side.

> My mind said, "Turn to the left"; so I turned left and went over on the West Side. I was trying to go across the bridge and I thought this was the last of me. So there was an old man, Ben Whitley, sittin' on his back porch, and he told me, "Come here, boy. What are you crying about?" I said, "I was on a freight train and I couldn't get off. This is where they stopped me at." He said, "Hell! It's good they didn't let you off. They brought you to a good place. You'd have

been down in Mississippi now." (I didn't tell him I was from Mississippi. He could just look at me and tell.)

For about the next five years, Bukka worked off and on for Ben Whitley, at this elderly black man's large roadhouse where there was always work to be done. Bukka usually spent the winters working at the roadhouse in St. Louis and the summers doing farm work with his family in Mississippi. As a result of his trips to St. Louis, he was a more sophisticated youth than most of his Delta contemporaries, and the independence was complementing his development as a leader. Transportation back and forth from the Delta to St. Louis was no problem: the freight trains ran both ways, and Bukka was adept at swinging aboard.

The roadhouse job had other real advantages. For one thing, the schools in St. Louis were certainly better than the poor "normal" schools that the State of Mississippi provided for young black children in the 1920s. Through Old Ben's encouragement to go to school, Bukka's educational level rose. From the first, however, St. Louis's main attraction was the roadhouse itself:

> The first night they had a ball there. I'd never seen nothing like that in the country. And them pretty girls come there dressed up and they was doing that two-step and that shimmy! I had to go to my room, I couldn't stand that shimmy! And pretty soon I played along pretty good. Old Ben done put me out there on that piano.

Since Bukka had played pump organ back when he was living with his uncle on the Delta, playing a piano was not entirely new to him. Even so, he needed some help; so Ben Whitley hired an elderly local musician to polish Bukka's style. It was the only formal training that he ever received in music, and it is doubtful that it lasted very long; yet Bukka remembered it clearly, for his teacher gave him more than just musical training, he gave him lessons in practical professional musicianship.

> There was this old man. His name was Johnny Thomas and he was a music teacher. Piano player, guitar player, even sax — he could instruct you in all of that. His family had been playing from way back, and he seemed like about eighty-six to me.
> So the days I wouldn't be doing anything, he'd come over to Old Man Ben's; his son would bring him over, and he'd sit sometimes two or three hours helping me. And he was so interested in me. He seen I was trying to make up for being a poor boy who didn't know

nothing. And I had to believe in what he said because he was the guy that taught the music.

See now, he separated this stuff into "sit down and listen music" and "dance music." If you be playing a bar and the folks is sitting and listening, then a slow blues may be just right. But if people want to dance, then that won't do. You got to know how to back up a black bottom or a trigger toe or a waltz. Listening music and dance music, them is two different kinds of feelings and two different kinds of music.

Bukka's recording career was to be built basically on the blues, but outside the recording studio, he played many styles on both piano and guitar. The lessons of old Johnny Thomas in St. Louis were not forgotten.

Bukka also played the guitar in St. Louis. He must have been developing his hard percussive attack on the strings at this time, for broken strings began to be an increasing problem. Rather than spend his hard-earned cash replacing strings, Bukka practiced on a piece of wire strung up on a wall and held tight with bridges made from forks. He would pluck with his right hand and slide a bottleneck held in the left hand along the wire to vary the pitch. This instrument is commonly played by black children in Mississippi, and Bukka had probably seen it back home. It seems to have influenced his guitar playing, since he usually played the bottleneck on one string only of the guitar, the high E string. In his teens, Bukka returned year-round to the sandy dirt of Mississippi, but the things he had seen and heard in the big city remained in his mind.

At the age of sixteen Bukka married, getting a new Stella guitar from his father as a wedding present. His wife's name was Jessie Bea, and she was six years older than Bukka. The marriage was a short one, lasting less than three years. Bukka worked hard at a variety of jobs around Houston, Mississippi, where he and Jessie Bea were living. He sharecropped, played music at night, and apparently helped make moonshine whiskey on the side. In the winter of 1928, Jessie Bea was suddenly taken sick. Bukka didn't know that her appendix had burst, but he knew that she was terribly sick. He took her to the little hospital at Houston and helplessly watched her die.

I'll always have this in me until I die. I feel bad, you know. There wasn't nobody at the hospital — she didn't have none of her people at the hospital. She had some nice peoples and they had a car, but the water was up and there wasn't a phone. The only way I could have went over there was to ride a mule forty-five miles.

With no family ties, Bukka began to travel. In early 1929 he went back to St. Louis. Ben Whitley was sick and needed help with the roadhouse. As a nearly full-grown nineteen-year-old, Bukka made himself useful in the big city for several months, then returned to Mississippi to help at home when word came that his mother was ailing. It was a difficult time for him; he was experiencing the full force of the basic stuff from which the blues are formed.

For two years Bukka simply "knocked around." He farmed on shares part of the time, played music when the opportunity presented itself, and ran with a fairly tough crowd. The manufacture and sale of moonshine whiskey was an important part of this phase of his life. He even worked as a general roustabout and part-time musician for the Silas Green Traveling Circus in 1929. "I had always wanted to get in with Silas Green," he recalls, "but it turned out to be more work than I thought it was." As a result, Bukka's contract with the traveling show was short, about three weeks. For the time being, he did not remarry, but several women went in and out of his life.

A turning point of sorts came for Bukka when he got a chance to record. At that time Victor, Columbia, Okeh, Paramount, and Vocalion were among the major companies to enter early the field of "race" records, recordings that catered to the musical tastes of blacks. In Memphis many race records were cut in hotel rooms, auditoriums, and small storefronts rented for a few days or weeks. Advertisements were sent out that "the man" from Victor or Vocalion was in town and that anyone interested in recording was to go see him. In Bukka's case the agent was Ralph Lembo. Bukka was farming at Swan Lake and playing in various Delta joints when he was approached by Lembo, a white businessmen from Itta Bena, Mississippi, who owned a furniture store that sold phonographs and records to the local blacks. It was an extension of this business that prompted him to act as a local talent scout for various record companies. In 1927 and 1928, for example, he had arranged sessions with Columbia and Paramount Records for Mississippi blues singer Rubin Lacy and preachers C. F. Thornton and Frank Cotton. Lembo had a contract to produce four records (eight sides) with an agent who was in Memphis a few weeks for Victor Records; he saw Bukka with a guitar walking the road outside his store and invited him into his office to play some pieces. Bukka was scared, but he soon relaxed after accepting Lembo's offer of some bourbon whiskey, no doubt a rare sight in those Prohibition days. Lembo liked Bukka's music and offered him a chance to record some pieces in Memphis. The twenty-year-old Bukka jumped at the chance. On Saturday morning, 24 May 1930, Bukka and a guitar-playing friend named Napoleon Hairiston found themselves waiting beside the dirt road that ran from the little community of Swan Lake to Webb, Mississippi. Ralph Lembo came along in a "brand new Studebaker" with several other musicians already aboard. Bukka recalled that there were two young white men who soon got out, evidently objecting to riding with blacks in a car. At any rate, Bukka, "'Poleon," and a thoroughly inebriated black preacher whom Bukka remembered as "Old Man Fountainathie" accompanied Lembo to Memphis. The preacher was probably Reverend M. H. Holt, who is known to have recorded at this session.

The next Monday morning, Bukka and Napoleon appeared at the Memphis Municipal Auditorium where the man from Victor had set up his temporary studio. Ralph Lembo was there, but "Old Man Fountainathie" was nowhere to be found, having drunk a bit too deeply of the spirits the night before. Lembo thought the problem over. "I've got four records, I've got to have eight songs. Why don't you boys just make them all yourselves." Since the contract called for several sides of a religious nature, Lembo suggested that Bukka try his hand at preaching. "Well," said Bukka, "I can't preach, I ain't no preacher." With that option closed, Lembo hit on another idea: "How about religious songs?" As long as music was wanted, Bukka felt he could oblige; consequently, the session was arranged. A woman whom Bukka remembered as "Miss Minnie" was brought in to provide the high voice characteristic of Negro church singing, and four religious sides were cut. Just before these, Bukka and Napoleon recorded ten secular pieces, most of them blues. Bukka was vague as to just how much he was paid for the session; he variously reported such figures as $240 and $400 plus a new guitar.

At any rate he seemed to be satisfied. He was more concerned with the release of a record that his friends and relatives could hear than with the money.

> I was green as grass in the spring of the year. I'd have been just as satisfied if he had given me a quarter as if he'd give me half a million dollars. But he was an honest man. He give me just what he said he would give me and he gave it to me right then. I like a man who does business that way.

Four of the fourteen songs from the session were released, two religious (Victor V38615) and two secular (Victor 23295), all under the name of Washington White. Reverend Holt showed up for the session and recorded four sermons, all of which were issued on two records, thus fulfilling Ralph Lembo's need for eight sides. All of Bukka's performances were outstanding, and we can only regret today that the other ten pieces he recorded were never issued. The two religious pieces, "I Am in the Heavenly Way" and "Promise True and Grand," are performed in a style that was common among street singers and in the Sanctified and Holiness churches. Bukka sings the melody in a bass register that often becomes an almost incoherent growl, while "Miss Minnie" in a higher voice sings along with him in a rough heterophony on some of the lines and adds vocal responses to others. It was a style recorded by a number of husband and wife gospel teams of the period, such as Blind Willie and Angeline Johnson and Charlie Patton and Bertha Lee Patton. Bukka plays a strongly rhythmic and percussive guitar in open D tuning, often following the song's melody with his bottleneck, while Napoleon adds to the driving rhythm with his guitar. On "I Am in the Heavenly Way," a piece that Bukka continued to perform throughout his career, one of the guitarists snaps the bass strings, adding to the piece's already heavily percussive sound.

The two secular pieces issued from this session are equally brilliant. "The New 'Frisco Train" has Hairiston singing single blues lines over a rushing rhythm played on the two guitars. The spaces between these lines are filled by Bukka's wry spoken comments and superb bottleneck playing. The rhythm of the guitars and the special bottleneck effects actually imitate the sounds of a train. Songs of this sort were an important ingredient in the early folk blues. The folklorist Howard W. Odum described similar "train songs" from his fieldwork in northern Mississippi just after the turn of the century. Bukka's "Panama Limited" also describes and imitates a train, but unlike the impressionistic text of Hairiston's piece, it tells a reasonably coherent story. Most of the vocal part is spoken over a repeated guitar figure played on the first three strings.

After the session Bukka returned to farming in Mississippi. The release of these four sides gave him status in the small Delta communities of Mississippi. It may be, however, that his own assessment of that status was greater than was healthy for his career. When asked if he ever recorded for Ralph Lembo again, he answered: "No, after that I was just moving too fast for him. He couldn't catch me." In point of fact, however, Bukka did not record for seven years; his one known attempt to record during that period was abortive.

Bukka did continue to play and sing regularly during the early thirties. He enjoyed the work as well as meeting other regional musicians and learning from them. During these years, much of his time was spent in the vicinity of Houston, Mississippi. His mother was growing more and more ill (she died in 1933), and his father needed help with the farm. Father and son began playing together regularly for the first time during these years. Whenever Bukka remarked on his father's musicianship, he did so with great respect.

By 1932 Bukka had also begun playing with George "Bullet" Williams, an Alabama musician living at the Delta town of Glendora, "as fine a harp blower as ever drawed his mouth across the harp." Williams' experience was broader than Bukka's. He had made some records back in 1928 for the old Paramount Record Company, cutting them in Chicago. He also knew many of the Delta musicians who had gone north and "made it." Williams was a great harmonica player, as his recordings attest, and it is a shame that he and Bukka never recorded together. But he was also an alcoholic, and as Mississippi was legally a dry state, he often drank such substances as shoe polish and rubbing alcohol. Frequently he would become sick when the two played together but would go on making music until he passed out. In 1934 Bukka married a niece of Williams named Susie Simpson. They began to farm near Aberdeen, Mississippi, in the hill country near Bukka's birthplace, and eventually Bukka lost track of Bullet Williams. He assumed that Williams went insane or died shortly thereafter from the effects of his drinking.

Apparently 1934 was the year that Bukka attempted to revive his recording career. He had a good idea. His father and he were playing together quite often for local parties and clubs. Why not go to Memphis and see if one of the companies would record them as a father-and-son team? It was an interesting thought, and folklorists today would love to be able to study such a record; but the idea met with difficulties from the start. Bukka's father was elderly and very much a part of rural Mississippi. The thought of a trip to Memphis terrified him. Nevertheless, Bukka slowly talked the old man around to his point of view; and finally, in the fall when the cotton was in, the two men started for Memphis. Since neither man had money to spare for the trip, their means of transportation was obvious:

> Well, we was hoboing, you see. I didn't want to fool with no passenger train, so we just rode along on the freights. That first night came along and we was pulled over on a siding and Daddy said he's going home. He's had about enough. So I says, "Go on home if you want to. I'm going to Memphis." Well the train commenced to roll and I looked out in the dark and I seen a big man running down the track. I thought for a minute somebody was after me until I seen that fiddle case swinging from his hand. Then I knew it was my daddy coming along after all.

Bukka managed to get his father to Memphis safely and even to get him settled into a cheap boarding house known as "Suzette Bottoms" in a ghetto area near the Memphis-Arkansas bridge, but at that point his luck ran out. Bukka had heard that the man who recorded for Okeh was to be at the Haupt Music Company on Main Street; but when he went to the store, he was told that the agent had gone to Jackson, Mississippi, and wasn't expected to return for a week. The secretary at the store was not very hopeful about recording prospects either. It was a staggering blow. Bukka simply could not afford to wait around for a week. His father's meals alone would exhaust their capital in a few days. Bukka recalled, "He was a big man and he ate like a big man. He didn't think nothing of eating twenty or thirty biscuits at a setting." The man at the boarding house was nice about the whole thing and told them that they could stay as long as they needed to; but Bukka reluctantly decided to give up. "I couldn't wait that long, and I didn't want to stay away from my wife that long either; so we stayed a day or two and came back. Now there ain't too many things about my life that I regret, but I have a sorrow in my heart that I never got to record with my daddy."

In 1934, when this episode probably took place, the recording industry was having very hard times. A quick study of any standard discography covering this period will reveal that few race records were being cut in the early thirties. Bukka need not have felt too badly about this particular failure, but it did indicate to him a certain truth. The recording industry was not going to be very lucrative for him at any time in the immediate future. As a result, he began to turn to other things.

From the mid-thirties until 1937, Bukka did a great deal of wandering. His marriage to Susie did not exactly end, it just "ran out" as his travels took him farther and farther away for increasingly long periods of time. He wandered all over the country. He stayed for a while in St. Louis; he stopped in Cincinnati, Cleveland, and Baltimore; he even went as far north as Buffalo, New York, for a while. When asked what he was doing during these travels, his answer was simple—"hoboing":

> I had to see the world; but, man, that traveling can get you down. It was hoboing, sleeping on this railroad track—off from it, you know—boiling roasting ear of corn in a bucket. I had my sugar in my pocket and I just drank hot water. Wherever I seen a pear tree or an apple tree I could get to, I would go and fill my pocket up and get back on the freight train and start to playing that old guitar. That would get the other hoboes in a good mood, and pretty soon we'd make up some kind of a meal together. Man, I'm telling you, I couldn't see no other way but to keep going.

Bukka did all sorts of things to make money during the mid-thirties. He pitched semiprofessional baseball for a couple of seasons with the Birmingham Black Cats. Always a good natural athlete, Bukka remembered his baseball pitching career with gusto, and, according to his own memories, he was good. "They didn't see nothing, but they hear the wind! I got proof. There is fellows living around here that knows. Fred Quinn in Mississippi, he was playing first base. He know. I had a ball I called a 'Hudson.' And the man that caught would say, 'Bukka going to throw his "Hudson" today.' I never remember us getting beat but twice."

Sometime during this period, Bukka fell in with a traveling show for a while. It was not much of a show and the pay was not very good, but it was headed the same way that Bukka wanted to go, so he went along. It was a tough little outfit, but Bukka was tough, too. The show featured an old man who claimed he was Jesse James. As Bukka described it, the old fellow just sat there and answered people's questions. If anyone could prove that he was not Jesse James, that person supposedly won a prize of $500. Nobody ever claimed the prize. Bukka remembered that the old man looked mean and that his manager carried a .45 caliber pistol. Bukka was playing at a fair of some sort near "Jesse James's" tent when the old man came over to him:

> He said, "Young man, you're a hit musician." And he wanted to know could I play "John Henry," and I told him I could play it pretty good; so he went for that. And he gave me five dollars right there and fifteen dollars a week, which was pretty good for them days. So I stayed with him for a few weeks, but I didn't like the looks of his show very much; so I dropped off and didn't go back.

It was probably in 1935 that Bukka made his first trip to Chicago. He recalled setting out from St. Louis with another musician, the legendary Peetie Wheatstraw, and settling in for a stay on the Windy City's South Side. Bukka had been listening to stories about the great music in Chicago for years; finally he was to hear and be a part of it. Within a short time he had made friends among the professional musicians on the South Side. There were "Big Bill" Broonzy, "Washboard Sam," and Memphis Slim. Memphis Minnie was also in town often, and Bukka was able to hear her. Tampa Red was living on the South Side, and he and Bukka became friends. Musically, it was an exciting town, but financially it was pretty hard. Very few of the musicians could actually make a living with their craft. Most had to find other work to make ends meet; Bukka was no exception. His answer to the problem was to go into professional boxing.

A boxer could make good money in Chicago during the depression if he was good. Bukka fought about twenty professional fights and seems to have done well in most of them. As in his other roles, he developed his own personal style; for example, he had a special punch which he named the "sledgehammer." He remembered fans calling, "Drop that sledgehammer on him, Bukka!" Eventually, however, his luck ran out when he was matched with a man considerably larger than he. It must have been in 1937 (although Bukka's memory put it much later) that he found himself in the ring with "a boy named Charles from Alabama." "Charles was a heavyweight—Bogalusa, Alabama [Tuscaloosa? Bogalusa, Louisiana?]. A big black boy, rough as a bull. I know Charles was going to whop me because my feelings dropped as soon as I seen him. You can just tell when you got your load. You can tell. He was mighty big and his back was that wide. I knew he wasn't used to eating nothing but peas and cornbread, you know."

Bukka was badly beaten and although he did fight a few times after that, his professional boxing career was ended. It was probably just as well. Had he continued, he surely would have ruined his hands, and the world would have been denied some of the finest and most sensitive blues guitar playing ever put on record.

In the summer of 1937, Bukka was back in Mississippi for a visit. By now he had been to the big cities, made records, and fought professional fights. He must have excited the envy of the local men, and it is certain that he was attractive to the local women. The combination was a dangerous one. Bad feelings arose, and before many weeks had passed, Bukka was involved in a shooting scrape.

> I was going to play at a park for a cousin of mine, Mark Davisson. And I just went to Aberdeen to get some strings, you know. And me and Wes Quinn was headed back to Houston to hitch a ride over to Davisson's, and them boys was layin' there for me. And they set out to start something. And there was this one boy who had it in for me pretty bad.
>
> Well, I had a .38 Colt in there and I let it loose. And I just shot him where I wanted to shoot him. Broke his thigh. Them others was gone around the corner.

That event in Bukka's life was pivotal; it meant that he was to spend some time in prison. Even so, it has been blown out of all proportion by many blues writers. For example, as recently as 1969 the noted English blues writer, Paul Oliver, in *The Story of the Blues*, wrote that Bukka killed a man "in a muddled fracas" (p. 121) and was sentenced to a long prison term. Oliver also states that his release was obtained after two years by his music agent, Lester Melrose. None of this fits the facts as Bukka related them. Bukka did not kill a man. He shot a man, as he said, "where I wanted to shoot him." In Mississippi in those days such a scrape between two blacks was common enough to elicit little reaction from the courts. Bukka was, in fact, sentenced to two years. He served this time and was duly released. It is true that he was under contract to Lester Melrose of Vocalion Recording Company, and Melrose does seem to have secured one favor for him — Bukka was allowed to make a short trip to Chicago to do one recording session before his prison term began. (Oliver says that he jumped bail to attend the session, but if this were true it seems likely that his stay in prison would have been longer and considerably more unpleasant than it was.)

The short recording session took place on 2 September 1937. It yielded only two songs, both with Bukka on guitar accompanied by a second unknown guitarist. The song that Bukka thought would sell best was a blues number about Pine Bluff, Arkansas, and a woman who was waiting there for his return. The lyrics had a coherent theme, and Bukka played some fine bottleneck guitar, but the record's other side was actually the hit. "Shake 'Em On Down" sold thousands of records and became a standard piece in the repertory of many blues singers in Mississippi and the Chicago area. "Big Bill" Broonzy, who had originally brought Bukka to Lester Melrose's attention, recorded a similar version a few months later that sold even better than Bukka's. Others — including Big Joe Williams, Robert Petway, and Stick Horse Hammond — modified the basic idea, creating "Break 'Em On Down," "Ride 'Em On Down," and "Truck 'Em On Down." In the manner of many folk blues, Bukka's song consisted of a series of traditional verses that were not clearly related to a single theme. They were joined together by a refrain repeated in every stanza. The fine melody and strong performance, along with the suggestive lyrics, made this piece just the sort of thing that was in demand at the rent parties and clubs of Chicago late in the depression.

SHAKE 'EM ON DOWN
Words and Music by Washington White

Guitar: standard tuning, E position.

Get your night-cap, ma-ma, and your gown. Ba - by, 'fore day we gon - na shake 'em on down. Hey, done stopped hol - ler'n. Oh, must I shake 'em on down. I done stopped hol-ler'n now. Must I shake 'em on down.

Get your nightcap, mama, and your gown.
Baby, 'fore day we gonna shake 'em on down.
Hey, done stopped holler'n. Oh, must I shake 'em on down.
I done stopped holler'n now. Must I shake 'em on down.

Too much of jelly to be throwed away.
Save this jelly for some old rainy day.
Hey, done stopped holler'n. Oh, must I shake 'em on down.
I done stopped holler'n, mama. Must I shake 'em on down.

Fix my supper, let me go to bed.
This white lightning done gone to my head.
Hey, must I holler, or must I shake 'em on down.
I done stopped holler'n, mama. Must I shake 'em on down.

4. I ain't been to Georgia, but I been told.
Georgia women got the best jelly roll.
It's done stopped holler'n. Oh, must I shake 'em on down.
I done stopped holler'n, mama. Must I shake 'em on down.

5. See, see, mama, what you done done.
Made me love you. Now your man done come.
Hey, done stopped holler'n. Oh, must I shake 'em on down.
I done stopped holler'n, mama. Must I shake 'em on down.

6. Baby got something, don't know what it is.
Make me drunker than a whiskey still.
It's done stopped holler'n. Oh, must I shake 'em on down.
I done stopped holler'n. Must I shake 'em on down.

For what it was worth, Bukka could go back to face his prison term in Mississippi knowing that he had produced a hit song. The years in prison are worth considerable investigation, for

they changed Bukka. His perspective on life deepened percepti-
bly, and his music became a true art while he was at Parchman
Farm. This is not to imply in any way that he enjoyed the prison
experience, for he emphatically did not. On the other hand, he
was not brutalized by it and he did learn from it. When asked
what he did while at Parchman, Bukka grinned and said, "Well,
mostly I played guitar." It seems that word of his arrival at the
farm got out in advance and the inmates and guards pooled their
money to buy him a guitar and even formed a band. The camp
director realized that Bukka's music could be used to boost mo-
rale and encouraged Bukka's playing.

> When I got to Camp Ten, that guitar was there. The sergeant
> commenced getting an instrument before I got there. They had a
> bass violin, a regular little band. Pete Paine, the Jackson boys,
> Skeeter and all of them were there, you know. They could play.
> They was hard players.
> I said, "There ain't no way in the devil I could beat that rap with
> y'all up here pulling me to come." And the sergeant, Sergeant Valen-
> tine, say, "Ain't nobody going to get Bukka till his two years is out.
> He does this camp too much good."
> I could go all over the place by myself. I was trusted. But it still
> wasn't like home.

For the most part, Bukka was not required to do heavy work
in the fields. The little band that was formed around him was in
constant demand and moved from camp to camp on the huge
farm bringing a little comfort to the men. As time went on, they
even gained a fame of sorts outside the prison fields. When on
one occasion the governor of Mississippi visited Parchman, the
little band was trotted out to play for his entertainment. Bukka
was introduced to the governor and remembered the conversation in this way: "'Are you Booker T. Washington White? You
don't know how many people have been down here trying to get
you turned loose. But your sergeant and your captain say,
"Don't turn him loose, he do too much good here."' So I got to
keep it up for two years." Bukka spent hours practicing guitar
runs, alone on his bunk in the evenings when the work was done,
and he even taught the camp captain's son to play guitar.

In 1939 Bukka had one short recording session while still in
prison. The folklorist Alan Lomax appeared at the farm with his
recording equipment in the back of his car. He was surveying

Southern folk music on a government grant for the Library of Congress. Lomax asked prison officials if there was any music worth recording at Parchman, and, of course, Bukka was quickly produced. Bukka recorded two songs for Lomax. He sang a nice version of the old standard "Po' Boy" with bottleneck guitar accompaniment and another song that he later claimed was inspired by his second wife Susie. This other piece, "Sic 'Em Dogs On," has an unusual single-line melody that Bukka duplicates on bottleneck guitar behind his singing. Between some of the verses he plays this bottleneck part as an instrumental chorus.

"SIC 'EM DOGS ON."
© 1974 Biograph Records, Inc.
USED BY PERMISSION, courtesy of Biograph Records, Inc.
Guitar: open D tuning.

Yes, I'm goin' down-town and tell the chief po-lice you sic-cin' your dogs on me.

Yes, I'm goin' downtown and tell the chief police you siccin' your dogs on me.

She went to running, running and crying. She said, "Listen, daddy, I ain't gon' do it no more, I ain't gon' do it no more."

You done got my money. Now you tryin' to sic your dogs on me.

That's all right, little girl, how you do me. You gon' see it again.

I'm gonna tell the chief you suc your dogs on me, told me you didn't want me around.

6. Oh, listen, Chief, she done got my money, now siccin' her dogs on me.

7. She went to running and crying, said, "Sic him, Butch and Paul; Fido, he won't bite."

8. Won't you take me back? I won't do it no more, baby. Don't sic your dogs on me.

9. She said, "Listen, daddy, don't you drive me, don't you drive me around."

"Sic 'Em Dogs On" was first-class blues and of a quality that Lomax was fortunate to record. Bukka, however, called a halt. As a professional, Bukka was accustomed to being paid for his services, and the government's folklorist was not offering any compensation. This was one of the few experiences that Bukka regarded as exploitative. Whether or not he was purposely taken advantage of by Lomax, Bukka felt that he was forced to record because of his position as a prison inmate. He seldom made his music without compensation.

Bukka spent a great deal of time during his years at Parchman simply watching the people around him. In spite of his relative comfort, he was terribly lonely; and watching others in similar or worse circumstances seemed to dispel his loneliness. Bukka had always been a struggler, a survivor who met life head-on without bitterness. In prison he was continuing to learn acceptance of things he could not change. At Parchman he came into direct and prolonged contact with good and evil. He saw bad men who had a good side, and he learned to accept the fact of death in a straightforward, simple way. He was developing a sense of tragedy.

> Every kind of peoples out in the free world is down there on Parchman. The best kind, white and black, lawyers, schoolteachers, some of the worst too. They all down there. There sure be some millionaire guys there, but they can't get out. That Kinnie Wagner, he stayed there till he died.
>
> I sometimes get to thinking about Kinnie. He was a musician from his heart. He was crazy about music. He didn't play nothing himself, but he would sit and listen to my music for the longest time. He'd say, "Play 'Po' Boy' " or "Play that 'Streamline Train,' " and sometimes he'd cry.
>
> He couldn't go free. They couldn't free him. He done killed four Tennesseans and maybe a couple more in Missouri. He shot a guard at Parchman while I was there. Shot him right between the eyes with a high-powered Winchester. [Actually Wagner shot a guard in 1927, ten years before Bukka entered Parchman; Bukka is also in error regarding the other shootings.] They couldn't do nothing to him 'cause he already had life. Nobody like the guard nohow.
>
> Kinnie would stand and listen to you play guitar all day long.

Two years in prison could have left ruinous scars on a less powerful personality than Bukka's. The loneliness and brutality could have embittered him to a point where further creative work would have been impossible. Instead it matured him. His ideas became deeper and more complex. Bukka emerged from prison with a head full of some of the finest classic blues songs ever written, and within a few months he would complete one of the greatest recording sessions in the history of the blues.

When Bukka got out of Parchman prison in 1939 his immediate thought was to get back to Chicago. Two years earlier he had been on the brink of a real career with Lester Melrose as his manager, and he wanted to pick up those threads if he could. Melrose had a reputation for honesty among black musicians in the Chicago area, and he had been well pleased with Bukka's short recording session in 1937. If Bukka could reestablish that contact, perhaps his days of wandering, riding freight trains, and working at odd jobs would be over. After a short visit with his family at Houston, Mississippi, Bukka hopped a freight train north and duly presented himself at Melrose's office on Chicago's South Side.

Bukka must have wanted a recording session badly, for he had even written out the words to several songs he intended to do. They were the same things that he had heard other, more successful bluesmen doing, songs like "Prowling Ground Hog" and "Sitting on Top of the World." They were not the blues that he had in his head, but who would want to listen to those? He showed his carefully handwritten pages to Melrose and the result was quite unexpected.

> I got there and showed Melrose all my songs I had writ out, and he got out a book and showed me who had put them out. He said, "You see. You couldn't make a quarter. They'd sue you from the first to the end." He said, "Now Booker, I'm going to give you a meal ticket and a room at a hotel. I'll give you two days to come up with something of your own." So help me God, I got down to it.

Now he had no choice. The blues he carried in his head, blues derived from being locked up in prison for two years, would have to do. He went to the hotel room that Melrose provided and went to work. Two days later he had the lyrics to a dozen songs. They were some of the finest blues ever to be recorded. The symbolism, the conceptions, the style were pure Delta, and they ranged in tone from boisterous to deeply tragic. The easy suggestive phrases, the commercial formulas were purged. What remained was art—clean, simple, direct lyrics in the best blues tradition. Melrose took one look and was convinced. His reaction was emotional:

> I never had a man, black or white, kiss me dead on the mouth before; but that's what he done. He say, "Lord man, you done 100 percent. I've been on this job thirty-five years and I never seen a man do what you done in two days." He said, "Just how the hell did you get

it? Where did it come from? When you came up here before, you had what all the other folks had. You was doin' Peetie Wheatstraw and Tampa Red and all the others. But this stuff is Booker White all the way!"

The recording session was arranged within a few days. On Thursday, 7 March 1940, Bukka went to the little studio that Lester Melrose maintained on Chicago's South Side and sang his songs. His guitar was a big Gibson borrowed from his friend "Big Bill" Broonzy because his own little Stella did not record well and Big Bill's "cut through better." Bukka wanted some kind of a rhythm background, so Melrose brought in a washboard player. Some discographers have suggested that this was George Washington, also known as "Oh Red," but Bukka always insisted it was the popular recording artist "Washboard Sam." Sam could be gotten cheaply and he did lay down a nice rhythm. The recording equipment was basic, and the room was spartan. Bukka was paid $17.50 per side (the two-day session yielded twelve sides), and Washboard Sam was paid a flat fee of $20. Bukka also received $33 for his travel home, but that was all. If these figures are correct, one of the greatest recording sessions in the history of the blues cost $263.

The relationship between men and women is dealt with in the majority of blues, and many blues singers seldom venture beyond this subject at all. Bukka's 1940 session broke dramatically with this pattern and remains a remarkable example of the breadth of subject matter and imagery that the blues can encompass. His first and last songs dealt with trains. In "Black Train Blues" the singer's lover has deserted him and he stands helplessly by the track, unable to escape because he lacks the money for a ticket. "Special Stream Line," on the other hand, is a monologue with train imitations on bottleneck guitar similar to those in "The Panama Limited" as Bukka had recorded it ten years earlier.

Three of the songs, or fully one-quarter of the entire session, dealt with aspects of the prison experience. "When Can I Change My Clothes" was one of them and was done on the first day. Critics have universally regarded it as one of the best of all of Bukka's blues. The musical pattern was familiar; in fact, it was almost identical to Bukka's earlier hit, "Shake 'Em On

Down," but the words cut much deeper and the images were much finer.

. Never will forget that day when they had me in Parchman Jail.
Wouldn't no one even come and go my bail.
I wonder how long before I can change my clothes.
I wonder how long 'fore I can change my clothes.

. So many days I would be sitting down.
I would be sitting down looking down on my clothes.
I wonder how long before I can change my clothes.
I wonder how long 'fore I can change my clothes.

. So many days when the day would be cold,
They would carry me out in the rain and cold.
I wonder how long before I can change my clothes.
I wonder how long 'fore I can change my clothes.

4. So many days when the day would be cold,
You could stand and look at the convicts' toes.
I wonder how long before I can change my clothes.
I wonder how long 'fore I can change my clothes.

5. So many days I would be walking down the road.
I could hardly walk for looking down on my clothes.
I wonder how long before I can change my clothes.
I wonder how long 'fore I can change my clothes.

6. Never will forget that day when they taken my clothes,
Taken my citizen clothes and throwed 'em away.
Wonder how long before I can change my clothes.
I wonder how long 'fore I can change my clothes.

To many blacks of that era, clothes symbolized one's status in the world. Prevented from owning fine houses, unable to dabble in stocks and bonds or to eat in nice restaurants, the clothes and the car often summed up a man's position. For Bukka, clearly, beautiful clothing was terribly important. The loss of his outer garments had hurt deeply, and from that hurt he had fashioned a powerful metaphor of the stripping away of personal pride which takes place within prison walls.

Bukka also sang knowingly about the psychological effects of deep trouble. In "Sleepy Man Blues" he explored the lethargy that accompanies a situation that the mind cannot cope with. It is one of the few blues to treat the subject of mental illness in some depth. Bukka took the song's beautiful melody from Leroy Carr's 1935 hit of "When the Sun Goes Down." Bukka's lyrics were originally about being out of money and worried, but he decided to revise them, placing the main emphasis on the theme of worry. It is obvious that his prison experience had set him back and caused him to think deeply about the direction of his life.

> I was troubled then. I was troubled in mind then and worried. Things that I desired, wanted to come true, was holding me back, and I couldn't see when would it [come true], and so I just made that song up. . . . I was blue and I was a little worried, and I found that number there, and I got satisfied. Everything was okay then.

SLEEPY MAN BLUES
Guitar: standard tuning, G position.

1. When a man get trouble in his mind, he
     want to sleep all the time.
   When a man get trouble in his mind, he
     want to sleep all the time.
   He knows he can sleep all the time, till
     trouble won't worry his mind, won't
     worry his mind.

2. I'm feeling worried in mind, and I'm trying
     to keep from crying.
   I'm feeling worried in mind, and I'm trying
     to keep from crying.
   I am standing in the sunshine to keep fro
     weakin' down, keep from weakin' dow

3. I want somewhere to go, but I hate to go
     town.
   I want somewhere to go to satisfy my
     mind.
   I would go to town, but I hate to stan
     around, hate to stand around.

4. I wonder what's the matter with my rig
     mind. My mind keep me sleeping all
     time.

I wonder what's the matter with my right mind. My mind keep me sleeping all the time.
But when I had plenty money, my friends would come around, would come around.

5. If I had my right mind, I would write my women a few lines.
If I had my right mind, I would write my women a few lines.
I will do most anything to keep from weakin' down, keep from weakin' down.

The guitar playing behind songs such as these was simple: a steady beat with a little ornamentation from Washboard Sam to keep things moving. Since Bukka was perfectly capable of playing very complex guitar patterns, it seems obvious that his choice in these cases was conscious. He had something to say and he did not want it obscured by fancy guitar work. The result is classical simplicity.

In "Strange Place Blues," recorded the same day, Bukka, shifting his concern to the ultimate human experience, sang movingly about his mother's death and the feelings that had filled him at that time. The title "Strange Place Blues" appears to have been supplied by Melrose in the hope that it would make the record sell better. Bukka never called the song by that title. He always referred to it as "I Am Looking for My Mother's Grave," a much more direct although less commercial name.

On the first day of the session he recorded another prison song, "Parchman Farm Blues," a piece sung from the viewpoint of a newly sentenced lifetime prisoner. Bukka played a highly percussive guitar in the key of D in D minor tuning (d A F D A' D') behind his singing with a beautiful bottleneck break after the second stanza. The song seems to sum up all the bitterness that he and the other prisoners felt about their condition.

PARCHMAN FARM BLUES

= 92→98

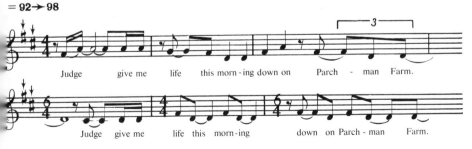

Judge give me life this morning down on Parchman Farm.

Judge give me life this morning down on Parchman Farm.

1. Judge give me life this morning down on
   Parchman Farm.
   Judge give me life this morning down on
   Parchman Farm.
   I wouldn't hate it so bad, but I left my wife
   this morn.

2. Oooh, good-bye, wife; all you have done
   gone.
   Oh, good-bye, wife; all you have done gone.
   But I hope some day you will hear my
   lonesome song.

3. Oooh, listen, you men, I don't mean no
   harm.
   Oh, listen, you men, I don't mean no harm.

If you want to do good, you better stay o
of Parchman Farm.

4. We go to work in the morning just the
   dawn of day.
   We go to work in the morning just the
   dawn of day.
   It be the setting of the sun; that's when th
   work is done.

5. I'm down on old Parchman Farm, and I
   sure want to go back home.
   I'm down on old Parchman Farm, but I
   sure want to go back home.
   But I hope some day I will overcome.

The second day's recording yielded two more classic blues in which the basic concerns were sickness and death. "High Fever Blues" was inspired by the death of a girl friend, Mary Johnson, from jaundice. Bukka changed the story, however, so that the singer was the one who was sick. The song records the thoughts of a man "taken down with the fever" who can't sleep and who wishes for his lover to come and "drive away" his fever. It's an old metaphor for the ardor of love but one that Bukka used to good effect.

One of the finest songs from the second day of recording was the hard-driven "Fixin' to Die Blues." Here was Bukka at his best. The song was inspired by a friend and fellow guitarist who went into a coma and died in 1938, evidently in Parchman. Bukka recalled, "He was looking funny in his eyes. They were all white. I got to wondering how a man feels when he dies." Bukka made the song into a complex consideration of the plight of a family man who faces death (perhaps an unconscious projection

of the family Bukka had never quite been able to put together);
and it was accompanied by fast, intricate guitar rhythms and
bottleneck figures that drove the song forward.

FIXIN' TO DIE
Words and Music by Booker White
© Copyright 1965 by MCA Music, A Division of MCA Inc.,
New York, New York. USED BY PERMISSION. ALL RIGHTS RESERVED.
Guitar: open G tuning.

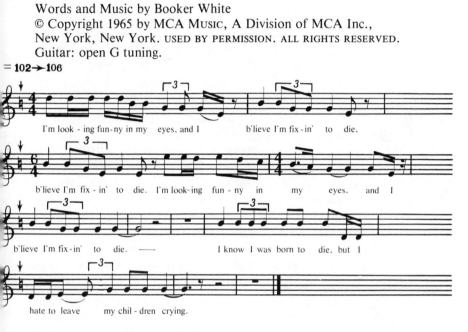

I'm looking funny in my eyes, and I b'lieve
    I'm fixin' to die, b'lieve I'm fixin' to die.
I'm looking funny in my eyes, and I b'lieve
    I'm fixin' to die.
I know I was born to die, but I hate to
    leave my children crying.

Just as sure as we live today, sure we's born
    to die, sure we's born to die.
Just as sure we live, sure we born to die.
I know I was born to die, but I hate to
    leave my children crying.

Your mother treated me, children, like I
    was her baby child, was her baby child.
Your mother treated me like I was her
    baby child.

That's why I tried so hard to come back
    home to die.

4. So many nights at the fireside, how my
    children's mother would cry, how my
    children's mother would cry;
So many nights at the fireside, how my
    children's mother would cry,
'Cause I told their mother I had to say
    good-bye.

5. Look over yonder on the buryin' ground,
    on the buryin' ground.
Look over yonder on the buryin' ground.
Yonder stand ten thousand, standin' to see
    'em let me down.

6. Mother, take my children back before they let me down.
   let me down, before they let me down. Ain't no need of them screamin' and cryin
   Mother, take my children back 'fore they on the graveyard ground.

By considering the lyrics of blues songs in the late 1930s, one can make a convincing case for Bukka's originality. Most commercially recorded blues songs by 1940 were popular music aimed at a common denominator of taste within the black audience. They were designed to accompany rent parties or dancing, and their primary concern during this period was the relationship between men and women, often described in terms more explicit than those that would dominate mainstream popular music thirty years later. The bluesman often bragged about his conquests and thus spoke the dreams of his audience. But much of the music had developed a dull sameness by 1940. The musical forms were generally well-worn, and many of the sexual allusions were becoming hackneyed. Bukka's lyrics and often his music achieved a freshness by returning to basics. His songs of familial love and death, backed on occasion by complex polyrhythms on the guitar, were something that Chicago's ghetto dwellers had not heard for a long time; and the songs sounded strange.

Bukka was also moving onto ground seldom trod when he sang a song that protested the system of justice in the United States. Overt protest songs were rare within the blues tradition; yet Bukka's "District Attorney Blues" was such a song. The implications might have been lost on white audiences, but to black listeners the message was clear. The district attorney, who would have been invariably white in this period, represented white justice, and he was surely "hard on a man."

DISTRICT ATTORNEY BLUES
Guitar: standard tuning, E position.

- ney   sure is hard   on a man.   He   will   take

a   wom - an's   man   and   leave   her cold in   hand.

. District attorney sure is hard on a man.
He will take a woman's man and leave her
   cold in hand.
District attorney sure is hard on a man.
He will take a woman's man and leave her
   cold in hand.

. District attorney sure is hard on a man.
He have caused a many mens to be in some
   distant land.
District attorney sure is hard on a man.
He have caused so many womens to be
   cold in hand.

District attorney sure is hard on a man.
He ain't no woman, but he sure will take a
   woman's man.

District attorney sure is hard on a man.
He will take a woman's man and leave her
   cold in hand.

4. District attorney sure is hard on a man.
He can tell, if he will, when he gonna take
   a woman's man.
District attorney sure is hard on a man.
Well, he'll take a woman's man and leave
   her cold in hand.

5. District attorney sure is hard on a man.
He taken me from my woman and caused
   her to love some other man.
District attorney sure is hard on a man.
He will take a woman's man and leave her
   cold in hand.

It may be that Bukka's own second marriage finally dissolved
once and for all while he was in Parchman Prison (it was not a
subject that he discussed willingly); there is certainly plenty of
evidence for this conclusion in the songs he recorded just after
the prison experience. But Bukka was not simply writing an autobiography in sound when he cut those twelve sides in March
1940; he was engaged in an activity which is the essence of art —
externalizing his own experiences and observations and making
them into universal themes that involve the feelings and thoughts
of his people.

The core of the music produced during the two-day session in
Chicago dealt with the themes that we have been discussing:
love, death, loneliness, persecution; but there were also several
blues songs that dealt with more positive themes. On the first
day, Bukka recorded the assertive "Good Gin Blues" with its
good-natured acceptance of life as long as the singer is kept well

supplied with his favorite drink. The second day of the session yielded two more songs in the positive vein. "Aberdeen Mississippi Blues" and "Bukka's Jitterbug Swing" were happy, fancy pieces, offering Bukka a chance to show that his hands were capable of producing incredible intricacies with a guitar. These are Delta blues songs of as great complexity as the blues medium could support.

The 1940 recording session was the artistic high point of Bukka White's career. In a sense, it culminated the blues movement of the 1920s and 1930s. Simon Napier has accurately described the music that emerged from this session as "astonishingly beautiful." Relative to the aesthetic accomplishment, record sales seem almost unimportant. In fact, none of the numbers achieved the status of hits, and each is now a collector's item. The session was financially profitable to Bukka, however, since Melrose proved to be trustworthy in the business relationship with him; for years Melrose continued twice a year to send royalty checks, or statements if no records had sold. Even Melrose's daughter when she inherited the business continued to send Bukka a statement (and sometimes a check) twice a year.

For two years the wandering life continued. Bukka went back to Mississippi to see his wife Sue and his two children by that marriage; but the relationship was hollow, and he and Sue finally agreed to a permanent separation. (Bukka continued to visit her from time to time in Aberdeen, where she still lives.) Bukka lived with a number of women after his separation, but permanent legal obligations did not attract him. "Them two was enough of paper for me, you know," he wryly observed. "Wasn't no need of buying a cow if somebody just give you all the milk you want."

Bukka returned to Chicago for a while, playing small club dates with his own little four-piece band. In 1941 and 1942 he probably did fairly well, for his records, which were well-known, guaranteed him a good reception with black audiences. Further recording sessions eluded him, however. It was not a case of Bukka's running out of musical ideas; his mind continued to produce music throughout his life. Instead, it was a matter of shifting musical tastes among the urban blacks of Chicago. As the depression faded into memory under the economic onslaught of war spending, relative affluence brought social changes to black Chicagoans. They began to think of themselves as part of the urban community, not as displaced country people. Bukka's music was in the classic mode of country blues; thus, it was of the past — the very past that they had moved north to escape. His music was "country," while they were sophisticated city people. (Actually, Bukka was rather sophisticated himself, but his music remained rooted in the Delta.) For these reasons, Bukka's long-awaited career was never really launched in Chicago, and after two years he began to consider returning to the area he knew best. Certainly a steady job of some sort would look better to a draft board than the occupation "musician." Bukka was thirty-three and tired. He had children to support, and Chicago was not providing much employment. He even gave up music for a brief period, and in 1942 Bukka came to Memphis to stay.

> Well, I started settling down — commenced to driving my mules back to the barn about 1942. Memphis was the closest place to Mississippi which is my home, you know. And I always like it here — it's a nice town. Of course when I come down here they wouldn't let you play music at Handy Park [a small park on Beale Street dedicated to the memory of the composer W. C. Handy, known as the father of the blues]. The colored police would come along and run you out if you tried to play down there. But it was a nice town.

There was still a blues scene in Memphis when Bukka arrived to make the town his home, but it was fragmented and without much commercial focus. The local black musicians knew each other, of course, and often played small jobs together; but their music could no longer fully support them, if indeed it ever had in Memphis. Beale Street had been closed down during the 1930s when the interests of E. H. "Boss" Crump were no longer served by keeping its taverns and roadhouses open. The recording industry, never more than a tenuous part of the Memphis music scene, had left the city entirely. What remained was a loose pattern of small clubs scattered about the town, where a musician or a small band might work a couple of nights on the weekend; the occasional pickup job at parties for wealthy whites or house parties for blacks; and short-term engagements in the rural towns within easy driving distance of Memphis where country blues were still very well received. For Bukka, a "known" musician with records on the market, the musical situation was not bad.

There was work in Memphis if you knew how to get it, and he knew how.

Another attraction that the Bluff City had for Bukka was the presence of a musician whose styles and abilities interested him. Bukka had known Frank Stokes off and on for years and had always found him a stimulating musician. Stokes was in Memphis working as a blacksmith and playing a job now and then whenever something lucrative came along. Stokes was a legend in blues circles. With a partner named Dan Sane, he had formed the "Beale Street Sheiks" and had recorded more than thirty tunes between 1927 and 1929. With a new partner (Will Batts, a Memphis violin player) Stokes recorded eight more songs in 1929 and brought the total of his recorded songs to forty. Among these were some eight or ten songs that were not in the blues tradition, mostly humorous songs of the type used in traveling medicine shows. Stokes and Sane had traveled in the 1920s with various medicine shows and were known all over the United States as versatile entertainers. In short, Frank Stokes was a major musical figure from whom Bukka could learn. Stokes was also accustomed to working with a partner, and despite the dissimilarity of their guitar styles, Bukka was certainly musician enough to hold his own with the older man. For the next few years, Bukka did much of his playing around the Memphis area in the company of Frank Stokes.

Stokes's blacksmith business put him in contact with wealthy whites on a regular basis. Situated near the Shelby County Fair Grounds, his shop specialized in caring for the feet of the racehorses that ran there in those days. Often the owners of such expensive animals had large parties, and frequently Frank Stokes was called on to entertain the guests. Bukka liked to go along on such jobs. In later life Bukka described the scene without irony or any sense of the condescension involved.

> I got with Frank Stokes, and him and me got to playing for rich white folks' parties. And we wouldn't just play; they would have us stopping and talking and just carrying on for them. Man say, "Hell! Y'all ain't got to work yourself to death for no hundred dollars here." Said, "Rest some. Eat some. Drink some." It'd be like that; and lots of times I'd come home with a hundred, and Frank would have a hundred. Did I like Memphis? Man, I made a lot of money. I had to like it.

The jobs with Frank Stokes were musically satisfying as well, for Bukka loved to hear the old man play and could always learn a "lick or two" from him. Of course, he couldn't allow himself to think too much about his surroundings or the people being entertained, but such conditions were fairly normal for a bluesman at that time. Bukka also played at times with Jack Kelly and Willie Borum, two other veteran Memphis bluesmen who had made recordings in the 1930s.

The jobs might occasionally pay very well indeed, but they would not pay Bukka's rent or the child support on a regular basis, nor would they keep the local draft board from calling him. For these reasons Bukka worked for a couple of years as a laborer at the U.S. Defense Depot in Memphis and then found a much better job as a "fit-up" man with the Newberry Equipment Company. For the next twenty years it was his job to lay out and prepare large preformed pieces of steel for welders to join together into the huge tanks that were the company's specialty. In wartime such work was classified as vital to national defense; consequently Bukka's knowledge of World War II was mostly secondhand. He did claim, however, to have entertained the men on a ship bound for Japan at the end of the war, perhaps as part of a USO tour.

Life began to be easier for Bukka as he settled into a routine. He rented a little house on Spottswood Avenue in the Orange Mound section of Memphis. It was a comfortable place; and best of all, it was near Frank Stokes's blacksmith shop. He could see the old bluesman often; and when they had time in the evenings, they could play a little music together for their own enjoyment. It was a way of life that Bukka could have enjoyed for many years, but time was against him. Stokes was elderly yet still needed to work hard. His heart "give out" and he died around 1955.

Bukka continued to play music whenever he could find a paying audience. He recalled even making a trip to Chicago around 1952 to record as a guitar player with a group, but music was becoming more and more a sideline for him. He easily slipped into the position of "semiretired" musician, enjoying the status that it gave him within the community and occasionally helping a younger musician on his way up.

One younger musician whose early career was fostered by

Bukka is his cousin, B. B. King, today one of the most successful musicians in urban blues. Riley King, the man who was to become known as "B. B.," was sixteen years younger than Bukka and was a first cousin on his mother's side of the family. There was music in young Riley's family too. His mother played several instruments and sang; his grandfather was Jap Pulliam, an old blues guitarist from whom Bukka had learned some of his earliest "licks." Bukka had been interested in the musical development of young Riley King since the early thirties. Bukka described an early meeting with his cousin and remembered lending him a guitar. At the time, Bukka must have been about twenty-two; he was a hotshot young musician with a record out, playing hard blues at the local roadhouses and clubs. To six-year-old Riley he must have looked like the most successful man in the world:

> When B. B. was six years old, I went down in the Delta to Bird Cloud. (That's a mile the other side of Itta Bena.) Me and George "Bullet" Williams was playing a job at Itta Bena. Bird Cloud was a little, one-store town at the end of a road. (They all got to have a name, you know, 'cause that's where the people get their mail.)
>
> My Auntie Nora was living there, and Riley was about six. So I was sitting talking to my auntie and I looked over in the corner and seen that boy looking at my guitar and he looked so pitiful to me, just sitting there so quiet, and my mind — looked like something said — "Get that boy a guitar. He may come to be a good guitar player." I had me a little Stella guitar with me; so I handed it to B. B., and he said, "Thank you" real quiet, setting there on the floor.
>
> Well, the next time I saw that boy he done growed up to be a great big, half-grown man; and he was sharp with that Stella guitar!

Bukka did not see much of Riley during the years when Bukka was wandering the countryside; but after Bukka came to Memphis and settled down, the friendship was reestablished. When World War II had ended and American society began to sort itself out again, Riley King was living near Indianola, Mississippi, driving a tractor for one of the large cotton farms in the area and singing blues in the local clubs. He knew he wanted a career in music, but he was unsure of the direction to take. For a while he drove twenty-six miles several times a week to work as a part-time disc jockey for wGUM in Greenville, Mississippi. wGUM was a small station serving the local area, and only one-third of its broadcast time was aimed at the Negro population. Still, the station offered good experience and a place to start. It was in 1947 or 1948 that King made the decision to move to Memphis. In or around Indianola or Greenville he had advanced about as far as he could; and as Bukka told him, "You can't play music and drive a tractor." Riley's family was divided as to the wisdom of the move. His father, who was not musically inclined, opposed it; but his mother and Bukka's side of the family were in favor. Bukka listened to King's guitar work, decided that he had the makings of a career, and encouraged him. Bukka's influence won in the end—Riley and his young wife moved to Memphis, staying for several months at Bukka's house in Orange Mound while they got established.

Bukka helped the emerging young musician in several ways. In addition to giving him a place to stay, he also helped him obtain the equipment he needed to pursue a career in music. The old Stella guitar was nearly worn out by this time; so Bukka and Riley went downtown to the Haupt Music Company, and Bukka bought him a new Gibson guitar. Bukka's memory of this period emphasized the family aspects of the decision to give Riley a chance in music. "When B come here to get him a job and start playing music, his daddy told me I was a damned fool for going out there and spending for that stuff because B wasn't going to pay for it. Well, I said, I could see the good in it. I could see it, and everybody on our side of the family could see the good of it. See, B's daddy didn't play no music; so he never did see the good of it."

Bukka began to take his cousin around town. At the little clubs they listened to the music that was being played, absorbing styles and learning what was drawing good audiences. Down on Beale Street there were still blues shows every Saturday night at the Palace Theater. Sometimes these shows still featured a traveling group built around one of the established stars in blues. More often they resembled a local talent show with regional blues musicians as the main ingredient. Musicians simply went down to the theater and presented themselves. If the show's manager used them that evening, they were paid five dollars. Bukka was a fairly regular guest on these weekend shows and knew everyone around the Palace, including the announcer, a young man named Rufus Thomas who combined a smooth stage presence with a canny awareness of the direction that black music was headed. Appearing on these shows was no route to riches; but it kept Bukka's contact with the world of blues music alive, and he enjoyed it.

The Palace was no great shakes of a theater. It was dirty and vermin-infested, and the lighting system would have given the fire department nightmares if they had ever been interested in checking it; but in spite of all its faults, the Palace was as close to a blues music center as any place Memphis had to offer in 1947. Bukka took his cousin there many times. As they listened to the performers who walked out on the shabby stage and earned their five dollars, one fact became clear to Riley King. Black music was becoming electrified. The advent of the amplified electric guitar was working a revolution in the blues, and the gentle old acoustic guitar simply could not keep up. The strings of an electric guitar could be laid very close to the neck since volume was controlled at the amplifier and not so much by the force of hitting the strings; thus very fast runs were possible. Amplification made it possible to sustain notes longer; much heavier, more exciting bass string work was also technically possible with electrification.

Within a few months of arriving in Memphis, King was developing a style of his own, and the sound was electric. An electronic pickup was added across the sound hole of the big Gibson. Later trips to Haupt Music yielded an amplifier and a speaker, with Bukka dutifully cosigning each note. Credit was hard to establish for a black man in Memphis in the late forties, and Bukka's help in this matter was not unimportant. He later recalled that Haupt Music "had to call on the job and see did I really have a job at Newberry Equipment and could we pay for all this stuff." It was not easy, but Bukka was able to open some preliminary doors for his cousin. His position in the Memphis community might not have seemed very important; but it was established enough to secure some badly needed credit.

Bukka also helped Riley to obtain employment at Newberry Equipment Company. This job helped the financial situation considerably for a few months but did not move King closer to his goal, a career in music. Eventually, however, King began to find friends who could help even more. It may be that he met Nat D. Williams at the Palace Theater; it is fairly certain that he met Rufus Thomas there. Both men were on the threshold of influential careers in radio and would later help King. In 1948 Nat D. Williams became the leading disc jockey for WDIA, the largest radio station in the mid-South to have programming totally directed to black audiences. Nat D. probably introduced King to Don Kern (one of the white owners of the station), who offered King a job as a disc jockey upon learning of the young musician's previous experience in radio. By early 1949 Riley King was a popular radio personality billed to the public as "Blues Boy" King. Pretty soon "Blues Boy" shrank to simply "B.B.," and the name stuck. Even though B.B. had a job that gave him status within the black community, his career as a musician was still far from launched. Few Memphis blacks were aware that "Blues Boy" King was also an accomplished guitar player and blues singer. B.B. was smooth and assured in his radio style, but he found it difficult to play his music before large audiences. In strange, new situations, his basic shyness reasserted itself. Bukka liked to recall that he helped the man he called "Cousin B" to overcome this shyness.

For his cousin's first public appearance as a musician Bukka chose a setting that was rural enough to "feel natural" to B.B. yet important enough to give him some real exposure. It was a long-standing tradition in Memphis for the black community to leave the city for large-scale country picnics on the Fourth of July. City parks were for the most part closed to blacks, reserved for the celebration of white independence; therefore, they went to the country. Over the years, certain picnics had developed reputations among the black population for good food and good entertainment, and these were heavily attended. One of the largest and most popular of these traditional country picnics was held at the Owens family farm near Somerville, Tennessee. Very few Memphis Negroes would have been unfamiliar with the Owens Picnic, and as many as could attend did so. They came by carloads and by special buses to eat reasonably-priced barbecue sandwiches and listen to good music. Many of the region's best musicians played at Owens's farm, and on 4 July 1949 the popular radio disc jockey B.B. King was one of them.

B.B's performance went well that day. In fact, Bukka recalls that his cousin was the hit of the show. Thereafter, he was more than just a popular radio voice, he was a singer developing a reputation of his own within the world of black music. The timing of King's emergence was good, too; for the postwar blues scene (with its important offshoots into what was becoming known as rhythm and blues) was just in the process of taking shape. Unlike Bukka's art, which flowered as his own blues era came to an end, B.B's was only beginning to reach its strength at the dawn of the era of which he was to be a part. Soon his music was available on records, and over the years he recorded hundreds of blues with many hits among them. In the early fifties Cousin B moved to Chicago to be closer to the mainstream of postwar Negro music, and Bukka saw little of him after that. Bukka's role as a passer of the torch to B.B. had been fulfilled.

Bukka stayed in Memphis, laying out sheet metal for welders and playing music when there was a demand for it. He was now past forty, and the years had not been particularly easy on him. He was tired, and peace was more important than something abstract called success. Bukka did not even envy his younger cousin's success very much. His own life was lived much as he wanted it to be. He could afford the rent for his house and he ate fairly well. When he felt like it, Bukka also drank well.

Like most of the bluesmen of his generation, Bukka was a hard drinker. Drinking was a part of his entire adult life. Back in the days when Mississippi was a dry state, he and George "Bullet" Williams had made whiskey together and on occasion had probably strained Sterno (canned heat) to extract the alcohol. As his life slowed into predictable patterns, he naturally turned to the bottle more and more to provide a cushion against the drabness of each day. Too much may be made of this, however. Bukka was a very strong man physically and could always drink vast quantities of liquor without apparent effects. He never became dependent on alcohol; he simply liked it. Some writers have intimated that Bukka's career might have been more successful were it not for his drinking habits. This analysis seems to reverse cause and effect. Bukka's career was never highly successful because of its historical timing; if anything, his later heavy drinking was an effect of his somewhat blighted hopes, not a cause. It may be added that Bukka probably never missed playing an engagement as a result of excessive drinking.

The decade of the 1950s was a period of virtually total obscurity for Bukka. Its music was new, and he could not play it. The musicians were, for the most part, people he did not know.

Memphis developed into a center of the new recording industry with people such as Johnny Ace, Bobby Bland, and Junior Parker emerging as genuine stars within the national black musical community. Recording companies, many of them begun as small independent labels, created hit after hit in rhythm and blues. Bukka watched from the sidelines. He still played a job now and then and even used an electric guitar for a while. He remembered, for example, driving fairly often to Hughes, Arkansas, with a little band of "local boys" he had formed to play a club there that still featured the country blues. But there were few jobs for an old-time musician in Memphis during those years.

Bukka might have remained in obscurity had it not been for the resurgence of interest in country blues that swept the campuses of white colleges in the early sixties. This resurgence is a phenomenon much too large for detailed consideration here, but it may be summarily stated that folk music of all sorts was an important form of entertainment among college-age young people from the late fifties through the late sixties, and the rediscovery of the classic country blues tradition was very much a part of this resurgence. In the United States and in Western Europe as well, educated young people were coming to the realization that the travail of the black man in the American South had created a new art form. The country blues was being taken seriously again — twenty years after it had, for all practical purposes, ceased to exist as a popular musical form among the nation's black population.

In record-collecting circles and at universities in New York, Massachusetts, and California, earnest young men began to listen carefully to scratchy old Paramount, Victor, Okeh, and Vocalion records. They becan to realize that there were distinguishable styles, that a Texas bluesman like Blind Lemon Jefferson played differently from an Atlanta bluesman like Barbecue Bob. They realized that there was an identifiable Mississippi Delta style of blues, and many came to feel that the 1940 recordings by somebody named Bukka White were the epitome of this style. "Fixin' to Die Blues" was reissued on a record to accompany Samuel Charters' pioneering book *The Country Blues* (1959), and it was soon imitated by many young white guitarists, including Bob Dylan. By the early sixties Bukka's records were probably more widely known than they had been in 1940, but he was unaware of his increased recognition. The interest in blues as a subject for serious study had not penetrated the original heartland of the blues at all.

In 1963 two young white men "found" Bukka, who was still living in Memphis and working for Newberry Equipment Company, unaware that he had ever been "lost." John Fahey, then a struggling young guitarist and student at the University of California at Berkeley, and his friend, Ed Denson, also a student at the university, had listened to the old Bukka White records and had decided that Bukka was a musician worth trying to find. Since one of the best songs of Bukka's 1940 recording session had been titled "Aberdeen Mississippi Blues," they simply addressed a letter to "Booker T. Washington White (Old Blues Singer), c/o General Delivery, Aberdeen, Mississippi." It was a good guess. Bukka still had relatives around Aberdeen and he had kept in touch well enough that the letter was eventually forwarded to him in Memphis.

Bukka did not know quite how to react to a letter from people he did not know in faraway California, but he finally wrote them a friendly letter saying that he would be happy to talk to them if they were ever around Memphis. Fahey and Denson made a quick telephone call to Bukka in Memphis and left for the mid-South within two hours of receiving Bukka's reply. They found Bukka living in a rented room and were amazed to discover that he still played. Bukka, of course, had never stopped playing; he had just stopped receiving much recognition for it. His style, though somewhat affected by his attempts to change with the musical tastes of the fifties, was still basically the same as it had been when he recorded in 1940. At times he tried to imitate popular recorded blues singers, and the results were not very satisfying; but when he played the old songs, his playing and singing reverted to the classic Delta-blues style that had always been Bukka's strength. Fahey and Denson listened and decided that they must bring Bukka out of obscurity and present him to the new blues-loving audience, the white college students.

In the fall of 1963 Bukka traveled west, on the road again for the first time in twenty years. He played for folklore classes at the University of California at Berkeley and charmed the students. He did an engagement at the Los Angeles coffeehouse, the Ash Grove. In December of 1963 he enjoyed the special treat of crossing paths with his cousin, B. B. King, in Oakland, California. B.B. was playing at a place called Sweet's Ballroom; when Bukka came into the room and took a table near the stage, Cousin B responded with a moving tribute to the man who had helped him so much in the early days. Certainly, recognition of this sort was more satisfying to Bukka than the money the trip west put into his pocket.

Three LP albums of Bukka's music emerged while he was on the West Coast. Bukka re-recorded many of his early songs for Fahey and Denson; these were released under the title *Mississippi Blues: Bukka White* on their own label, Takoma Records. The Takoma album is distinguished both by its excellent selections and presentation and by the solicitous interest its producers took in Bukka's legal rights. Too often in recent years the field of blues has been blighted by collectors who take advantage of older singers, utilizing their songs for personal profits; however, Fahey and Denson copyrighted all of Bukka's songs in the name of B.T.W. White and thus insured Bukka against one form of exploitation. Two highly original albums were also cut for Chris Strachwitz, whose Arhoolie Record Company has represented to serious collectors for many years the finest in folk, blues, and jazz recordings. These two albums, *Bukka White: Sky Songs,* Volumes I and II, give students of the blues access to a different side of Bukka. Bukka's older blues are not there. Instead, the listener hears Bukka White as a maker of new songs, but one who continued to work in a folk tradition. Bukka composed on the spot many of the songs that Strachwitz recorded. "I just reach up and pull them out of the sky—call them sky songs—they just come to me," Bukka said. Longer and much looser than the earlier songs, often with unrhymed lines, Bukka's "sky songs" are nevertheless some of his most interesting productions. They show that his mind was still working, still creating.

"Single Man Blues," issued on the second Arhoolie album, can serve as a good example of Bukka's "sky songs." Much longer than the three-minute format imposed by the more commercially oriented record companies, it allows Bukka an opportunity to extend his imagination and storytelling skills to the fullest. It also features his rather simple but solid barrelhouse piano playing, a skill that Bukka never let get away from him. The lyrics should convince any listener that Bukka's abilities as a composer never declined during his period of reduced musical activity.

SINGLE MAN BLUES
Words and Music by Booker T. White
© by Tradition Music Company (BMI). USED BY PERMISSION.

1. I'm a single man, I'm a single man, I ain't
   doing nothing but going from hand to
   hand.
   I'm a single man, I'm a single man. Boys,
   I'm just going from hand to hand.
   When I find that little woman I love, I'll
   stop right still and hold her little hand.

2. I got the news early this morning, some
   women downtown looking for a good
   man.
   I got sad news this morning, bunch of
   womens downtown looking for a man.
   I went to the employer early this morning
   and found out. They say, "Yes, Booker,
   there's two or three here want to see
   you."

   Spoken: Play it out there now. I see three
   standing on the corner. Gonna check them.

3. Tell me y'all womens downtown trying to
   find a man don't have no girl.
   I'm gonna tell you before I carry you on
   home, I don't want no woman always
   having some other man in her arms.

4. I believe I'm gonna get up early morning
   with the sun. Babe, I'm gonna leave you
   asleep in my little bed.
   But, God knows, don't let me, when I
   come in late that evening, baby, see no
   fellow, have no other rounder laying
   around my bed.
   If I do, if I do, baby, I'm gonna call back
   the employer, tell the undertaker to
   please hurry on over here.

5. It's gonna be like a little 'tomic bomb,
   baby, if I see the sign of a man been
   around.

And I'm out yonder slaving from sun to
sun; some other rounder here in my bed.
I don't want y'all women to get the wrong
impression. Yes, I'm the man who's
looking for someone.

5. Babe, all you got to do late in the evening,
have the old red rooster on the stove
when I come.
All you got to do, to have the old red
rooster on, baby, and plenty dumplings,
baby, in the pot.
I'll bet you won't see no frown in my face.
I'll bet you I'll come in with smiles on me.

Spoken: Lay it out there now.

7. Lord, baby, now baby, now baby, you
ought to be thanking the Lord to find a
man like me.
I keeps you plenty food, baby, and I keep
good shoes on your little old feet.
All you have to do, baby, look pretty when
I come in, fool me, baby, like you love me.

8. My baby, she got little dreamy eyes. I hate
for her to look me dead in my sight.
My baby, she got them little pretty eyes.
Boys, I declare, I hate for her to look me
in my sight.

Every time my baby look at me, something
roll over me just like a flea.

9. I gets in the bed, gets in the bed trembling,
and I gets up the same old way.
I gets in my bed 'side of my baby trembling
just like a leaf on a tree.
I be saying to myself, "Lord, have mercy;
don't let this little angel child kill me."

10. She said, "Daddy, why do you keep on
shaking?" I said, "Why do you keep on
pulling on me?"
She said, "Daddy, why do you keep on
shaking?" I said, "Why that you keep on
pulling on me?
You done knowed the doctor already told
me you was gonna be the, the death of
poor me."

11. Baby, when you kissed me early this morning, it felt like zigzag had hit my bones.
Baby, when you throwed your arms around
me early this morning and kissed me, I
thought zigzag lightning had hit my
bones.
I tumbled out the bed and fell on my knees.
I said, "Lord, don't let me go."

There were many satisfactions in the trip to California, but after a few months Bukka began to grow restless. The people
around him were people he did not know, and California was not
his home. In early 1964 he returned to Memphis. The trip to California had not made him wealthy; he still lived in rented rooms.
But it had made a difference. He was no longer an obscure figure
veiled in the past. Now he was known, and people who wanted
to listen to his music knew where to find him.

Bukka continued to travel occasionally, and his travels took
him over much of the world. He appeared on a number of new
records, always with fine results. He never became rich, but he
did not ride the freight trains anymore either. He appeared in the
Newport Folk Festival in 1966 and sang at the Olympic Games in
Mexico City in 1968. In 1968 he also toured Europe for the first
time. He made other tours of Europe and recorded albums in
Germany in 1972 and 1975. He was one of the folk musicians

listed on the "Festival of American Folklife" tours sponsored by the Smithsonian Institution, and he made many college appearances on such tours. Once in a great while he was even asked to sing at one of the colleges in Memphis. These requests were rare, however, for Memphis has yet fully to recognize the blues in its midst as an art form.

Bukka liked to play dates at colleges. The money was good and he loved the young audiences.

> I have played lots of colleges. Now, a lot of people don't understand this kind of work. A coffeehouse ain't able to pay like a college. They're not able. They'll do the best they can, but they can't come up with what a college can. And I like them college kids too. Seems like they really want to understand what you're doing. Every song, I stops and tells them what tuning I'm in and talk about the song.
>
> I ain't going to sit up there and jump in and go to playing and them not know what tuning I'm in or nothing. I care for them. They want to learn and I want them to learn, 'cause I'm not going to be playing always and somebody ought to be picking this up.

Bukka had come a long way and had seen much. It was not all pleasant for him, but neither was it all bad. His little apartment on Mosby Street in Memphis was steamy and warm in the winter, and the television worked. On sunny days he liked to sit on a bench in his neighborhood at the side of a little grocery run by "the Chinaman" and swap stories with other older men of the area. He called the bench his "office," and anyone who wanted to find Bukka generally started there. Bukka realized that his work was seen as significant by many people around the world, and he took vast satisfaction in that awareness. When the mood was right, Bukka remained a wonderful musician carrying the sounds of classic Delta blues to new audiences and new generations. "It ain't a bad way for an old man to make a living," he would say with a wily grin.

Bukka had clearly mellowed over the years. His success and fame in later life, although not overwhelming, had probably removed much of the disappointment he had felt as a result of the failure of his earlier attempt at a musical career to bring him the rewards his artistry deserved. He had come to enjoy the young admirers at concerts and coffeehouses who nicknamed him "Big

Daddy" and who occasionally came to visit him in Memphis in an effort to absorb in a day or two what it had taken him a lifetime to learn. He was still strong and alert and in apparent good health, making a concert tour in 1976 at the age of 66, when he suffered a light stroke in Massachusetts. He spent a few weeks in the hospital there until he recovered sufficiently to return to Memphis. For a while it looked as if his life would return to normal, but more strokes followed. He suffered from diabetes in later years; and as it turned out, he also had cancer of the pancreas. It was of the latter that he finally died on 26 February 1977. Throughout the 1970s, whenever his concert appearances became less frequent, there were rumors that Bukka White had died. These were often published in blues magazines and probably did his career no good, but always Bukka would emerge to refute the rumors and play and sing as well as ever. Finally, sadly, it was not a rumor. The world had lost one of the greatest country blues singers. His career had begun in the golden age of country blues in Mississippi; when he died, more than five decades later, he had played an important role in America's folk music revival, and his music had received international acclaim.

BUKKA WHITE CHRONOLOGY

1909	Booker T. Washington White is born 12 November near Houston, Mississippi.
1918	Bukka gets his first guitar and begins learning songs from his father and other older local musicians.
ca. 1920	Bukka goes to the Delta to work on his uncle's farm, hears the legendary bluesman Charlie Patton.
ca. 1922	Bukka goes to St. Louis for the first time, learns to play piano there.
1925	Bukka marries his first wife, Jessie Bea. They farm near Houston, and Bukka plays music locally.
1928	Jessie Bea dies. Bukka moves to St. Louis, returns to Mississippi, and wanders.
1929	Bukka sharecrops, makes and sells moonshine whiskey, works as general roustabout and part-time musician for three weeks with Silas Green Traveling Circus.

1930– 1934	Bukka lives at Swan Lake in the Delta, sharecropping and making music, often performing with harmonica player George "Bullet" Williams.
1930	Bukka makes his first records in Memphis for Victor, performing with Napoleon Hairiston on two "train" pieces and with Miss Minnie on two gospel songs.
1934	Bukka marries Susie Simpson, "Bullet" Williams' niece, and moves with her to Aberdeen, Mississippi. He tries unsuccessfully to record with his father in Memphis.
1935– 1937	Bukka hoboes, pitches baseball, works in a traveling show, goes to Chicago, performs with local blues musicians there, has a career as a professional boxer.
1937	Bukka is given a two-year sentence to Parchman Farm for shooting a man in Aberdeen. Before serving his term, he goes to Chicago and records two blues songs for Vocalion. "Shake 'Em On Down" is a big hit. His marriage disintegrates.
1939	Bukka records two songs for folklorist Alan Lomax shortly before his release from Parchman.
1940	Bukka records twelve blues numbers for Vocalion and Okeh in Chicago. These represent the artistic high point of his career.
1940– 1941	Bukka travels between Mississippi and Chicago, pursuing his career in music.
1942	Having failed to find great success, Bukka settles in Memphis, taking a steady job and playing music part-time. His partners are Frank Stokes and other local musicians.
ca. 1942	Bukka and his wife Sue agree to a permanent separation.
1945– 1946	Bukka entertains troops briefly in the Pacific.
1948– 1949	Bukka helps his cousin B. B. King establish a career as a blues singer.
1950– 1963	Bukka is relatively inactive in music, performing on occasion mainly in the Memphis area.
1963	Bukka is "rediscovered" by two young blues enthusiasts and brought to California for concerts and new recordings.

1963– Bukka enjoys a second career on the folk music revival
1977   circuit as a concert and coffeehouse singer. He trav-
       els nationally and internationally and appears on a
       number of records, but continues to make Memphis
       his home.
1977   Following a series of strokes Bukka dies of cancer on
       26 February at age sixty-seven.

Conclusion

BY THOMAS G. BURTON

Come, my lord, and take the pipe. . . .
Cease, Muses, come cease the pastoral song.
— THEOCRITUS

No pastoral poets were they; but like their ancient predecessors, Tom Ashley, Sam McGee, and Bukka White inherited a song-craft, offered their own performance, and then passed on their lore to others. No great procession follows them because not any one of these three topped the crest or pointed out new heights, although each achieved a certain place and left his individual mark. Yet, as distinctive as each man is, their careers have so much in common that one might muse that each was given the same stage directions:

Enter an agrarian culture that is rich in traditional music; choose a family that embodies that tradition; learn from them their songs, their instruments, their feelings, and then join in with them when they play and sing together. Go when you are asked to play for parties and dances, and accept whatever pay you are given. Then, since you would rather sing and play than almost anything, try making a go of it on your music alone as much as possible — people genuinely enjoy your performances, and others no better than you seem to be doing well. Face the fact that your venture is not easy: times are hard, and the profession you have chosen is young and unsteady. Try everything available: find a partner or a band, go wherever you can draw a crowd — traveling show circuit, auditorium, theater, or radio station — wherever you can earn a dollar. Accept the pressures of having few opportunities but many obligations, for example, a family; and bring everything to bear — your background, your artistry, your contacts, your experience, your store from others. Try recording — that is the newest and most exciting thing on the scene — you can use the money, even though it will not be much; your name will become known; the recognition will increase your bookings; and you just might become a star. But realize finally that your success will not be great: the market for you and your kind of music does not last. Perform less and less; be your own patron more and more by doing other kinds of work, and move off center stage to make room for a new kind of musician. Assimilate some, compromise a little perhaps, but do not undergo the metamorphosis necessary to make you highly commercial. Recede into the wings, since you have become somewhat anachronistic; but come forward when an audience cries out for an encore and a spotlight is focused on you. Bow; then exit.

Selected Bibliographies

Child, Francis James. *The English and Scottish Popular Ballads.* 5 vols. Boston: Houghton Mifflin, 1882–98.
The Frank C. Brown Collection of North Carolina Folklore. 7 vols. Durham, N.C.: Duke Univ. Press, 1952–61.
Gower, Herschel. "Wanted: The Singer's Autobiography and Critical Reflections." *Tennessee Folklore Society Bulletin,* 39 (March 1973), 1–7.
Laws, G. Malcolm, Jr. *American Balladry from British Broadsides: A Guide for Students and Collectors of Traditional Song.* Philadelphia: American Folklore Society, 1957.
_____. *Native American Balladry: A Descriptive Study and a Bibliographical Syllabus.* Rev. ed. Philadelphia: American Folklore Society, 1964.
Lomax, Alan. *The Folk Songs of North America.* Garden City, N.Y.: Doubleday, 1960.
Malone, Bill C. *Country Music, U.S.A.* Austin: Univ. of Texas Press, 1968.
_____ and Judith McCulloh, eds. *Stars of Country Music: Uncle Dave Macon to Johnny Rodriguez.* Urbana: Univ. of Illinois Press, 1975.
Nettl, Bruno. *Folk and Traditional Music of the Western Continents.* Englewood Cliffs, N.J.: Prentice-Hall, 1965.
Shelton, Robert. *The Country Music Story.* Indianapolis: Bobbs-Merrill, 1966.

Shestack, Melvin. *Country Music Encyclopedia.* New York: Crowell, 1973.
Weatherford, W. D., and Wilma Dykeman. "Literature since 1900." In *The Southern Appalachian Region: A Survey.* Ed. Thomas R. Ford. Lexington: Univ. of Kentucky Press, 1962, 259-70.

TOM ASHLEY SELECTED BIBLIOGRAPHY

Correspondence

Acuff, Roy. Letter to Minnie M. Miller. 23 Dec. 1974.
Isley, Larry C. "Tex." Letter to Minnie M. Miller. April 1973.
Schlappi, Elizabeth. Letters to Thomas G. Burton. 24 Dec. 1974, 21 Jan. 1975.

Audio Tape Recordings

Blaustein, Richard. Fred Price Interview at Shouns, Tenn. Recorded 2 Oct. 1974.
Burton, Thomas G. Richard Blaustein Interview at Johnson City, Tenn. Recorded 10 Jan. 1974.
Burton, Thomas G., and Ambrose N. Manning. East Tennessee State Univ. Folk Festival. Recorded 7 Oct. 1966.
_____. Eva Ashley Moore Interview at Saltville, Va. Recorded 1969.
_____. Tom Ashley in Folklore Class at East Tennessee State Univ. Recorded 7 April 1966.
Fisher, Jim. Tom Ashley at Saltville, Va. Recorded fall 1965.
_____. Tom Ashley at Shouns, Tenn. Recorded 19, 26 Aug. 1965.
Miller, Minnie M. Arthel "Doc" Watson Interview at Deep Gap, N.C. Recorded 19 June 1973.
_____. Clint Howard Interview at Mountain City, Tenn. Recorded 20 June 1973.
_____. Fred Price Interview at Mountain City, Tenn. Recorded 12 April 1973.
_____. Hettie Osborne Ashley Interview at Shouns, Tenn. Recorded 29 June 1973.
_____. J. D. Ashley Interview at Mountain City, Tenn. Recorded 29 April 1973.
University of California, Los Angeles Folk Festival, 1963: Workshop No. 3 — Banjo, Old Style.

Video Tape Recording

"Hillbilly Music." *Lyrics and Legends*. Prod. Richard Burdick. WNET/13, New York, 1962 (black and white).

Other Sources

Baldwin, Robert. "Union Grove Lays It On." *Greensboro* (N.C.) *Record*, 19 April 1965.

"Caught in the Act: Ashley." *Melody Maker* (London), 7 May 1966, p. 20.

"Clarence Ashley." *Sing Out!* 17, No. 4 (Aug.–Sept. 1967), 30.

Cohn, Lawrence. "Newport Folk Festival 1963: The Recordings." *Saturday Review*, 16 Jan. 1965, pp. 70–71.

"Concerts, Hoots, Workshops Highlight UCLA Folk Festival." *Sing Out!* 13, No. 3 (summer 1963), 41–43.

Cooper, John. "This Is the Gen-u-ine Article, Folks." *Hull Times* (England), 14 May 1966.

"Country Music Makers Take Part in Chicago University Festival, Workshop." *Mountain City* (Tenn.) *Tomahawk*, 31 Jan. 1962.

"Critic Calls Ashley's 'Coo Coo Bird' a Work of Art — A Great Contribution." *Mountain City* (Tenn.) *Tomahawk*, 23 Sept. 1964.

Dallas, Karl. "Out of the Past, a Banjo Picker Supreme." *Melody Maker* (London), 30 April 1966, p. 8.

Earle, Eugene. "Discography." Notes to *Old-Time Music at Clarence Ashley's*. Folkways, FA 2355, 1961.

_____. "A Discography of Recordings by Dock Walsh and Garley Foster." Notes to *The Carolina Tar Heels*. Folk-Legacy, FSA-24, 1965, pp. 28–33.

"The Friends of Old Time Music." *Sing Out!* 11, No. 1 (Feb.–March 1961), 63–64.

Gibson, Jim. "Area Folks to Record Country Music Album." *Bristol* (Va.-Tenn.) *Herald Courier*, 19 Feb. 1961.

Gilbert, Anne. "Folk Music Trails Lead through the Appalachians." *Smyth County* (Va.) *News*, 7 May 1964.

Green, Archie. Notes to *The Carolina Tar Heels*. Folk-Legacy, FSA-24, 1965.

Grimes, Junius. "Goings On: Clarence Asheley [*sic*], One of the Greats." *Raleigh* (N.C.) *News and Observer*, 19 April 1965.

Gustafson, Robert. "Coffee House Circuit: From the Mountains." *Boston Globe*, 1 May 1966.

Hamill, Dorothy. "Tom Ashley: Meet the 'Country Feller' Who Taught a Few Tunes to Opry Star Roy Acuff." *Johnson City* (Tenn.) *Press-Chronicle*, 18 June 1966.

Hentoff, Nat. "Entertainment: Recording of Special Merit—Tom Ashley and Tex Isley." *Hi/Fi Stereo Review*, 17, No. 3 (Sept. 1966), 115.

Jones, Robert C. "Broadside: Clarence Ashley and Tex Isley—Folkways FA 2350." *Broadside*, 5, No. 16 (28 Sept. 1966), 18.

"Little Sadie." *Sing Out!* 14, No. 6 (Jan. 1964), 40.

Miller, Minnie M. "Tom Clarence Ashley: An Applachian Folk Musician." M.A. thesis, East Tennessee State Univ., 1973.

"Mountain Man Gains Fame as Folk Singer." *Elizabethton* (Tenn.) *Star*, 10 Feb. 1963.

"Music Club Features Folk Music." *Bristol* (Va.-Tenn.) *Herald Courier*, 19 Feb. 1963.

"Old Time Music at Clarence Ashley's (Folkways 2355)." *Little Sandy Review*, 12, pp. 36–39.

"Old Time Music at Clarence Ashley's Vol. 2 (Folkways 2359)." *Little Sandy Review*, 26, pp. 19–20.

Old Time Music at Newport, Notes to. Vanguard, 9147, 1963.

Pankake, Jon. "Clarence Ashley." *American Folk Music*. Minneapolis: Arts Council of Walker Art Center, March 1965.

_____. Notes to *Clarence Ashley and Tex Isley*. Folkways, FA 2350, 1966.

Plous, Fritz. "The Remarkable History of Tom Ashley's 'Coo-coo Bird.'" *Hootenanny*, Nov. 1964, p. 30.

Rinzler, Ralph and Richard. Notes to *Old-Time Music at Clarence Ashley's*. Folkways, FA 2355, 1961. Vol. 2, FA 2359, 1963.

Scanlan, Thomas. "Getting Right at the Guthrie." *University of Minnesota Ivory Tower*, 8 March 1965, pp. 15–17.

Schlappi, Elizabeth. *Roy Acuff: The Smoky Mountain Boy*. Ed. James Calhoun. Gretna, La.: Pelican, 1977.

Shelton, Robert. "Folk Group Gives 'Village' Concert." *New York Times*, 27 March 1961.

_____. "Old Time Rural Musician Finds a New Crop of Fans in the City." *New York Times*, 25 Oct. 1966.

Third Annual Old Time Fiddlers and Bluegrass Convention. Marion, Va.: Civitan Club, 1971.

"Walking Boss." *Sing Out!* 15, No. 4 (Sept. 1965), 7.

Wright, Mac. "Recording in 1920's Leads to New Album." *Johnson City* (Tenn.) *Press-Chronicle*, 12 Feb. 1961.

SAM McGEE SELECTED BIBLIOGRAPHY

Audio Tape Recordings

Wolfe, Charles. Sam McGee and Members of the McGee Family Interviews. Recorded 1972–75.

Other Sources

Calt, Stephen, Nick Perls, and Michael Stewart. Notes to *Mr. Charlie's Blues (1926-1938)*. Yazoo, L-1024, n.d.

Cicchetti, Stephen, and Fly Bredenberg. *Old-Time Country Guitar*. New York: Oak, 1976.

Clemons, Marvin. "Sam McGee from Tennessee." *Bluegrass Unlimited*, Oct. 1975, pp. 28-30.

Cohen, Anne and Norm. "Tune Evolution as an Indicator of Traditional Musical Norms." *Journal of American Folklore*, 86 (March 1973), 37-48.

Fleder, Robert. Notes to *Old-Time Mountain Guitar*. County, 523 (1972).

Hay, George D. *A Story of the Grand Ole Opry*. Nashville: George D. Hay, 1947.

McCormick, Mack. "Henry Thomas: Our Deepest Look at the Roots." Notes to *Henry Thomas: Ragtime Texas*. Herwin, LP 209, 1974.

Pankake, Jon. Notes to *The McGee Brothers and Arthur Smith: Milk 'Em in the Evening Blues*. Folkways, LP FTS 31007, 1968.

_____. "Sam and Kirk McGee." *Sing Out!* 14 (Nov. 1964), 46-50.

_____ and Mike Seeger. Notes to *The McGee Brothers and Arthur Smith*. Folkways, LP FA 2379, 1964.

Rinzler, Ralph, and Norman Cohen. *Uncle Dave Macon: A Bio-Discography*. JEMF Special Series, No. 3. Los Angeles: John Edwards Memorial Foundation (UCLA), 1970.

Russell, Tony. *Blacks, Whites, and Blues*. New York: Stein and Day, 1970.

Sawyer, Kathy. "Sam and Kirk Go Way Back." *Nashville Tennessean*, 15 Oct. 1967.

Schuller, Gunther. *Early Jazz*. New York: Oxford Univ. Press, 1968.

Seeger, Mike. Notes to *Grand-Dad of the Country Guitar Pickers*. Arhoolie, LP 5012, 1971.

Wolfe, Charles. *Grand Ole Opry: The Early Years, 1925-1935*. London: Old Time Music, 1975.

_____. "In Memoriam, Sam McGee." *The Devil's Box*, Dec. 1975, pp. 3-6.

_____. Notes to *Sam and Kirk McGee from Sunny Tennessee*. Bear Family (Bremen, West Germany), BF 15517, 1976.

_____. "Sam and Kirk McGee: Part 1." *Pickin' Magazine*, Oct. 1974, pp. 4-11.

_____. "Sam and Kirk McGee: Part 2." *Pickin' Magazine*, Nov. 1974, pp. 4-10.

_____. *Tennessee Strings: The Story of Country Music in Tennessee*. Knoxville: Univ. of Tennessee Press, 1977.

BUKKA WHITE SELECTED BIBLIOGRAPHY
by David Evans

Video Tape Recording

Booker White. Prod. Seattle Folklore Soc. in Cooperation with KCTS-TV, Seattle, Wash. (24 min., black and white).

Other Sources

Basiuk, Bo. "Interview with Bukka White — Memphis, August, 1975." *Blues Magazine*, 2, No. 6 (Dec. 1976), 20–30; 3, No. 1 (Feb. 1977), 16–31.

————. "The Music of Bukka White." *Blues Magazine*, 2, No. 6 (Dec. 1976), 41–49.

————. "Bukka White 1909–1977." *Blues Magazine,* 3, No. 2 (April 1977), 13–14.

Battaglia, John. "Bukka White 'Bottleneck Train Blues' Guitar Style." *Blues Magazine*, 2, No. 6 (Dec. 1976), 56–59.

Brake, Ed. "Post-War Discography." *Blues Magazine*, 2, No. 6 (Dec. 1976), 63.

Broonzy, William. *Big Bill Blues.* Rev. ed. New York: Oak, 1964.

Charters, Samuel B. *Sweet As the Showers of Rain.* New York: Oak, 1977.

————. *The Country Blues.* New York: Da Capo, 1975.

————. *The Bluesmen.* New York: Oak, 1967.

————. "An Inner Sense of Self — Bukka White." In *The Legacy of the Blues.* New York: Da Capo, 1977, pp. 33–46.

Denson, Ed. "The Re-Discovery of Bukka White." *Blues Magazine*, 2, No. 6 (Dec. 1976), 6–13.

Dixon, Robert M.W., and John Godrich. *Recording the Blues.* New York: Stein and Day, 1970.

Evans, David. "Afro-American One-Stringed Instruments." *Western Folklore*, 29 (Oct. 1970), 229–45.

————. "Booker White." In *Nothing but the Blues.* Ed. Mike Leadbitter. London: Hanover, 1971, pp. 248–55.

Fahey, John. *Charley Patton.* London: Studio Vista, 1970.

Ferris, William R., Jr. *Blues from the Delta.* London: Studio Vista, 1970.

Gentry, Claude. *The Guns of Kinnie Wagner.* Baldwyn, Miss.: Magnolia, 1969.

Godrich, John, and Robert M.W. Dixon. *Blues & Gospel Records 1902–1942.* London: Storyville, 1969.

Grossman, Stefan. *Delta Blues Guitar*. New York: Oak, 1969.

Keil, Charles. *Urban Blues*. Chicago: Univ. of Chicago Press, 1966.

Leadbitter, Mike. *Delta Country Blues*. Bexhill-on-Sea, England: Blues Unlimited, 1968.

_____ and Neil Slaven. *Blues Records: 1943–1966*. London: Hanover, 1968.

Lornell, Kip. "C. D. Dobbs." *Living Blues*, 16 (spring 1974), 27–28.

Melrose, Lester. "My Life in Recording." In *The American Folk Music Occasional*. Ed. Chris Strachwitz and Pete Welding. New York: Oak, 1970, pp. 59–61.

Misiewicz, Roger. "Booker T. Washington White — Pre–World War II Discography." *Blues Magazine*, 2, No. 6 (Dec. 1976), 61–63.

Mossel, Eric. "Bukka's Story." *Blues World*, 19 (April 1968), 10–11.

Napier, Simon. "The Story of Bukka White." In *Nothing but the Blues*. Ed. Mike Leadbitter. London: Hanover, 1971, pp. 246–48.

Oakley, Giles. *The Devil's Music: A History of the Blues*. London: British Broadcasting Corp., 1976.

Odum, Howard W. "Folk-Song and Folk-Poetry As Found in the Secular Songs of the Southern Negroes." *Journal of American Folklore*, 24 (1911), 255–94, 351–96.

Oliver, Paul. *The Story of the Blues*. London: Barrie and Rockliff, 1969.

Olsson, Bengt. *Memphis Blues and Jug Bands*. London: Studio Vista, 1970.

Richards, Roberta. "The Legendary Bukka White." *Blues Magazine*, 2, No. 6 (Dec. 1976), 38–40.

Whitely, Ken, and Bo Basiuk. "Aberdeen, Mississippi." *Blues Magazine*, 2, No. 6 (Dec. 1976), 50–53.

Discographies

First column: master and issued take numbers; numbers underlined indicate the take that was originally issued. Second column: title and instrumentation. Third column: release data, release numbers, and labels; record numbers in italics are LP reissues. Label names are abbreviated as follows: Ad, Adelphi; Al, Albatros; Arh, Arhoolie; Ba, Banner; BB, Blues Beacon; BC, Blues Classics; BF, Bear Family; BH, Blue Horizon; Bio, Biograph; Br, Brunswick; CBS, CBS Records; CC, Collectors' Classics; Ch, Champion; Chl, Challenge; Co, Columbia; Cor, Coral; Cq, Conqueror; Cy, County; De, Decca; Del, Delmark; DwG, Down with the Game; Fw, Folkways; Ge, Gennett; GHP, GHP Records; H, Herwin; Hist, Historical; MBA, MBA Records; Me, Melotone; MW, Montgomery Ward; OJL, Origin Jazz Library; Ok, Okeh; Or, Oriole; OT, Old Timey; Pe, Perfect; RBF, RBF Records; Ro, Romeo; Roun, Rounder; Rts, Roots; Si, Sire; Son, Sonet; SpC, Sparkasse in Concert; Tak, Takoma; Van, Vanguard; Vet, Vetco; V-Fw, Verve-Folkways; Vi, Victor; Vo, Vocalion; X, Xtra; Yaz, Yazoo.

TOM ASHLEY by Charles Wolfe and Stephen Davis

Recordings of 1928–1933

STARR PIANO CO. Richmond, Ind., 2 Feb. 1928
Clarence Ashley, vocal and guitar; with Dwight Bell, banjo.
(Challenge recordings as by Tom Hutchinson, Champion recordings as by Oscar Brown, Gennett recordings as by Tom Ashley.)

GE 13419	Ohio Lovers	unissued
GE 13420	Drunkard's Dream	unissued
GE 13421	You're a Little Too Small	Ge 6404, Chl 391, Ch 15525
GE 13422	Four Nights Experience	Ge 6404, Chl 391

VICTOR TALKING MACHINE CO. Atlanta, Ga., 11 Oct. 1928
Carolina Tar Heels: Dock Walsh, vocal and banjo; Clarence Ashley, vocal and guitar; Garley Foster, harmonica and guitar.

BVE-47159-1	There's a Man Goin' Around Takin' Names	Vi 40053, *GHP LP-1001*
BVE-47160-2	I Don't Like the Blues No How	Vi 40053, *GHP LP-1001*
BVE-47161-3	Lay Down Baby Take Your Rest	Vi 40024, *OT LP-101*
BVE-47162-3	Can't You Remember When Your Heart Was Mine	Vi 40219, *BF 15507*

_____. Atlanta, Ga., 14 Oct. 1928

BVE-47163-2	Roll On Boys	Vi 40024, *GHP LP-1001*
BVE-47164-3	You Are a Little Too Small	Vi 40007, *BF 15507*
BVE-47165-2	Peg and Awl	Vi 40007, Fw *FA2951*, *BF 15507*
BVE-47166-3	I'll Be Washed	Vi 40219, *BF 15507*

_____. Camden, N..J., 3 April 1929
Carolina Tar Heels: Dock Walsh, vocal and banjo; Clarence Ashley, vocal and guitar; Garley Foster, harmonica and guitar.

51067-2	My Home's across the Blue Ridge Mountains	Vi 40100, *GHP LP-1001*
51068-2	Hand in Hand We Have Walked Along Together	Vi 40177, *GHP LP-1001*
51069-1	The Train's Done Left Me	Vi 40128
51070-2	Who's Gonna Kiss Your Lips, Dear Darling	Vi 40100, *GHP LP-1001*
51071	Oh How I Hate It	Vi 40077, *GHP LP-1001*
51072-2	Rude and Rambling Man	Vi 40077, *GHP LP-1001*

51073-3	Somebody's Tall and Handsome	Vi 40128, *GHP LP-1001*
51079-3	The Old Gray Goose	Vi 40177, *GHP LP-1001*

COLUMBIA PHONOGRAPH CO. Johnson City, Tenn., 23 Oct. 1929
Byrd Moore and His Hot Shots: Byrd Moore, banjo and guitar;
C. T. Ashley, banjo and guitar; Clarence Greene, fiddle and
guitar.

149240-1	Frankie Silvers	Co 15536
149241-2	The Hills of Tennessee	Co 15536
149242-2	Careless Love	Co 15496
149243-2	Three Men Went A-Hunting	Co 15496, *OT LP-101*

Clarence Ashley, vocal and banjo.

149250-2	Dark Holler Blues	Co 15489, *Cy 525*
149251-2	The Coo Coo Bird	Co 15489, *Fw FA2953*
149252-2	Little Sadie	Co 15522
149253-2	Poor Omie	Co 15522

COLUMBIA PHONOGRAPH CO. Atlanta, Ga., 14 April 1930
Clarence Ashley, vocal and banjo.

150210-1 (194982)	The House Carpenter	Co 15654, *Fw FA2951*
150211-1 (194988)	Old John Hardy	Co 15654, *Cy 525*
150212	Ain't Got No Honey Babe	unissued
150213	Bitter Pill Blues	unissued
150214	Dear I Love You	unissued
150215	I Once Knew a Little Girl	unissued

VICTOR TALKING MACHINE CO. Charlotte, N.C., 28 May 1931
Haywood County Ramblers: probably Ashley, guitar and vocal;
Foster, guitar and harmonica; Walsh, banjo and vocal; Med-
ford, mandolin.

69369	All Bound Down	Vi 23779
69370	Short Life in Trouble	unissued
69371	Buncombe Chain Gang	Vi 23779

AMERICAN RECORD CORP. New York, 30 Nov. 1931
Blue Ridge Mountain Entertainers: Tom Ashley, guitar (-1);
Gwen Foster, guitar and harmonica (-2); Clarence Greene, fid-
dle (-3); Will Abernathy, autoharp and harmonica (-4); Walter
R. Davis, guitar.

11035	There Will Come a Time (-1)	unissued
11036	Penitentiary Bound (-1,-3)	Cq 8149

11037-1	Drunk Man Blues (-1)	Me 12538, Pe 12864, Ba 32630, Ro 5183, Or 8183
11039-2	Short Life of Trouble (-1,-3)	Cq 8149, Pe 12800, Ba 32427, Ro 5129, Or 8129
11040	Baby All Night Long (-1,-2)	Vo 02780

_____. New York, 1 Dec. 1931

11041-3	Cincinnati Breakdown	Pe 12805, Ba 32432, Ro 5134, Or 8134
11042-2	Honeysuckle Rag	Pe 12805, Ba 32432, Ro 5134, Or 8134
11043-1	Over at Tom's House	Cq 8103
11044-2	The Fiddler's Contest	Cq 8103
11045-1	Washington and Lee Swing	Cq 7942, Pe 12782, Ba 32356, Ro 5116, Or 8116
11046-2	Goodnight Waltz	Cq 7942, Pe 12782, Ba 32356, Ro 5116, Or 8116
11047-2	My Sweet Farm Girl (-1,-2)	Cq 7939, Pe 12779, Ba 32353, Ro 5113, Or 8113, Vo 02780
11048-3	I Have No Loving Mother Now (-1,-2)	Me 12425, Pe 12822, Ba 32478, Ro 5152, Or 8152

_____. New York, 2 Dec. 1931

11050-1	Haunted Road Blues (-1)	Cq 7939, Pe 12779, Ba 32353, Ro 5113, Or 8113
11051-2	Corrine Corrina (-1,-4)	Pe 12800, Ba 32427, Ro 5129, Or 8129
11052-2	Bring Me a Leaf from the Sea	Me 12425, Pe 12822, Ba 32478, Ro 5152, Or 8152
11053	Far across the Deep Blue Sea	unissued

AMERICAN RECORD CORP. New York, 5 Sept. 1933
Ashley and Foster: C. T. Ashley, vocal, banjo, and guitar;
Gwen Foster, vocal, harmonica, and guitar.

12959	Sideline Blues	Vo 02611
12960	Rising Sun Blues	Vo 02576
12961	Sadie Ray	Vo 02900
12962	Greenback Dollar	Cq 9112, Ok 02554, Vo 02554

| 12963 | East Virginia Blues | Vo 02576 |
| 12964 | You Are Going to Leave the Old Home | unissued |

_____. New York, 7 Sept. 1933

13967	One Dark and Stormy Night	Vo 02750
13968	Faded Roses	Vo 02666
13969	The Old Armchair	Vo 02647
13970	Let Him Go, God Bless Him	Vo 02666
13971	Bay Rum Blues	Vo 02611
13972	My North Carolina Home	Vo 02900

_____. New York, 8 Sept. 1933

13975	Ain't No Use to High Hat Me	Vo 02789
13977	Times Ain't Like They Used to Be	Ok 02554
13979	Down at the Old Road House	Vo 02750
13980	Go 'Way and Let Me Sleep	Vo 02789
13983	Frankie Silvers	Vo 02647

Recordings of the 1960s (Date and place are release data rather than recording data.)

Old-Time Music at Clarence Ashley's. Fw FA2355. New York, 1961.
Claude Allen; God's Gonna Ease My Troublin' Mind; Honey Babe Blues.

Old Time Music at Clarence Ashley's, Volume Two. Fw FA2359. New York, 1963.
Free Little Bird; Little Sadie; Tough Luck; Walking Boss; My Home's across the Blue Ridge Mts.; The Coo-Coo Bird; Rising Sun Blues; Shady Grove; Poor Omie; Amazing Grace.

Country Music and Bluegrass at Newport. Van 9146. New York, 1963.
Way Downtown; Maggie Walker Blues; The Girl I Loved in Sunny Tennessee; Lee Highway Blues.

Old Time Music at Newport. Van 9147. New York, 1963.
House Carpenter; Little Sadie; Coo-Coo Bird; The Old Account Was Settled Long Ago; Amazing Grace.

Clarence Ashley and Tex Isley. Fw FA2350. New York, 1966.
Can I Sleep in Your Barn Tonight, Mister? Rude and Rambling Man;

Whoa Mule; Faded Roses; Shout Little Lulu; The House Carpenter;
I'm the Man That Rode the Mule around the World; Wild Bill Jones;
The Little Old Log Cabin in the Lane; Cluck Old Hen; Frankie Silvers;
Prisoner's Song; Tom's Talking Blues; Little Hillside.

SAM McGEE by Charles Wolfe

VOCALION DIVISION, Brunswick-Balke-Collender Co. New York,
14 April 1926
Uncle Dave Macon, vocal and banjo; Sam McGee, guitar.

E2751-52	Rise When the Rooster Crows	Vo 15321, Vo 5097, *RBF RF-51, Vet 101*
E2753-54	Way Down the Old Plank Road	Vo 15321, Vo 5097, *Fw FA2953*
E2755-56	The Bible's True	Vo 15322, Vo 5098, *Vet 101*
E2757-58	He Won the Heart of My Sarah Jane	Vo 15322, Vo 5098
E2759-60	Late Last Night When My Willie Came Home	Vo 15319, Vo 5095, *De DL-4760*
E2761-62	I've Got the Mourning Blues	Vo 15319, Vo 5095, *RBF RF-51*
E2763-64	Death of John Henry (Steel Driving Man)	Vo 15320, Vo 5096, Br 112, Br 80091, Br BL-59001, Cor MH-174, *Cy 502, Hist 8006*
E2765-66	On the Dixie Bee Line (In That Henry Ford of Mine)	Vo 15320, Vo 5096, Br 112, *Vet 101*

Sam McGee, solo guitar.

E2767-68	Buck Dancer's Choice	Vo 15318, Vo 5094 *Yaz L-1024*
E2769-70	The Franklin Blues	Vo 15318, Vo 5094, *Yaz L-1024*

_____. New York, 16 April 1926
Uncle Dave Macon, vocal and banjo; Sam McGee, guitar.

E2774-75	Whoop 'Em Up Cindy	Vo 15323, Vo 5099
E2776-77	Only As Far As the Gate, Dear Ma	Vo 15323, Vo 5099
E2778-79	Just Tell Them That You Saw Me	Vo 15324, Vo 5100
E2780-81	Poor Sinners, Fare You Well	Vo 15324, Vo 5100, *Vet 101*

_____. New York, 17 April 1926
Uncle Dave Macon, vocal and banjo; Sam McGee, guitar.

E2792-93	Old Ties	Vo 15325, Vo 5104, *Hist 8006*

Sam McGee, vocal and guitar solo.

E2794-95	In a Cool Shady Nook	Vo 15325, Vo 5104
E2796-97	If I Could Only Blot Out the Past	Vo 15326, Vo 5101
E2798-99	Knoxville Blues	Vo 15326, Vo 5101, *Cy 523*

VOCALION DIVISION, BRUNSWICK-BALKE-COLLENDER CO. New York, 7 May 1927
Uncle Dave Macon and His Fruit Jar Drinkers: Uncle Dave Macon, vocal and banjo; Sam McGee, guitar; Kirk McGee and Mazy Todd, fiddles, except as follows: Kirk McGee, mandolin (-1), vocal (-2); Sam McGee, vocal (-3); Kirk McGee not present (-4); Mazy Todd not present (-5).

E4923-24	Bake That Chicken Pie	Vo 5148
E4925-26	Rockabout My Saro Jane	Vo 5152, Br 80091, Br BL-59001, Cor MH-174, *Cy 521*
E4927-28	Tell Her to Come Back Home	Vo 5153, *De DL-4760*
E4929-30	Hold That Woodpile Down (-2,-3)	Vo 5151, *RBF RF-51, Vet 101*
E4931-32	Carve That Possum (-2,-3)	Vo 5151, *De DL-4760, MW 236*
E4933-34	Hop High Ladies, The Cake's All Dough	Vo 5154, *Hist 8006*
E4935-36	Sail Away, Ladies	Vo 5155, Br 80094, Br BL-59000, Cor MH-174, *Cy 521*

_____. New York, 9 May 1927

E4944-45	I'm A-Goin' Away in the Morn (-2,-3)	Vo 5148, *De DL-4760*
E4946-47	Sleepy Lou	Vo 5156, *De DL-4760, Hist 8006*
E4948-49	The Gray Cat on the Tennessee Farm	Vo 5152, *Cy 521*
E4950-51	Walk, Tom Wilson, Walk (-4,-5)	Vo 5154
E4952-53	I'se Gwine Back to Dixie (-1,-5)	Vo 5157, *Cy 521*
E4954-55	Take Me Home, Poor Julia (-1)	Vo 5157, *Cy 521*
E4956-57	Go Along Mule (-2,-3)	Vo 5165, *RBF RF-51*
E4958-59	Tom and Jerry	Vo 5165, *De DL-4760*
E4960-61	Rabbit in the Pea Patch	Vo 5156, *Cy 521*
E4962-63	Jordan Is a Hard Road to Travel	Vo 5153, *RBF RF-51, Vet 105*
E4964-66	(untraced)	
E4967-68	Pickaninny Lullaby Song (-5)	Vo 5155

_____. New York, 11 May 1927

The Dixie Sacred Singers: Uncle Dave Macon, banjo and vocal; Sam McGee, guitar and vocal; Kirk McGee, vocal; Mazy Todd, fiddle, except as follows: Kirk McGee, fiddle (-1), mandolin (-2); Mazy Todd not present (-3).

E4969-70	Are You Washed in the Blood of the Lamb? (-2)	Vo 5158
E4971-72	The Maple on the Hill (-2)	Vo 5158
E4973-74	Poor Old Dad (-2) (released as by Uncle Dave Macon and McGee Brothers)	Vo 5159
E4975-76	Walking in the Sunlight (-2)	Vo 5160, *Cy 521*
E4977-78	Bear Me Away on Your Snowy Wings (-2)	Vo 5160
E4979-80	The Mockingbird Song Medley (-1) (released as by Uncle Dave Macon)	Vo 5161
E4981-82	Shall We Gather at the River (-3)	Vo 5162, *De DL-4760*
E4983-84	When the Roll Is Called Up Yonder	Unissued
E4985-86	In the Sweet Bye and Bye (-2)	Vo 5162
E4987-88	God Be with You Till We Meet Again	Unissued

McGee Brothers or McGee Brothers and Todd: Sam McGee, vocal (-1), guitar (-2), banjo-guitar (-3); Kirk McGee, vocal (-4), fiddle (-5), mandolin (-6), banjo (-7); Mazy Todd, fiddle (-8); Uncle Dave Macon, banjo (-9), vocal (-10).

E5014-15	Old Master's Runaway (-2,-4, -7,-8) (Vo 5167, 5166, 5170, and 5172 released as by Uncle Dave Macon and McGee Brothers)	Vo 5167, *Cy 542*
E5016-17	Charming Bill (-2,-4,-5,-8,-9)	Vo 5166, *BF 15517*
E5018-19	A Flower from My Angel Mother's Grave (-2,-4,-6)	Vo 5166, *BF 15517*
E5020-21	C-H-I-C-K-E-N Spells Chicken (-1,-2,-4,-5)	Vo 5150, *BF 15517*
E5022-23	Salty Dog Blues (-2,-4,-5)	Vo 5150, *BF 15517*
E5024-25	Salt Lake City Blues (-2,-4,-5)	Vo 5169, *Cy 541*
E5026-27	Rufus Blossom (-1,-2,-4,-7,-8)	Vo 5170, *BF 15517*
E5028-29	Ragged Jim (-2,-4,-6)	Vo 5170
E5030-31	Someone Else May Be There While I'm Gone (-2,-4,-5)	Vo 5167, *BF 15517*
E5032-33	Hannah, Won't You Open the Door? (-2,-4,-5)	Vo 5169
E5034-35	My Family Has Been a Crooked Set (-1,-2,-7)	Vo 5171, *BF 15517*

E5036-3<u>7</u>	The Tramp (-1,-2,-6)	Vo 5171, *BF 15517*
E5038-<u>3</u>9	You've Been a Friend to Me (-1,-4,-9,-10)	Vo 5172
E5040-4<u>1</u>	Backwater Blues (-2,-9,-10) (released as by Uncle Dave Macon and Sam McGee)	Vo 5164

BRUNSWICK DIVISION, BRUNSWICK-BALKE-COLLENDER CO. Chicago, 25 July 1928
Uncle Dave Macon, vocal (-1), banjo (-2); Sam McGee, vocal (-3), banjo-guitar (-4), guitar (-5), banjo (-6).

C2125, A, B	From Earth to Heaven (-1,-2,-4)	Br 329, *RBF RF-51*
C2126, A, B	The Coon That Had the Razor (-1,-2,-4)	Vo 5261
C2127, A, B	Buddy, Won't You Roll down the Line (-1,-2,-3,-4)	Br 292, *Fw FA 2953, Hist 8006*
C2128, A, B	Worthy of Estimation (-1,-2,-4)	Br 266, *Cy 521*
C2129, A, B	I'm the Child to Fight (-1,-2,-3,-4)	Br 292, *De DL-4760, Hist 8006*
C2130, A, B	Over the Road I'm Bound to Go (-1,-2,-4)	Br 329, *RBF RF-51, Cy 542*
C2131, A, B	Uncle Dave's Banjo Medley	Rejected

Sam McGee, vocal solo with banjo-guitar.

| C2132, A, B | Easy Rider | Vo 5254, *BF 15517* |
| C2133, A, B | Chevrolet Car | Vo 5254, *Cy 541* |

Uncle Dave Macon, banjo and vocal; Sam McGee, banjo (-1).

| C2135, A, B | Uncle Dave's Favorite Religious Melodies (-1) | Rejected |

Sam McGee, vocal solo with guitar.

| C2137, A, B | As Willie and Mary Strolled by the Seashore | Vo 5310, *BF 15517* |
| C2138, A, B | The Ship without a Sail | Vo 5310, *BF 15517* |

OKEH PHONOGRAPH CORP. Jackson, Miss., 17 Dec. 1930
Uncle Dave Macon, banjo and vocal; Sam McGee, banjo-guitar.

404754	Tennessee Red Fox Chase	Ok 45507, *Vet 101*
404755	Wreck of the Tennessee Gravy Train	Ok 45507, *RBF RF-51*
404756	Oh Baby, You Done Me Wrong	Ok 45552
404757	She's Got the Money Too	Ok 45552
404758	Oh Lovin' Babe	Roun 1028
404759	Mysteries of the World	Ok 45522, Roun 1028
404760	Round Dice Reel	Unissued

404761	Come On Buddie, Don't You Want to Go	Roun 1028
404762	Go On, Nora Lee	Roun 1028
404763	Was You There When They Took My Lord Away	Ok 45522

STARR PIANO CO. Richmond, Ind., 14 Aug. 1934
Uncle Dave Macon and the McGee Brothers: Uncle Dave Macon, banjo and vocal; Sam McGee, guitar; Kirk McGee, guitar (-1), banjo (-2).

N-19651	Thank God for Everything (-1)	Ch 16805, Ch 45105, De 5373
N-19652	When the Train Comes Along (-2)	Ch 16805, Ch 45105, De 5373, *RBF RF-51, Vet 103*
N-19653	The Train Done Left Me and Gone (-2)	Unissued

McGee Brothers: Sam McGee, guitar and vocal; Kirk McGee, banjo and vocal.

| N-19655 | Brown's Ferry Blues | Ch 16804, Ch 45033, De 5348, *Cy 542* |

Uncle Dave Macon and the McGee Brothers.

| N-19656 | There's Just One Way to the Pearly Gates (-2) | Unissued |
| N-19657 | The Grey Cat (-2) | Unissued |

_____. Richmond, Ind., 15 Aug. 1934
Sam McGee, guitar solo with vocal.

| N-19660 | Railroad Blues | Ch 16804, Ch 45033, De 5348, *Cy 511* |

Uncle Dave Macon and the McGee Brothers.

N-19662	The Good Old Bible Line (-1)	Unissued
N-19663	Don't Get Weary Children (-2)	Ch 16822, Ch 45048, De 5369, MW 8029, *Cy 515*
N-19664	He's Up with the Angels Now (-2)	Ch 16822, Ch 45048, De 5369, MW 802

LP Albums

FOLKWAYS RECORDS. Nashville, Nov. 1957
The McGee Brothers and Arthur Smith. FA 2379. Sam McGee,

vocal and guitar or banjo (-1); Kirk McGee, banjo and guitar (-2); Arthur Smith, fiddle (-3) and occasional vocal (-4).

Cumberland Gap (-3); Roll On Buddy; Needlecase (-1); Buck Dancer's Choice (Sam, guitar solo); Sally Long (Sam, guitar solo); Rock House Joe; Polly Ann (-3); Hell among the Yearlings (-3); Kilby Jail (-3,-4); Coming from the Ball; Dusty Miller (-3); Sixteen on Sunday (-3); Snowdrop; Railroad Blues (Sam, guitar solo); House of David Blues (-3,-4); Green Valley Waltz (-3,-4); Guitar Waltz (Sam, guitar solo); Knoxville Blues (Sam, guitar solo); Jim Sapp Rag (-1, solo); Whoop 'Em Up Cindy (Sam, banjo-guitar; Kirk, banjo); Hollow Poplar (-3); Bile 'Em Cabbage Down (-3).

STARDAY RECORD CO. Nashville, ca. June 1961
The McGee Brothers. SLP 182. Sam McGee, guitar and vocal; Kirk McGee, banjo or guitar and vocal; Jerry Rivers, fiddle; Jesse Poteete, bass.
Roll On Buddy; Hung Down My Head and Cried; Freight Train Blues; Roll Along Jordan; My Gal's a Highborn Lady; Comin' from the Ball; Chittlin' Cookin' Time in Cheatham County.

The Crook Brothers. SLP 182. Herman Crook, harmonica; Sam McGee, guitar; Jerry Rivers, fiddle; Lewis Crook, banjo; Goldie Stewart, bass.
Black Mountain Rag; Soldier's Joy; Ragtime Annie; Lost John; Liberty; Will the Circle Be Unbroken.

FOLKWAYS RECORDS. Newark, ca. July 1965
The McGee Brothers and Arthur Smith. FTS 31007. Sam McGee, vocal and guitar or banjo-guitar (-1); Kirk McGee, banjo or fiddle (-2); Arthur Smith, fiddle (-3), occasional vocal (-4), and occasional banjo (-5).
Single-Footing Horse (-3); Widow Haley (-3); Charming Bill; Milk Cow Blues; Memphis Blues (-1); Boogie (-1); Amos Johnson Rag (-1, Sam, banjo-guitar solo); Redwing (-1,-3); Under the Double Eagle (-1,-3); Don't Let Your Deal Go Down (-1,-3); Evening Shade (-3); Pig at Home in the Pen (-3,-4); Peacock Rag (-3); Milk 'Em in the Evening Blues; Late Last Night (-1); Keep a Light in Your Window Tonight; Uncle Buddy (-5); Lafayette (-2,-5); Drummer Boy (Sam, guitar solo); Easy Rider (-1); Chinese Breakdown (-1); Dance All Night with a Bottle in Your Hand (-3); Whistling Rufus (-3); Sally Johnson (-3); I've Had a Big Time Tonight (-3).

ARHOOLIE RECORDS. Franklin, Tenn., Nov. 1969 and Oct. 1970
Sam McGee. Arh 5012. Sam McGee, vocals, guitar, banjo, and

banjo-guitar; Clifton McGee, second guitar; Goldie Stewart, bass.

Sam McGee Stomp; Fuller Blues; Burglar Bold; Dew Drop; Jesse James; Ching Chong; Blackberry Blossom; Wheels; How Great Thou Art; When the Wagon Was New; Franklin Blues; Penitentiary Blues; Pig Ankle Rag; Railroad Blues; Buck Dancer's Choice.

MBA RECORDS. Franklin, Tenn., ca. 1972
Sam McGee. MBA-606-S. Sam McGee, guitar and vocals; Clifton McGee, rhythm guitar; Elmer Boswell, bass and occasional vocal (-1).

Flat-Top Pickin' Sam McGee (-1); Buck Dancer's Choice; Won't Happen Again; Victory Rag; When the Wagon Was New; Uncle Fuller; Wheels; Under the Double Eagle; Railroad Blues; Shut the Door; Sally Long; Cabbage Head; Franklin Blues; Knoxville Blues; Sam's Other Side; Little Texas Waltz.

MBA RECORDS. Franklin, Tenn., ca. 1972
Sam and Kirk McGee. MBA-607-S. Sam McGee, lead guitar and vocal; Kirk McGee, rhythm guitar and vocal, banjo (-1); Clifton McGee, guitar; Elmer Boswell, bass.

Southern Moon; Waiting for a Letter; Snow Drop (-1); The End of Forever; Farewell Blues/Alabama Jubilee/Just Because; Will the Circle Be Unbroken; Snow Bird; Milk Cow Blues; Y'All Come; San Antonio Rose; If I Had My Life to Live Over; Whispering Hope.

DAVIS UNLIMITED RECORDS. Franklin, Tenn., Aug. 1975
Sam McGee. DU-33021. Sam McGee, guitar and vocals; Jim DeFriese, rhythm guitar and occasional vocal (-1); Bill Lowery, mandolin and occasional vocal (-2); J.P. James, bass (-3).

There Is a Fountain; Farther Along; How Great Thou Art; Life's Railway to Heaven (-1,-2); Whispering Hope; Where No One Stands Alone; Wayfaring Stranger; Amazing Grace; What a Friend We Have in Jesus (-2,-3); Where the Roses Never Fade; I'm S-A-V-E-D; God Be with You Till We Meet Again.

BUKKA WHITE by David Evans

All of Bukka White's 1937 and 1940 recordings have been reissued on Co C 30036, *Bukka White/Parchman Farm.*

MEMPHIS, 26 May 1930
Washington White: vocal and guitar; Napoleon Hairiston, guitar, and vocal (-1); Miss Minnie, vocal (-2).

59995	The New 'Frisco Train (-1) (is labeled WHITE AND HAIRISTON and has Hair-iston on vocal and guitar, White on guitar with spoken comments)	Vi 23295, *Yaz 1009*, *Rts RSE-2*
59996	The Panama Limited	Vi 23295, *OJL 5, Yaz 1026*, *Rts RSE-2*
59997	The Doctor Blues	Vi unissued
59998	Mississippi Milk Blues	Vi unissued
59999	Women Shootin' Blues	Vi unissued
60000	Mule Lopin' Blues	Vi unissued
62501	Stranger Woman Blues (-1)	Vi unissued
62502	Jealous Man Blues (-1)	Vi unissued
62503	Mama Ain't Goin' to Have It Here (-1)	Vi unissued
62504	Dirty Mistreatin' Blues (-1)	Vi unissued
62505	Over Yonder	Vi unissued
62506	I Am in the Heavenly Way (-2)	Vi V38615, *OJL 12*, *Rts RSE-2*
62507	Trusting in My Saviour	Vi unissued
62508	Promise True and Grand (-2)	Vi V38615, *OJL 13*, *Rts RSE-2*

CHICAGO, 2 Sept. 1937
Bukka White: vocal and guitar; another guitarist.

C-1996-2	Pinebluff, Arkansas	Vo 03711, Cq 9072, Co 30139, *Rts 3*, *Co C 30036*
C-1997-1	Shake 'Em On Down	same as above

STATE PENITENTIARY, PARCHMAN, MISS., 24 May 1939. Recorded for the Archive of American Folk Song, Library of Congress, Washington, D.C.
Washington (Barrelhouse) White: vocal and guitar.

2678-A-2	Sic 'Em Dogs On	H 92400, 201, *Rts 32*
2678-B-1	Po' Boy	H 92400, 201, *Rts RSE-2*

CHICAGO, 7 March 1940
Bukka White: vocal and guitar; probably Washboard Sam, washboard.

WC-2977-A	Black Train Blues	Vo 05588, *Rts 2*, *Co C 30036*
WC-2978-A	Strange Place Blues	Vo 05526, *RBF 9*, *Co C 30036*

WC-2979-A	When Can I Change My Clothes	Vo 05489, *DwG 1*, *Co C 30036*
WC-2980-A	Sleepy Man Blues	Ok 05743, *RBF 11, CC 3*, *Co C 30036*
WC-2981-A	Parchman Farm Blues	Ok 05683, *Rts 3*, *CBS 66218, Co C 30036*
WC-2982-A	Good Gin Blues	Ok 05625, *BC 6*, *Co C 30036*

Chicago, 8 March 1940

WC-2987-A	High Fever Blues	Vo 05489, *DwG 1*, *Co C 30036*
WC-2988-A	District Attorney Blues	Ok 05683, *Rts 3*, *Co C 30036*
WC-2989-A	Fixin' to Die Blues	Vo 05588, *RBF 1*, *Co C 30036*
WC-2990-A	Aberdeen Mississippi Blues	Ok 05743, *RBF 11*, *Co C 30036*
WC-2991-A	Bukka's Jitterbug Swing	Ok 05625, *BC 6, X 1035*, *Co C 30036*
WC-2992-A	Special Stream Line	Vo 05526, *OJL 5*, *Co C 30036*

Recordings Since 1963

(All of the following except Tak 31364 are 12″ LPs. The albums on Takoma, Arhoolie [except F 1018], Blue Horizon, Blues Beacon, Biograph, and Sparkasse in Concert feature Bukka's music throughout. The remainder have one to five tracks by him.)

Mississippi Blues. Tak 1001 (reissued as *Legacy of the Blues, Vol. 1,* Son SNTF 609). Memphis, 1963.
"World Boogie"/"Midnight Blue." Tak 31364, 45 rpm. Memphis, 1963.
Sky Songs, Vol. 1. Arh F 1019. Berkeley, 8, 25, and 26 Nov. 1963.
Sky Songs, Vol. 2. Arh F 1020. Berkeley, 25 and 26 Nov. 1963.
Bad Luck 'n Trouble. Arh F 1018. Berkeley, 25 Nov. 1963.
Living Legends. V-Fw 3010. New York, 1966.
1968 Country Blues Festival. Si SES 97003. Memphis, 20 July 1968.
Memphis Hot Shots. BH 7-63229. Memphis, 21 July 1968.

On the Road Again. Ad AD 1007S. Memphis, 7 and 10 Oct. 1969.

The Memphis Blues Again, Vol. 2. Ad AD 1010. Memphis, probably 1969.

Baton Rouge Mosby Street. BB 1932 119. Munich, 27 Oct. 1972.

Tennessee Blues, Vol. 1. Al VPA 8240. Probably Memphis, 22 Dec. 1972.

Big Daddy. Bio BLP 12049. West Memphis, Ark., July 1973.

Bukka White. SpC 1/75. Bremen, West Germany, 11 March 1975.

Index of Song Titles

References to music are signified by an "m," and references to lyrics by a "w."

General Index

This book was composed on the Compugraphic Phototype-
setter in Times Roman. Friz Quadrata was selected for display.
The book was designed by Jim Billingsley, typeset by Metri-
comp, Inc., Grundy Center, Iowa, printed offset by Thomson-
Shore, Inc., Dexter, Michigan, and bound by John H. Dekker &
Sons, Grand Rapids, Michigan. The paper on which the book is
printed was manufactured by S.D. Warren Company.

UNIVERSITY OF TENNESSEE PRESS / KNOXVILLE